ANGRY, BORED, CONFUSED

ANGRY, BORED, CONFUSED

A CITIZEN HANDBOOK OF AMERICAN POLITICS

MICHAEL J. KRYZANEK

BRIDGEWATER STATE COLLEGE

Westview Press

A Member of the Perseus Books Group

Copyright © 1999 by Westview Press, A Member of the Perseus Books Group

Published in 1999 in the United States of America by Westview Press, 5500 Central Avenue, Boulder, Colorado 80301-2877, and in the United Kingdom by Westview Press, 12 Hid's Copse Road, Cumnor Hill, Oxford OX2 9JJ

Library of Congress Cataloging-in-Publication Data
Kryzanek, Michael J.
  Angry, bored, confused : a citizen handbook of
American politics / Michael J. Kryzanek
    p. cm.
  Includes bibliographical references and index.
  ISBN 0-8133-6884-7 (hc.) — ISBN 0-8133-6885-5 (pbk.)
    1. United States—Politics and government. 2. United States—
Politics and government—1993– —Public opinion. 3. United States—
Social conditions—1980– —Public opinion. 4. Public opinion—
United States. 5. Political culture—United States. I. Title.
JK271.K795   1999
320.973—dc21
                                                                    98-55173
                                                                    CIP

The paper used in this publication meets the requirements of the American National Standard for Permanence of Paper for Printed Library Materials Z39.48-1984.

10   9   8   7   6   5   4   3   2   1

To my mother
Mary Kryzanek

CONTENTS

TABLES AND ILLUSTRATIONS

Tables

Figures

Boxes

I'm mad as hell, and I'm not going to take it anymore.

—Peter Finch in Network

Frankly my dear, I don't give a damn.

—Clark Gable to Vivien Leigh in
Gone With the Wind

Who are those guys?

—Paul Newman to Robert Redford in
Butch Cassidy and the Sundance Kid

PREFACE

I am sure you have played the word association game—a word is stated, and you answer with the first word that comes into your mind. If you try the word association game using "American government" as the starting point, the responses will likely be distressing. I play this game in my classes on a regular basis, and I have yet to elicit responses that suggest my students feel much in the way of trust, support, and hope when it comes to the American government. The responses usually range from "corrupt" to "sleazy" to "bribes" to "scandals." Rarely do I get responses like "effective," "common good," or "honest." My students' responses reflect the deep-seated and disturbing belief among Americans that the politicians who lead their government are self-serving, money-grubbing connivers who run this country to benefit special interests and ultimately themselves.

In my classes, I try my best to give a balanced picture of American government, with its flaws and its opportunities, but I often run up against the latest newspaper headline or television news program that reinforces the perception that all is not well in Washington. I tell the students that they must see government as made up of human beings, some of whom use their power and authority to advance the interest of the people, and others who can be easily tempted by the perks of their office. Unfortunately, my modest cheerleading for what is good about American politics runs up against the constant drumbeat of scandal and petty partisanship. Wherever I look I find evidence that confirms that Americans have tuned out and turned off. Here is just a sampling of that evidence:

54.2 percent of the voting age population cast ballots in the presidential election in 1996, the lowest level since the

Census Bureau began compiling figures in 1964. In 1998, voter turnout was 36 percent, the lowest turnout in an off-year election since 1942.

25 percent of Americans feel that they can trust the U.S. government most of the time; this is down from 71 percent in 1964.

21 percent of the American public expressed confidence in the U.S. Congress in 1995.

40 percent of Americans polled in 1996 could not name the Vice President of the United States, 94 percent could not name the Chief Justice of the Supreme Court.
(Answer—Albert Gore and William Rehnquist.)

In 1998, 26.7 percent of college freshmen said that "keeping up with political affairs is very important." In 1966, 57.9 percent said so.[1]

These bits of data lend credence to my choice of the title for this book. It would appear that Americans are indeed angry, bored, and confused when it comes to their view of government. They may not be angry, bored, and confused all at the same time, but it is a safe bet that their feelings about American government can be described by at least one of these adjectives. Unfortunately, these negative terms reflect one aspect of the reality of public life in the 1990s, which further feeds the current cultural malaise that accents all that is wrong with this country.

Yet the people that I interact with, whether in the classroom or in my daily walk through life, are not simply angry, bored, and confused. Americans are smarter than many pundits give them credit for. Yes, a negative streak shows up in the political data, but there is something else as well; there is a quest for answers, for straight talk about government. If Americans have anything in common in their attitude towards their government, it is that they are full of questions about the hows and whys of their democratic institutions and their elected leaders. They see the work of government every day in their

[1]Sources: Gallup Report, 1995; *New York Times*/CBS News Surveys; *Washington Post* Survey, 1995; Higher Education Institute, 1998.

pay stubs, in the warning label on the side of the cigarette package, in the signs on the highway, and in the soldiers who parade down their streets. But more often than not they still ask in exasperation why their taxes are so high or why the government regulates their private lives or why government spends money in one area of national life and not in another.

Government for many Americans has become incomprehensible and distant. With numbers like a federal budget of $1.7 trillion, 5,000 pages of IRS regulations, and 2.8 million employees working in hundreds of departments, agencies, and bureaus, Americans are simply overwhelmed by the scope of their government. Then when petty partisan wrangling in Congress, campaign finance scandals, and the all-too-frequent sexual escapades of politicians are thrown in the mix, the result is a recipe for anger, boredom, and confusion. Nevertheless, it is the thirst for answers, for straight talk, that best identifies the public side of Americans.

I have no illusions about this book turning Americans away from being angry, bored, and confused about their government. I do believe, however, that it is necessary to begin approaching the explanation of American government in ways that are accessible to the average citizen, without being negative. When American government is presented to a general audience, whether in mainstream books, the electronic media, or the local newspaper, the presentation usually takes a "what's wrong with America" approach, and pounds the reader into submission with countless examples of how our government is going to hell in a hand basket.

What is missing is an old-fashioned question-and-answer handbook. Nothing fancy, nothing overwhelming, and nothing designed to make matters even more unclear. *Angry, Bored, Confused* attempts to be such a simple handbook, asking and answering the questions that are actually on the minds of the American people.

The forty questions that make up *Angry, Bored, Confused* come from my experiences in the classroom, my work as a newspaper columnist for a number of years, and my experience as a local cable talk-show host (a regional version of the *McLauglin Group*, the *Capital Gang*, and *Washington Week in Review* all mixed together). With my ear close to the ground, I believe that I have been able to compile a body of questions and answers that bring to the fore what really is on the mind of Americans when it comes to their government. These forty questions are organized into eight chapters that correspond to key aspects of our national government, its origins, and its current dilemmas. The questions are direct, and the answers are relatively brief. This is not an oversize college textbook or a tell-all negative narrative. It is rather a medium-sized citizen handbook that can help deal with the negativity and confusion about politics that has gripped our country.

As with any writing project, there are many who must be thanked for their inspiration and their assistance. To all my anonymous readers, I want to give my thanks for their helpful comments. To my department colleagues, Victor DeSantis, George Serra, Shaheen Mozaffar, Polly Harrington, Chris Kirkey, and Mike Ault, I want to make my acknowledgments for their support and professional assistance, particularly during those hallway conversations and coffee breaks when American government was the topic. In particular I want to express my thanks to George Serra, who painstakingly read the manuscript and offered many helpful suggestions. To the best secretary in the world, Sharon Hines, I want to give my thanks for always being there to help out a nervous author. Thanks also to Silvine Marbury Farnell for her fine copyediting. And to my editor, Leo Wiegman, who is always the epitome of professionalism, many thanks. I especially want to thank my wife, Carol, who remains my compass, guiding me through family and work and gently reminding me what's important. And to my three daughters, Laura, Kathy, and Annie, who likely will not become political scientists, thanks for showing their love for the house political scientist. Finally, I want to thank my mother, Mary Kryzanek, who every Sunday scoured the newspapers for articles on American government that her son could use in his book. There is no more loyal fan than Mary Kryzanek and no more passionate supporter of our government. To her I owe an eternal debt of gratitude.

Michael J. Kryzanek

Angry, Bored, Confused

1

THE FOUNDATIONS OF AMERICAN GOVERNMENT

At this auspicious period, the United States came into existence as a Nation, and if their Citizens should not be completely free and happy, the fault will be entirely their own.

—*George Washington in his Farewell Address*

What Are the Ideas and Ideals that Our Government Was Founded On?

Most important events that have influenced the course of history had their origins in a set of ideas, a vision of how government should treat its citizens. The French Revolution, for example, gained important momentum and legitimacy because of the writings of Jean-Jacques Rousseau, which called for a government of the "General Will" and emphasized the importance of a social contract between the people and their leaders. So too with the Russian Revolution and the bold attack against the Old Regime by the Bolshevik Communists. Revolutionary leaders such as Lenin and Trotsky were avowed students of Karl Marx, heavily influenced by Marx's *Das*

Kapital with its tirades against capitalism and its call for a workers' revolution.

In many respects the evolution of the American political system, from the impassioned calls by Patrick Henry to "give me liberty or give me death," to the inspiring "We the People" introduction to the Constitution, has underscored the importance of ideas in the formation of our nation. Early political leaders in the colonies were impressed by the writings of European political thinkers who emphasized the importance of expanding democratic rights and forming a new relationship between citizens and their state.

The first European thinker of prominence to cast his shadow on events in the colonies was Thomas Hobbes, whose emphasis on the individual and property rights was a powerful justification for the movement for independence. Although Hobbes's view of governance was rather authoritarian, he moved the thinking of his time away from reliance on monarchical rule, viewing each individual as controlling his own destiny. Then there was John Locke, who advocated a government of consent and frequently used the words "inalienable rights" in his commentaries. Many of Locke's ideas found their way into the Declaration of Independence and the Constitution. Our early leaders were also impressed by the French writer Montesquieu, who talked about the importance of separating powers in government to ensure that power was not abused. Creating a governing system that would protect the rights of citizens and counteract the excesses of power would always be a guiding vision in the thinking of the men who shaped our government.

In fact, if there is one attitude that defines the intentions of the founders of the United States, it is a profound mistrust of men with power. Throughout the writings and deliberations of our early leaders, it is clear that they were concerned that government control the excesses of those who occupied political office. It is not that they viewed man as inherently bad; in fact there is a surprising level of confidence in the ability of ordinary men to manage their own public affairs. But there is always grave apprehension over the potential for abuse of power. Democratic governance was on the horizon, but the early leaders of this country were nevertheless wary of the potential abuses that might accompany democratic rule.

The best way to describe many of the Founding Fathers is not so much as thoughtful democrats, but rather as savvy pragmatists. And indeed, all of them joined to their talk of grand ideas such as liberty and democracy and rights and freedom, a strong concern for less romantic details, such as how to win a war against a formidable foe, how to fashion a workable constitution that would satisfy all the colonies, and how to keep the fledgling nation together when so many forces were at work for separation.

Although the break with England and the founding of a new country is enshrined forever as one of the great moments for our democracy, it must be remembered that the establishment of the United States was the work of men of considerable means and conservative inclinations. They saw the need for a new relationship between the people and their leaders, but they were reluctant to fully embrace democratic principles and practice. Their primary concern was to end the taxation policies of the Crown, which were draining the colonists. When the colonists raised the cry of "no taxation without representation," the objection to the way England's taxes were taking money out of the pockets of merchants and traders played as big a role as the concern for the right to vote. Some historians would even say that the individualistic and democratic ideas of thinkers like Hobbes, Locke, and Montesquieu served mostly as handy propaganda tools to use against the British, who were desperate for money to fight their foreign wars.

Because the movement for American independence was largely controlled by the landed and business elites, there was little pressure on leaders to move beyond the grandiose language of democracy to the actual implementation of a democratic republic. Historians and political scientists have debated for years about the motives of the Founding Fathers as they waged war against the British and laid out the governmental ground rules for a new nation. For years the common view was that desires to preserve wealth and status and to increase economic opportunity were the driving forces behind independence. Later there was the view that the new nation was founded by political pragmatists interested above all in keeping the nation together. More recently, there has been a return to the economic argument, but with more emphasis on economic stability rather than economic self-interests. But whatever the motivations, it is clear that the Founding Fathers were neither wide-eyed theorists nor revolutionary romantics.

Even though concern over the distribution of governing power and the economic future of a new nation may have been foremost on the minds of the Founding Fathers, it is important not to discount the role of democratic ideas in the establishment of this country. Franklin, Jefferson, Madison, and Washington clearly took a profound interest in the writings of those European thinkers who were calling for more popular participation in government. Jefferson and others like him were in fact vigorous proponents of democratic rule and individual rights, and Madison and others like him at least recognized that a new constitution would not win favor unless it made concessions to the new democratic thinking. The result was a fortuitous melding of principle and practicality, ideas and action, that is at the heart of the American independence movement and the formation of the constitution.

Those who focus on the philosophical component of this blend usually turn to James Madison and his famous treatise on democracy in *The Federalist Papers, no. 10*. Madison, in what is generally considered a brilliant piece of persuasive writing, told his readers that the most dangerous threat to democracy was "factions"—small groups of citizens whose major objective was to advance their narrow interests at the expense of the vast majority. Madison in clear and certain terms opted for a majoritarian democracy based on elected representatives.

In Madison's view, the best form of government ensured that the interests of the people as a whole would not be stymied by the interests of minority factions. At the same time, however, Madison wanted to avoid creating a "tyranny of the majority." He suggested that the ideal governing system would create a tension between multiple factions and be structured in such a way that minority opinion and rights would not be overwhelmed by the majority. In short, Madison wanted a governing system of balance and limitation so that policy decisions would be arrived at with caution and consensus. Madison is thus a firm advocate of federalism with its allocation of some powers to the central government and others to the state government. He was also in favor of creating a republican form of government in which a popularly elected assembly would not be the only center of power, but would be one of three separate power centers. Always fearful of power and suspicious of powerful leaders, Madison's *Federalist no. 10* reveals the heart of what has become our unique approach to governing.

While Madison's technical approach to governing in *Federalist no. 10* has become the most widely recognized contribution to American political philosophy, the passionate views of Thomas Jefferson remain forever at the core of our positive beliefs about government and our relationship to government. To refresh memories, a few lines from Jefferson's historic work, the Declaration of Independence, will suffice:

> We hold these truths to be self-evident, that all men are created equal, that they are endowed by their Creator with certain inalienable Rights, that among these rights are Life, Liberty and the pursuit of Happiness . . . That to secure these rights, Governments are instituted among Men, deriving their just powers from the consent of the governed. That whenever any Form of Government becomes destructive of these ends, it is the Right of the People to alter or abolish it, and to institute new Government, laying its foundation on such Principles and organizing its powers in such form, as to them shall seem most likely to effect their Safety and Happiness.

In that short excerpt from the Declaration of Independence, Jefferson lays out the basic principles of American democracy—equality, popular sovereignty, and, of course, liberty. Jefferson's major contribution to American political philosophy is that he provided an important balance to the many Founding Fathers who were primarily interested in structure and process. Although no fuzzy romantic, Jefferson recognized that governing is not only about rules, but also about vision. People need to be assured that the new government they are being asked to support will give them more than procedures. To Jefferson, governing was as much about inspiration as about organization.

There is much to the observation that a country is a reflection of the people who were there at the beginning. In the case of the United States, the people who were there at the beginning were men convinced that change was in the wind and that they had an obligation to seize the opportunity to move their colonies in a different direction. Being practical men, the Founding Fathers would not idle over grand principle or promise heaven on earth. Rather they would lead an independence movement and later construct a constitution designed to bring stability and avoid the excesses of absolute power.

Box 1.1   *Tocqueville's America*

From May of 1831 to February of 1832 Alexis de Tocqueville, a French aristocrat, traveled the length and breadth of the United States. During his travels Tocqueville wrote down his impression of America, Americans, and American democracy. The end result of his travels and analysis was the classic *Democracy in America*, which has remained the definitive work on the United States during its formative years. Tocqueville made many cogent observations on the young United States and its people. Below is Tocqueville's description of how Americans view the importance of philosophy, which also describes the way we think and act as citizens.

> I think that in no country in the civilized world is less attention paid to philosophy than in the United States. The Americans have no philosophical school of their own; and they care but little for all the schools into which Europe is divided, the very names of which are scarcely known to them. Yet it is easy to perceive that almost all the inhabitants of the United States conduct their understanding in the same manner, and govern it by the same rules; that is to say, without ever having taken the trouble to define the rules, they have a philosophical method common to the whole people. To evade the bondage of system and habit, of family-maxims, class-opinions, and, in some degree, of national prejudices; to accept tradition only as a means of information, and existing facts only as a lesson to be used in doing otherwise and doing better; to seek the reason of things for one's self, and in one's self alone; to tend to results without being bound to means, and to aim at the substance through the form; — such are the principal characteristics of what I shall call the philosophical method of the Americans. But if I go further, and seek amongst these characteristics the principal one which includes almost all the rest, I discover that, in most of the operations of mind, each American appeals only to the individual effort of his own understanding.

There are pieces of philosophy in the foundations of our governing system, if by philosophy we mean a view of man (generally untrustworthy), an outlook on life (liberty is an essential quality of being human), and a vision of the future (democratic governance is essential for national development), but what American political philosophy has come to mean has more to do with a practical approach to creating a country that would be able to survive in the face of hostile foreign powers and divisive internal forces. This "how to" approach has been an essential element of our national psyche, seen in our support for practicality, bargaining, and compromise. Jefferson's words in the Declaration of Independence may serve as a valuable classroom memorization exercise, but we are a people molded in the image of those Founders who were interested in making the country work properly, while at the same time feeling uplifted by noble ideas.

How Did the Constitution Get Written and Accepted?

The U.S. Constitution is the longest running governing document in existence. While many democratic countries have torn up their basic rules countless times and started over again, the United States continues to run its public affairs with a system that was fashioned over two hundred years ago. The handiwork of the Founding Fathers is a piece of history that approaches sacredness in this country. When tourists walk past the Constitution in the National Archives Building in Washington, invariably they whisper as if they know they are in the presence of greatness. Although longevity does not mean perfection, the Constitution should be viewed as a model of how to craft a governing structure that can stand the test of time.

The Constitution may be our holy document now, but that outcome would have been hard to predict back in 1787 when the Founding Fathers sat down to write a governing plan. When representatives from twelve of the thirteen colonies (Rhode Island sent no representatives) met in Philadelphia, much divided the delegates, and great uncertainty existed over the prospects for reaching an agreement. All the delegates really knew was that they could not continue to govern an independent nation with bills to pay and powerful enemies under the existing governing structure, the Articles of Confederation. With no executive, no taxing power, and no means of linking thirteen colonies into a nation, the Articles of Confederation had outlived its usefulness and had to be replaced with a governing system that offered the United States the means through which it could prosper and protect itself.

But finding a suitable replacement for the Articles of Confederation was a daunting task for the delegates. On a more abstract level, the delegates disagreed over how much democratic governance the new Constitution ought to permit, with some preferring a return to monarchical rule and others urging greater guarantees for citizen rights. Associated with this debate was the issue of whether this new country would accent its ruralness or its urbanness, whether governing power would reside in the state governments, which were tied more closely to the land, or in a central government, which would likely have a more urban and cosmopolitan worldview.

On a practical level, the delegates were also at odds over issues of popular representation in the legislative branch and the distribution of power among the various states. States with larger populations, such as New York, Pennsylvania, and Virginia, were lined up against smaller states, such as Delaware, New Jersey and Georgia, over who would have the dominant voice in the new government. Big state interests versus small state interests would be a nasty source of division at the Constitutional Convention. After a few weeks of deliberations in the heat of summer, it became clear to the delegates that they might not be able to agree on a Constitution and that their new nation might never attain the unity so vital for economic development and national security.

The constitution-makers in Philadelphia were no amateurs in the drive for independence and national governance. Most of the "best and the brightest" were there—George Washington, Benjamin Franklin, James Madison, and Alexander Hamilton—along with some lesser knowns such as Roger Sherman and William Patterson, who would play key roles in the unfolding drama. The best and the brightest, were men with property, wealth, and national reputation. In many respects, they had the most to lose if they failed to take their young country to the next level of governance.

Before the conclave began, James Madison of Virginia put together a kind of constitutional roadmap laying out his vision of how a nation must be governed. Madison, like many of his colleagues, was no radical interested in shaking up the existing socio-economic relations. Rather Madison wanted to move away from the weakness of the Articles with as little disruption and controversy as possible. But despite the confluence of great minds and great plans, it became obvious from the start that there was more that separated the delegates than unified them. Despite universal agreement that the Articles of Confederation had proved incapable of creating a national system of governance, the formation of a new system brought to the surface a range of fears and concerns that could not be easily dismissed.

Perhaps the key stumbling block at the Constitutional Convention was the issue of how to allocate seats in the legislature. Representation in the legislature was viewed by the delegates as critical, since that is where the policy-making power of the new country would reside. If seats were allocated according to population, then the more populous states would have greater representation than the less populous states. This was an intolerable situation for the smaller states, who were adamant in their opposition to a representation system that created an inequality of voice and power among the states. Nevertheless, the advocates of representation tied to population controlled the Convention. Edmund Randolph of Virginia, in close association with James Madison, introduced a proposal at the start of the Convention which advocated a strong central government based on a single national executive and a two-house legislature (a lower house based on population and an upper house elected by the other house). The Virginia Plan, as it came to be called, dominated the early debate in Philadelphia.

The Virginia Plan, however, only verified the fears of those delegates from smaller states who viewed strong central government with suspicion. The representation plan of Randolph and Madison served as confirmation that the populous states were intent on creating a governing document that would limit the autonomy of the smaller states and weaken their ability to influence the direction of the new country. As a result, in June of 1787, after the debate bogged down in a storm of charge and countercharge, William Patterson of New Jersey offered a second plan that was in large part a fine tuning of the Articles of Confederation. Patterson's alternative stressed the importance of one vote–one state and proposed a collective executive who would be hamstrung by a powerful legislature. Despite the fact that the Patterson plan did not gain much support, it was clear that the Convention delegates were confronted with a serious division of interests and vision. As the hot summer dragged on, the delegates began to fear the worst—that they would leave Philadelphia without a constitution.

Thankfully, the opposition between the big states and the small states proved amenable to compromise. Roger Sherman, one of the delegates from Connecticut, was able to cut through the impasse. The so-called Connecticut Compromise created a House of Representatives based on an allocation of seats reflective of population and determined by popular vote (excluding slaves, Indians, women, and men without property) and a Senate, which would have two representatives from each state elected by the state legislature. The Sherman alternative gave something to each side—to the larger states, a legislative body that was democratic in that it represented existing population patterns, and to the smaller states, a legislative body that assured equity for all the states by giving all the same representation.

With the delegates agreeing to this compromise, the Convention adjourned for eleven days. When the delegates returned on August 6, a Committee of Detail had already worked out a number of other compromises. For example, they made the executive and judicial branches subordinate to the legislature (a concession to those concerned over a domineering central authority), and they addressed the slavery and trade issues of the Southern states by agreeing to count only three-fifths of the slave population (thereby lessening the tax burden of the slave states) and prohibiting export taxes (thereby protecting the lucrative export trade in agricultural products). What had seemed a hopeless deadlock in July had produced a working document that was gaining support and momentum.

On September 17, 1787, the delegates produced a constitution. Of the remaining forty-two delegates, thirty-nine approved the document, while three refused, citing objections over what they feared would be excessive central government power. Even though such an achievement must have led to a celebration, the delegates knew that their work really had just begun. Article 7 of the Constitution required that nine of the thirteen states would have to endorse the new governing system in order to formally establish its legitimacy. The delegates were convinced, however, that in order to ensure that the Constitution would be accepted throughout the country and respected as a lawful document, ratification from all thirteen states would be necessary. Thus began the arduous task of convincing state legislatures and the general citizenry that the new constitution, with its accent on central power, limited democracy, and restrained decision-making institutions, was the best governing system that could be achieved.

For some states the decision about ratifying the Constitution was easy. Delaware took but four months to ratify by a unanimous vote (thus permitting the state to place the logo "The First State" on its automobile license plates) and was joined a few weeks later by Pennsylvania, New Jersey, Georgia, and Connecticut. These early victories emboldened the supporters of the Constitution but did not blind them to the opposition in states such as Virginia, New York, North Carolina, and Rhode Island. The arguments against ratification were expressed by individuals known as the Anti-Federalists. The Anti-Federalists (Patrick Henry, Samuel Adams, and at times Thomas Jefferson) restated their concern over what they believed would be excessive central government power and advocated locating governing control in the states. The Anti-Federalists also criticized the failure of the delegates to provide sufficient individual liberties in the original document.

The state of New York was viewed as critical to the successful completion of the ratification process. The fight for ratification in New York spurred James Madison, Alexander Hamilton, and John Jay into action. Individually they authored a series of essays under the pseudonym of Publius and published them collectively as the *Federalist Papers*. The *Federalist Papers* were designed to explain the value of strong central government and the need for majoritarian government. The papers attributed to James Madison, *Federalist no. 10*, which addressed the dangers of factional division and majority rule, and *Federalist no. 51*, in which he supported a system of separation of powers, have become classic representations of the arguments in favor of the new constitution.

Although there was no scientific analysis of the motivations behind the final vote in New York, historians view the *Federalist Papers* as critical in swaying public opinion in favor of ratification. On July 26, 1788, by a margin of 30–27, the delegates in New York ratified the Constitution. North Carolina, which previously had voted against ratification, waited till November of 1789 to lend its support, and Rhode Island, always the independent voice in this process, signed on only in May of 1790. By this time, George Washington had already been president for one year.

And so the difficult journey from independence to constitutional democracy came to an end. Instead of thirteen former colonies speaking to the world in thirteen different voices, the Constitution established the United States of America and created a governing system based in law and committed to democratic principles. The work of the Founding Fathers will forever be enshrined in our national psyche as brilliant lawmaking. To fashion a constitution that brought together disparate factions with contrary interests was an enormous achievement. Moreover, the fact that the delegates to the Philadelphia convention delivered a Constitution that was basically democratic in nature, at a time when the rest of the world was run by kings, queens, and despots, set the United States on the course of popular rule that today is the envy of the world.

Yet the work done in the summer of 1787 was only a beginning. The Constitution got this country going, but it left many unanswered questions and many unresolved disputes. Despite its greatness, the Constitution was not a document for all time or for all people. One critic of the Constitution, Thurgood Marshall, the first black Supreme Court justice, reminded Americans during the bicentennial celebration of the Constitution that in his view the work of the Founding Fathers in 1787 was "defective from the start, requiring several amendments, a civil war, and momentous social transformation to attain the system of constitutional government." Marshall's words serve to remind us all that the Constitution was not and is not a final governing document, but rather a means to an end.

What Is Actually in the Constitution?

The system of government that the Founding Fathers created and then promoted can best be described as a complex web of powers and restraints. The terms that are often associated with the structures and processes laid out in the Constitution, such as separation of powers, checks and balances, veto, advise and consent, and supremacy clause, suggest that governing the United States was purposely designed to be a competitive venture filled with obstacles and limitations. The Constitution provided its elected leaders with the means to run a country, but there would be no blank check to ramrod legislation through, assume emergency executive powers, use the courts as a mere legitimizing body, or control the destiny of the individual states. The governing system created by the Constitution rather requires solutions to public policy issues worked out gradually through compromise.

The Constitution is a very simple, straightforward, and short document. A brief preamble lays out the mission statement of the new government—"to form a more perfect Union, establish Justice, insure domestic Tranquillity, provide for the common defence, promote the general Welfare, and secure the Blessings of Liberty to ourselves and our Posterity." The Preamble, which begins with those memorable words "We the People," establishes the Constitution as a democratic document and separates the United States from the world powers of the time, whose governing goals were quite different from those of this new, upstart nation.

Unlike the constitutions of many other countries, the U.S. governing document is not loaded down with laundry lists of specific tasks or promises. The Constitution is not an exercise in problem solving or social engineering. Moreover, many of the powers and responsibilities listed in the Constitution raise immediate questions or beg for further explanation. Reading the seven operative articles could easily leave one with the feeling that the writers were either men of exceptional brevity or had consciously made a decision to create a governing system that would require further interpretation and application. As we shall see, the Founding Fathers were indeed from the no-nonsense school of writing, but more importantly they recognized that a constitution, in order to meet the test of time, had to be written in a way that allowed for flexibility and innovation.

Article 1, which defines the organization and powers of the legislative body, points clearly to the Founding Fathers' view that the two-house Congress would carry the main burden of governing the nation.

The most important part of Article 1 is Section 8, which identifies the powers of the Congress. From the most critical powers, the ability to levy and collect taxes and to declare war, to more mundane responsibilities such as coining money and establishing post offices, Section 8 is intended to send the message that the new Congress will be the focal point of governance. Furthermore, Section 8 ends with a phrase, often termed the "elastic clause," which expands the specific powers by stating that Congress has the power "to make all laws which shall be necessary and proper for carrying into execution the foregoing Powers."

Considering how visible and central the President is in modern day America, it is interesting to note that the Constitution writers were not eager to provide the chief executive with extensive powers and responsibilities. Article 2 makes clear that the President is in charge of foreign relations and that, with his title of commander in chief, he is the civilian head of the armed forces. But other than heading the executive branch (which in the early days of the country was quite small) and addressing Congress on the State of the Union, the President of the United States is a secondary figure in the tripartite governing system. Moreover, Section 4 of Article 2 on the Presidency makes the office even less formidable, or attractive, as the Constitution lays out the grounds for impeachment for treason, bribery, and high crimes and misdemeanors.

If the executive branch is given a reduced role in the affairs of state, the judicial branch is presented as a mere afterthought, suggesting that the Founders viewed the judiciary as the weakest of the three branches. Article 3 is even shorter than Article 2, and is more a discussion of judicial organization than judicial power and responsibility. Section 2 does provide a listing of what areas of judicial responsibility shall be given to the federal courts—all cases affecting federal officials, controversies in which the United States is a party, conflicts between two or more states, and disputes between citizens and states. The Supreme Court was seen by the Founders as primarily an appellate body, except in cases involving high public officials and states, in which it has original jurisdiction. It was to take the bold genius of the Supreme Court's third Chief Justice, John Marshall, to chart a more independent and expansive role for the judicial branch.

Although most of the attention of Constitutional interpreters has been on the first three articles, it is Articles 4 and 6, which describe the relationship between the central government and the states, that have been the most controversial. Article 4 presents the essential elements of federalism in the new United States of America. In general terms, federalism is defined as a system for organizing the relationship between the central governing authority and the local units of government. Federalism as practiced in the United States means that there is a power-sharing arrangement between the national government and the individual states, with some powers held exclusively by the national government, some powers held exclusively by the state governments, and some powers held concurrently.

Article 4 establishes what can best be described as "rules of sameness," establishing the manner in which citizens of one state are to be treated in the others. Citizens are to receive "full faith and credit" for all public acts, records, and judicial proceedings from all states. Citizens are to be granted all privileges and immunities in all the states, and no citizen can use one state as sanctuary in order to avoid facing prosecution in another. Even more important is Section 4, which establishes that the central government takes it upon itself to ensure a republican form of government to all the states, to protect the states from invasion, and to guarantee domestic tranquillity. This last responsibility has meant that the national government has the responsibility to use the military or its agents to enforce federal laws, court decisions, and executive orders.

The crux of the controversy between the federal government and the states, however, comes later on in the Constitution in Article 6, in which it is made explicit that the central authority is supreme. The supremacy clause in Article 6—"This Constitution and the Laws of the United States, which shall be made in pursuance thereof, and all Treaties made, or which shall be made, under the authority of United States, shall be the supreme law of the land"—has been the source of historic debates, decades of posturing, and an inevitable constitutional meltdown with the Civil War.

The ratification of the Constitution merely masked the ongoing dispute over how much autonomy state governments were going to be able to exercise and how aggressive the national government would be in advancing its central authority over the country. The supremacy clause is one of those constitutional statements that does not hedge or wander off into generality. It states that the federal government is supreme. This power grab by the federal government not only forced North against South but also initiated a never-ending debate between state capitals and Washington on issues ranging from the distribution of federal moneys to environmental regulations to the setting of speed limits on interstate highways.

While we are on the matter of change, the Constitution does address the issue of how to make changes, corrections, and additions to the document. Article 5 presents a number of ways in which amendments to the Constitution can be introduced and approved. The most frequently used method is to have a proposed amendment approved by a two-thirds vote in both houses of Congress and then have three-fourths of the state legislatures ratify the amendment. This method has been utilized in all but one of the twenty-seven amendments. The Twenty-first Amendment repealing Prohibition (the Eighteenth Amendment) started with a two-thirds vote in both houses of Congress but was then ratified by conventions in three-fourths of the states.

The Constitution has not been tampered with extensively since its ratification. The major revision occurred but a few years after ratification when ten amendments were added. The Anti-Federalist camp had complained from the beginning that the Constitution did not offer the American citizens sufficient personal freedoms in the form of guarantees of protection from the government. As a result the Bill of Rights was quickly added to the Constitution, in what most historians feel is the most important revision to the document in its existence. More on this later.

After the Bill of Rights, the remaining seventeen amendments are a mix, ranging from procedural adjustments, such as moving the inauguration from March to January and forbidding more than two presidential terms, to more substantive changes, such as freeing the slaves, giving women and eighteen year olds the right to vote, and authorizing Congress to lay a tax on income (clearly the most dreaded of the constitutional changes). Two amendments canceled each other out—one requiring prohibition (the Eighteenth) and one ending prohibition (the Twenty-first). The most recent amendment, the Twenty-seventh, which was ratified in 1992, actually had been held in suspension since 1789, when James Madison felt that members of Congress should not vote for their own salaries until an election had "intervened." The amendment initially got a chilly reception and was approved by only a handful of state legislatures. In 1982 a student in Texas came across the suspended amendment and worked tirelessly to have it ratified. Finally, after ten years, the Twenty-seventh Amendment was passed by the Michigan legislature, the thirty-eighth state to do so.

The fact that after over two hundred years the Constitution has undergone minimal change is a testament to the ability of the decision-making institutions it created to respond to political issues and crises without the need for promulgating a new governing document. Many observers feel that the strength of the Constitution is in its lack of attention to the details of government. When there is a particularly thorny issue with the potential for disagreement, the Constitution lapses into generality and vagueness. The assumption is that the government will define itself in relationship to the times.

The great American historian Henry Steele Commager once said that the Constitution was "the greatest monument to political science in literature." Commager, like many students of the Constitution, has strong feelings about this very short document. Average Americans, however, only have some vague idea of their basic law, mainly because they have never taken the time to read it. My conclusion is in the form of a simple request—take maybe an hour of your time and sit down and read the document that has had perhaps the most profound effect on your public life. The Constitution is no steamy novel, but it is the key that unlocks the door to understanding how we have come to be Americans.

How Has the Constitution Changed over the Years?

One of my early memories of studying the Constitution was a professor who made the distinction between the "Real Constitution" and the "Living Constitution." According to my professor, the real Constitution is the original document, untouched by legislative application,

Box 1.2 Key Language from the Constitution

Article 1, Section 1   All legislative power herein granted shall be vested in the Congress of the United States, which shall consist of a Senate and a House of Representatives.

Article 1, Section 2   No person shall be a Representative who shall not have attained to the age of twenty-five years and been seven years a citizen of the United States, and who shall not, when elected, be an inhabitant of the state in which he shall be chosen.

Article 1, Section 3   No person shall be a Senator who shall not have attained the age of thirty years, and been nine years a citizen of the United States, and who shall not, when elected, be an inhabitant of that state for which he shall be chosen.

Article 1, Section 8   The Congress shall have Power To lay and Collect Taxes, Duties, Imposts and Excises, to pay the Debts and provide for the common Defense and general Welfare of the United States; but all Duties, Imposts and Excises shall be uniform throughout the United States.

To borrow Money on the credit of the United States;
To regulate Commerce with foreign Nations, and among the several States, and with the Indian Tribes;
To establish an uniform Rule of Naturalization, and uniform Laws on the subject of Bankruptcies throughout the United States;
To coin Money, regulate the Value thereof, and of foreign Coin, and fix the Standard of Weights and Measures;
To provide for the Punishment of counterfeiting the Securities and current Coin of the United States;
To establish Post Offices and post Roads;
To promote the Progress of Science and useful Arts, by securing for limited Times to Authors and Inventors the exclusive Right to their respective Writings and Discoveries;
To constitute Tribunals inferior to the supreme Court;

(continues)

Box 1.2   (continued)

To define and punish Piracies and Felonies committed on the high
   Seas, and Offenses against the Law of Nations;
To declare War, grant Letters of Marque and Reprisal, and make
   rules concerning Captures on Land and Water;
To raise and support Armies, but no Appropriation of Money to
   that Use shall be for a longer Term than two Years;
To provide and maintain a Navy;
To make Rules for the Government and Regulation of the land
   and naval Forces;
To provide for calling forth the Militia to execute the Laws of the
   Union, suppress Insurrections and repel Invasions;
To provide for organizing, arming, and disciplining, the Militia,
   and for governing such Part of them as may be employed in the
   Service of the United States, reserving to the States respectively,
   the Appointment of the Officers, and the Authority of training
   the Militia according to the discipline prescribed by Congress;
To exercise exclusive Legislation in all Cases whatsoever, over
   such District (not exceeding ten Miles square) as may, by Ces-
   sion of Particular States, and the Acceptance of Congress, become the Seat of the Government of the United States, and to
   exercise like Authority over all Places purchased by the Consent of the Legislature of the State in which the Same shall be,
   for the Erection of Forts, Magazines, Arsenals, dock-Yards
   and other needful Buildings;–And
To make all Laws which shall be necessary and proper for carrying into Execution the foregoing Powers, and all other Powers
   vested by this Constitution in the Government of the United
   States, or in any Department or Officer thereof.

 Article 2, Section 2   The President shall be the Commander in Chief
of the Army and Navy of the United States and of the militia of the several states . . . ; he may require the opinion in writing of the principal
officer in each of the executive departments, . . . and he shall have the

(continues)

Box 1.2   *(continued)*

power to grant reprieves and pardons for offenses against the United States, except in case of impeachment.

He shall have the power, by and with the advice and consent of the Senate, to make Treaties, provided two-thirds of the Senators present concur and he shall nominate, and by and with the advanced consent of the Senate, shall appoint ambassadors, other public ministers and consuls, judges of the supreme Court and all other officers of the United States.

Article 2, Section 4   The President, Vice President and all civil officers of the United States, shall be removed from office on impeachment for, and conviction of treason, bribery, or other high crimes and misdemeanors.

Article 3, Section 1   The judicial power of the United States, shall be vested in one supreme court, and in such inferior courts as the Congress may from time to time ordain and establish.

Article 4, Section 2   The citizens of each state shall be entitled to all privileges and immunities of citizens in several states.

Article 6   The Constitution, and the laws of the United States which shall be made in pursuance thereof, and all treaties made, or which should be made, under the authority of the United States, shall be the supreme law of the land.

executive administration, and judicial interpretation. The living Constitution on the other hand is the flexible and durable system of governance based on a document that for two hundred years has been made "alive" by Congress, the President, and the Courts, in response to the ever changing character of American society.

Perhaps the most important step in the development of the Constitution was the addition of the Bill of Rights within the first years after ratification. The Constitution was woefully weak on personal rights and protections from government power, giving citizens some relatively minor concessions in terms of criminal procedures—the habeas corpus protection (citizens can expect that when charges are lodged against them, those charges will be publicly made in a court of law) and the prohibition of bills of attainder (no law can be passed to send a citizen to jail). Pressure mounted quickly to add amendments to the Constitution that would provide more substantive rights and protections for American citizens. The result was the Bill of Rights, the first ten amendments to the Constitution. Most of us take the Bill of Rights for granted, but it is without question the shining star of constitutional development.

The Bill of Rights can be separated into two areas, guarantees of personal liberty and guarantees of judicial protection. The First Amendment is often viewed as the centerpiece of the Bill of Rights because of its broad and undefined granting of freedoms of religion, speech, press, and assembly. With one short statement in Amendment One, the American people were granted a bonanza of rights that have allowed them to worship their own god, express themselves with almost complete freedom, gather and report news and opinion free of government censorship, and petition government, confident that public authorities will not interfere. Because of the importance of the First Amendment to our way of life, it may be helpful to see the exact words as written by the Founders: "Congress shall make no law respecting an establishment of religion, or prohibiting the free exercise thereof; or abridging the freedom of speech, or of the press; of the right of the people peaceably to assemble, and to petition the Government for a redress of grievances." Although the First Amendment clearly and concisely defines the basic personal rights of the American people, the interpretation of these rights has occupied much of the federal judiciary's time, as endless calls for applying the amendment to specific circumstances have been directed to the Court.

The Second Amendment grants another right, the right to bear arms. This right has also generated much controversy, since there is a qualifying phrase in the amendment suggesting that only the militia has the right to bear arms—"A well-regulated Militia being necessary to the security of the State, the right of the people to keep and bear arms shall not be infringed." Whether the authors of the amendment really meant to limit the right to bear arms to the militia has been the subject of vigorous debate. Nevertheless, the political tradition in the United States has been to view the right to bear arms as a personal liberty rather than part of the job description of the militia. As a result of the Second Amendment, we are a nation of gun owners, proud of this right and passionate about threats to infringe on it.

As for the remainder of the Bill of Rights, it is evident that the Founding Fathers, when pressed to incorporate rights into the Constitution, were suspicious of the police and the power of the judicial authorities to deny citizens a fair shake in the courts. As a result, the remaining amendments forbid the military from entering private citizens' homes, deny the police the right to search a citizen and seize his property without a warrant, require due process in criminal proceedings, ban double jeopardy and self-incrimination, guarantee a speedy trial by a jury of one's peers, and restrict excessive bail and punishment. To say that the Bill of Rights concentrates on providing alleged criminals with strong protections from government would not be an exaggeration. In many respects the First Amendment, despite its enormous implications for individual liberty, is overshadowed by the criminal rights contained in the remaining amendments.

It is interesting to note that once the Bill of Rights was added to the Constitution, it took some years for the power of these guarantees to have an impact on the way Americans lived and used the court system. In the early days of the Republic, the political elite was focused on a range of issues related to institutional power. The Bill of Rights was seen more as a concession and an afterthought rather than a goldmine of legal interpretation and application. Gradually, however, the Bill of Rights would begin to take center stage, as each of these rights was extended (the official term is incorporated) to the states through a series of Supreme Court decisions. Perhaps the most important case in the incorporation process was *Gitlow v. New York*, in which the Supreme Court in 1925 upheld the right of freedom of speech against a state government under the due process clause of the Fourteenth Amendment. By nationalizing the Bill of Rights and requiring states to be held to the same constitutional standards as the federal government, the Supreme Court transformed the Bill of Rights into a powerful tool for expanding individual liberties and strengthening protections against unwarranted government power.

But if the Bill of Rights took years to become established as a powerful tool of personal liberty and protection, the debate over where the supreme power lies in our government quickly occupied the agenda of presidents, members of Congress, and Supreme Court justices. In the growing dispute over who would have ultimate authority, Chief Justice John Marshall became a central figure. Almost from the onset of the new government, Marshall exerted the authority of the Court to define what the Constitution meant. In the most significant decision affecting court power, *Marbury v. Madison*, Marshall established the power of judicial review—the right of the Court to declare acts of Congress unconstitutional. The Supreme Court, by asserting its authority in the process of national policy-making, sent a message to the other two branches that it did not intend to play a minor role in guiding the governing system through its early years.

With its role established, the Court tackled a series of issues at the heart of government power. In *McCulloch v. Maryland*, in which the state of Maryland was locked in a dispute over taxing the national bank, Justice Marshall came down solidly on the side of the federal government, stating that the United States Congress, under its enumerated powers in the Constitution, had the right to establish a national bank and that the bank could not be subjected to taxes levied by a state government. The forcefulness of the language used by Marshall sent an early signal to the country that the national government had the authority to make national policy and that the states had limited authority.

Following upon the McCulloch decision, Justice Marshall tackled the issue of commerce and in particular the commerce clause in the Constitution. The issue this time was the right of the state of New York to grant an exclusive contract to a steamship owner on the Hudson River. The state of New Jersey also entered the fray with its own attempt at controlling the steamship business on the Hudson. In the *Gibbons v. Ogden* decision, Marshall found that Congress had the right to control interstate commerce and that New York could not claim the exclusive right to control commerce on the Hudson. Again, the national government came out the victor, and the states were sent a message that the powers granted the central government of a United States of America in the Constitution would be upheld by the Supreme Court.

As the central government asserted its power in financial and commercial concerns, another more serious issue was rising to the surface—slavery. Although slavery, its moral legitimacy, its economic necessity, and the possibility that it might spread as the country grew were powerful political issues, they also involved important constitutional issues dealing with individual rights and states' rights that cried out for resolution. In the highly controversial *Dred Scott* decision in 1857, the Supreme Court under Justice Roger Taney decided that Dred Scott, a slave who challenged his status as property, was not to be considered a citizen. Taney wrote that slaves "were never thought of or spoken of except as property" in the Constitution. The *Dred Scott* decision not only spoke in support of slavery but also in the process limited the ability of Congress to control the spread of slavery to the territories, a clear victory for states' rights.

The Court's siding with the states on the issue of slavery, making it possible for slavery to expand westward, is often considered one of the stimuli for the Civil War. Where the Marshall Court was able to interpret the Constitution as strengthening national authority, the Taney Court was reluctant to limit state power in the area of slavery.

In fact, on issues of race in the United States the interpretation of the Constitution by a series of Justices gave little hope to African Americans seeking relief from onerous discrimination after the Civil War. The so-called Civil Rights Cases in the late 1880s limited the ability of Congress to address discrimination in public accommodations. Later, in the landmark *Plessy v. Ferguson* case in 1892, the Court established the standard of "separate but equal" for facilities used by African Americans. In effect the Court stated that separate facilities for African Americans did not violate the equal protection clause of the Fourteenth Amendment. It was not until 1954, with the *Brown v. Board of Education of Topeka, Kansas* decision, in which the process of integrating public schools "with all deliberate speed" was mandated, that the Constitution became colorblind, and interpreters of constitutional language concentrated on equal citizenship rather than on states' rights.

Another area of importance that tells much about the living constitution is presidential power and the response to that power by the Congress and the Supreme Court. The United States has had its share of strong presidents who have tested the limits of the constitution. George Washington, for example, made a significant contribution to defining presidential power by putting down the Whiskey Rebellion in Pennsylvania, which was a challenge to the taxing authority of the federal government. Washington also moved quickly to assert the responsibility of the president in foreign relations by negotiating the Jay Treaty with Great Britain and establishing a policy of neutrality in the ongoing war between France and Great Britain.

Although there were aggressive presidents who followed Washington, few broke new ground in expanding the power of the office or redefining Article 2 of the Constitution. Thomas Jefferson is credited with establishing a critical role of the presidency in Congress, Andrew Jackson was the first president to exercise his veto power to thwart Congress, and Abraham Lincoln, faced with the threat posed by Southern secession, assumed emergency powers that stripped Americans of basic constitutional guarantees such as habeas corpus. Many of the presidents in post–Civil War United States were content to avoid confrontations with the other two branches of government or reluctant to initiate constitutional controversies that were designed to expand the powers of the chief executive.

It was not until Franklin Delano Roosevelt assumed office during the Depression that new ground was broken in defining the constitutional powers and responsibilities of the president. Roosevelt's New Deal program, which was a bold attempt to pull the country out of the economic doldrums, ran into immediate opposition from the Supreme Court. The Court, in a number of cases brought by states and businesses, struck down a series of Roosevelt's legislative acts as unconstitutional. The Court feared that Roosevelt had overstepped his power by infringing on the economic rights of the business community. Roosevelt felt strongly that as president he had the responsibility to use executive power to address a serious national crisis. Roosevelt was so infuriated by the use of judicial review by the Court that he tried unsuccessfully to increase the number of Justices from nine to fifteen. Although this attack on the Court ultimately failed,

Roosevelt had shown his willingness to use the power of his office to advance presidential authority.

The transformation of the constitutional definition of presidential power initiated by Franklin Roosevelt continued with his successors, but with mixed results. President Harry Truman's attempt to nationalize the steel industry during the Korean War was thwarted by the Supreme Court as an illegal use of presidential power. Lyndon Johnson, on the other hand, used his power as commander in chief to expand U.S. involvement in Vietnam without a congressional declaration of war. Johnson's successor, Richard Nixon, will go down in history as presiding over the greatest constitutional crisis in the country since the Civil War brought on by the Watergate scandal. By the time Nixon was forced out of office in 1973, the Supreme Court had demanded that the president release the transcripts of damaging White House tape recordings, Congress had initiated impeachment hearings, and the nation was engulfed in a daily barrage of media reports on abuse of presidential power.

The presidents who followed Nixon served in a new atmosphere of constitutional checks and balances. During the Ford and Carter presidencies, Congress sought to exercise more control over executive authority. The Reagan administration was quite successful in working with Congress on domestic policy, but the Iran-Contra scandal of the late 1980s, in which key White House aides broke laws and ignored Congressional restraints, again tested the limits of executive power under the Constitution. The Bush and Clinton presidencies have been involved in quite different constitutional controversies. In the case of Bush, the Panama invasion and the Persian Gulf War once more raised the issue of the warmaking powers of the president and the role of the Congress. In the case of Clinton, the Supreme Court's decision to permit the sexual harassment suit against the President by Paula Corbin Jones to proceed showed that a sitting chief executive is not above the law in civil suits. As the United States heads into the twenty-first century, the power relationship between the three branches of government appears to be settling into a period of balance, with no one branch exercising dominance and no clear signs of new power trends emerging.

The final area of constitutional development is in the broad field of personal rights. Although extending the Bill of Rights to the states began in the 1920s, it is in post–World War II America that issues of privacy and personal protection have taken center stage, with the drive to establish and then expand a woman's right to an abortion. Interpreting the Constitution as providing all citizens a right to privacy, the Supreme Court in a landmark decision in 1973 (*Roe v. Wade*) held that a woman had the right to an abortion during the first trimester of pregnancy. Since that decision, the Court has been the target of right-to-life advocates and constitutional strict-constructionists. The former abhor the new right, the latter see the Court as finding a right in the Constitution that is not there.

While applying this right of privacy to reproductive options and now also to homosexual relations has dominated the field of individual liberties, a number of other important legal battles have been fought around the proper interpretation of the First Amendment. Rarely does the Supreme Court finish a year of decisions without addressing issues related to defining how the freedoms of religion, speech, press, and assembly apply to specific situations and conditions in contemporary America. In the area of religious freedom, the Court has taken a consistently tolerant approach, protecting even what most would agree are fringe religions and religious practices. In the area of freedom of speech, the Court has recognized the dangers of unchecked speech when that threatens national security and domestic order, but has nevertheless supported the right of Americans to speak out and to express themselves. In the area of press freedom, the Court has been reluctant to limit the ability of newspapers, the electronic media, and now Internet providers to provide information to their customers free of government intervention or censorship. And finally, the Court has come down solidly on the side of the right of citizens to peaceably assemble and present their grievances to government, even if those citizens are advocates of racist, anti-government, or other extremist views.

Observers from outside the United States often ask why the United States has had only one constitution in its history? They marvel at the resiliency of the document and the ability of the governing system it instituted to weather crises, scandals, and threats to the political order. Much of the answer lies in the ability of the Constitution to remain alive, in the ability of the government it established to respond to new challenges without forcing the country to resort to wholesale reconstruction of the governing system. Of course the credit for keeping the Constitution alive goes not only to the political leaders and the institutions they head, but also to the American citizens who still revere this document and are wary of replacing it.

Box 1.3   Some Important Facts About the Bill of Rights

- Representative James Madison proposed a series of amendments to the Constitution. Madison introduced his proposed amendments in the House of Representatives in May, 1789. Originally twelve amendments were proposed.
- The Bill of Rights was ratified by the states on December 15, 1791, but the first two amendments were voted down. Failed Amendment One would have required that at least one representative be allocated in Congress for every 50,000 citizens. At that rate, Congress today would have 5,000 members. Failed Amendment Two would have required that no salary raise for members of Congress could take effect until after the next election of Congress. This proposal eventually became the Twenty-seventh Amendment.
- New Jersey was the first state to ratify the Bill of Rights, Virginia the last.
- The United States was the first country to have a formal, written bill of rights as part of its fundamental law.
- Public opinion polls consistently show that fewer than 50 percent of Americans can identify the Bill of Rights as the first ten amendments to the Constitution.
- For a time during the nineteenth century the federal copy of the Bill of Rights was in the basement of the State Department along with a sword owned by a Haitian emperor and six ancient Japanese swords. It later was moved to the National Archives.
- Of the fifteen original copies of the Bill of Rights, two were lost or destroyed. The only original copy on permanent display is in the National Archives.

Is the Constitution Democratic?

The direct answer to this question is maybe. Certainly the language of the Constitution with its "We the People" beginning suggests that the intent of our governing document was to create a political system, a democratic republic, that would firmly establish the involvement of the American people in the affairs of their new country. But closer inspection of the document and the content of the discussion of the delegates in Philadelphia raises a number of questions about the democratic character of the Constitution and the commitment of the political elite to implement a democratic governing system. For example, John Adams was quoted as saying in Philadelphia in 1787, "Democracy never lasts long. It soon wastes, exhausts, and murders itself. There never was a democracy yet that did not commit suicide."

The first visible sign that the authors of the Constitution writers were lukewarm in their commitment to democratic participation comes in Article 1, Section 2, which defines the relationship between representation and taxation. As stated earlier, one of the key stumbling blocks at the Constitutional Convention was the status and future of slavery in the new nation. At issue was how to count slaves for the purposes of state tax allotments for the national treasury. But beneath the debate over representation was the more serious issue of slavery and its acceptance within the United States. The constitution-makers decided that the total slave population would be divided by three-fifths; that number would then be used to determine state population and ultimately tax allocation. African Americans were not only denied citizenship (later to be changed with the Fourteenth and Sixteenth Amendments), they were viewed with such disregard that the political elite actually treated them as less than whole human beings in order to reach a compromise between Northern and Southern interests.

Following closely on the heels of the three-fifths resolution is the position taken by the Founding Fathers in Article 1, Section 3, which defines the composition and responsibilities of the Senate. Rather than have the Senators elected directly by the people in each state, the Constitution directs each state legislature to chose the two senators. Although the House of Representatives is clearly seen as being made up of members directly elected by the citizens from each state, the Founding Fathers viewed the Senate as an "upper body" that would serve as a brake on the potential excesses of the "lower body." The Senate, for example, was given the important duties of ratifying foreign treaties and approving executive and judicial appointments, two powers extremely critical for an emerging country beset with external threats and still feeling its way internally.

The case against a democratic constitution grows stronger when the manner in which the President is elected is presented in Article 2, Section 1. This segment of the Constitution describes what has come to be called the electoral college, a complicated and controversial device designed to ensure that the chief executive would not be directly elected by the American people. The electoral college, in its most simple terms, is a system of indirect election in which each state is assigned electors based on the number of representatives and senators. These electors, who were originally intended to be members of the elite political class, would be required to cast their votes for president one month after the popular vote was taken. As envisioned by the authors of the Constitution, the electoral college would be the final arbiter of presidential selection, with the electors' vote from each state being transported to Congress for the final tally and the final result. What happened on the first Tuesday after the first Monday in November every four years was viewed as of lesser importance than what happened in each state capital as the electors met to participate in the "real" election for president.

During the early years of the nation, the electoral college was indeed the locus of presidential selection. In many respects the electoral college made sense, since without modern means of communications and travel it was very difficult for the American citizenry to vote for a national candidate. But from the start the electoral college created a convoluted and flawed process of presidential selection that begged for reform.

One major problem was that delegates voted separately for the president and vice president, thus creating the possibility that the top two executives of the government would have different philosophies and perhaps even be personal enemies. The situation came to a head in the election of 1800, in which Thomas Jefferson and Aaron Burr received equal votes for president. As required by the Constitution, the House of Representatives was called in to settle the tie vote, in this case in favor of Thomas Jefferson. As might have been expected, Aaron Burr did not go on to become a functioning vice president. This problem inherent in the voting system of the electoral college was solved with the Twelfth Amendment, which created what is now known as a presidential ticket—the president and vice president run as one rather than separately, and the electoral votes are cast for this ticket.

Despite the indirect nature of presidential election, the people did participate in the selection of the electors, and a gradual movement away from defining the electoral college as an independent voice separate from the people did take place. In the election of 1792, nine states used a legislative appointment method for choosing electors. By 1824 only six of twenty-four states used legislative appointment, and by 1832 the United States was firmly abiding by a method of election in which the people voted for electors who were firmly committed to a particular presidential ticket. In spite of this democratization of the presidential selection process, however, the complicated nature of the electoral college continued to cause problems and call into question the commitment to popular rule in the United States. In 1876, Rutherford B. Hayes won the presidency when the House of Representatives decided in his favor, even though he had 250,000 fewer popular votes than his opponent. In 1888, Grover Cleveland lost to Benjamin Harrison, despite the fact that he had 100,000 more popular votes than Harrison. Harrison had won a majority of electoral votes. In both cases the will of the people was overridden because of the nature of electoral college procedures.

Today the electoral college is often viewed as an anachronism that stands in the way of direct election of the president. Choosing the president still comes down to how many electoral votes candidates receive (270 wins the prize), and whether a candidate can fashion a strategy in which he wins in as many states as possible. But at least it is now understood that the electors, who come to the state capital to vote one month after the general election, are representatives of the people and have an obligation to cast their ballot to reflect the popular will.

The establishment of the electoral college as a kind of aristocratic intermediary in presidential elections was not the only evidence of caution about democracy on the part of the Founding Fathers. Voting eligibility was left up to the state legislatures, and the leaders in these bodies were opposed to extending the franchise beyond white males with proven financial means, as evidenced by ownership of property and payment of taxes. It was not until the presidency of Andrew Jackson that eligibility to vote was extended to all white males. The passage of the Nineteenth Amendment in 1920, which granted women the right to vote, was a huge step forward in extending suffrage, achieved only after years of struggle by women's groups.

Although former slaves had been given the right to vote with the Fifteenth Amendment in 1870, segregationist policies, primarily in the South, limited voting opportunities for many African Americans. With the Twenty-fourth Amendment in 1964 outlawing the poll tax, the Voting Rights Act of 1965, and the forceful implementation policies of the Federal government in the years that followed, African Americans gradually became free of obstacles to casting their democratic ballot. The most recent extension of suffrage came in 1971 with the passage of the Twenty-sixth Amendment, which granted those from eighteen through twenty the right to vote.

Any consideration of how democratic the Constitution is must mention that very strange date for the presidential election. Think about it a second—why the first Tuesday after the first Monday in November to call the people to cast their ballot? The decision certainly had much to do with the end of the harvest season and the need to avoid interrupting commerce with a presidential election. But by placing the election in early November the Founding Fathers contributed to a lessening of interest in presidential selection simply because of the inconvenience of the date. In the early days of the Republic, the first Tuesday after the first Monday in November may have been a wise choice, but in the twentieth century this date has created a whole host of problems. First, there is the choice of Tuesday, a work day in the middle of the week when most adults are up to their eyeballs with the demands of office and home. Second, this time in November is usually the beginning of the cold and flu season. One pollster actually found out that as much as 7 percent of the electorate is sick on Election Day. Then there is the weather. Most elections in November are held when the prospects of cold, rain, and dampness are high. Asking people to leave the comfort of their homes to choose a president becomes a little more difficult when it's just plain lousy outside.

Many European democracies schedule elections in May or June or September, when the weather is better, and pick a date on a weekend or declare a national holiday. We, however, cling to that first Tuesday after the first Monday in November and are reaping the sad results of declining participation. Periodically there is talk of a constitutional amendment to move the election to a more attractive date, but such efforts go nowhere. Of course commitment to democratic participation should overcome all of these calendar and climatic restraints, but what started out as a response to agricultural and commercial needs has ended up as a constitutional limitation to popular involvement in the most important decision made by citizens in this country.

Because the Constitution is a living document that undergoes change in order to meet contemporary needs and concerns, the issue of whether our governing document is being interpreted and applied properly in order to enhance democratic participation is frequently addressed. For example, during the 1960s, as population shifts from urban to suburban neighborhoods were under way, there was great concern that state legislatures, which were responsible for settling the boundaries of voting districts, were apportioning those representative districts in an improper and undemocratic fashion. In a key Supreme Court decision in 1964, *Baker v. Carr*, the Justices stated that mal-appropriation of legislative seats violated the equal protection clause of the Fourteenth Amendment by denying proper representation in states with shifting populations.

The focus on representation in the 1990s has been on legislatively created districts that enhance the chances of minority candidates, particularly African Americans, winning election to the House of Representatives. After the 1990 census the state of North Carolina created a rather strange congressional district that connected a string of African American communities in an obvious attempt to ensure the election of a minority candidate to Congress. In 1993 the Supreme Court struck down the minority district approach as in

Box 1.4   What Is Pluralism?

The United States is defined as a federal republic, which simply means that the government is organized around a number of state entities and that democracy is representative in nature, but with popular participation. Although defining the United States as a federal republic is helpful, it says nothing about how our governing system works and how the people participate in governing. Over the years political scientists have used the term pluralism to better describe what kind of a democratic system we have in this federal republic of ours. Here are the essential elements of our pluralistic democracy.

1. Public decisionmaking is achieved primarily through elite interaction instead of popular participation.
2. The principal elites belong to both governmental institutions and private sector organizations. The general public often plays only a peripheral role in this interaction.
3. This elite interaction is fairly complex and fragmented with many governmental and private sector players. For the general public to play the game they must work through the government elites or form their own specialized group.
4. Because the playing field is complex and fragmented, the interaction requires that elites engage in bargaining and compromise in order to attain their policy objectives.
5. The elite players are forever changing, with new elites rising to the surface and challenging the established power holders. Elections are one way of changing the government elites, but the private sector elites change due to factors such as resources, reputation, leadership, and policy success.
6. The public policy decisions that are arrived at by government do not necessarily represent the majority will of the people. A powerful elite can attain its objective despite being a minority and fostering a minority position. Public policies that advance the common good or the people's needs are never assured under this system.

violation of the Voting Rights Act of 1965 because it denied the constitutional rights of white citizens. In 1995 the Court struck down a similar redistricting arrangement in Georgia. All in all seven minority-created districts were declared unconstitutional. Although minorities criticized the decision as weakening the prospects of African Americans and Hispanics being elected to Congress, the newly designed districts created in the wake of the Supreme Court decisions actually did continue to send members of minorities to Congress.

Is the Constitution a democratic document? Perhaps the answer is that over time the Constitution has become more democratic by expanding the base of participants and by ensuring that participation would be equitable and fair. What started out as a document that raised many democratic eyebrows with its restrictions and barriers to direct popular participation has evolved into an ever stronger foundation for popular involvement in the election of public officials. *Democracy* roughly translates from the Greek into "rule by the common people." After over two hundred years the Constitution today does indeed offer the common people the means through which they can participate in their government. Whether they choose to do so is another matter.

A Few Books You Should Read

Banning, Lance. *The Sacred Fire of Liberty: James Madison and the Founding of the American Republic*. Ithaca: Cornell University Press, 1995. A new approach to understanding the mindset of Madison and the formation of the Constitution.

Beard, Charles. *An Economic Interpretation of the Constitution of the United States*. New York: Macmillan, 1913. A classic but controversial examination of the Founding Fathers.

Becker, Carl. *The Declaration of Independence*. New York: Vintage, 1942. Still the premier account of this important document.

Bernstein, Richard. *Amending America: If We Love the Constitution So Much Why Do We Keep Trying to Change It?* New York: Time Publishing, 1993. A contemporary look at the politics and process of amending the Constitution.

Fleming, Thomas. *Liberty: The American Revolution*. New York: Viking, 1997. This volume, a companion to the popular PBS series of the same name, is a highly readable and thoroughly interesting account of pre- and post- revolutionary America. More than 200 illustrations add to the attractiveness of this book.

Madison, James, Alexander Hamilton and John Jay, *The Federalist*. Edited by Jacob E. Cooke. Middletown, Conn.: Wesleyan University Press, 1961. A must read for all Americans interested in the foundations of their government.

Storing, Herbert J. *What the Anti-Federalists Were For: The Political Thought of the Opponents of the Constitution*. Chicago: University of Chicago Press, 1981. An important contribution to the literature on the arguments against the Constitution.

Wood, Gordon. *The Creation of the American Republic*. Chapel Hill: University of North Carolina Press, 1969. Good background on the ideas that shaped the Constitution.

2

THE AMERICAN PEOPLE AND AMERICAN GOVERNMENT

... that government of the people, by the people, for the people, shall not perish from the earth.

— President Abraham Lincoln, Gettysburg Address

Who Are the American People—and What Are They Thinking About Politics?

Politics at its heart and soul is about people—people choosing their leaders, people demanding something of government, people trying to influence the direction of public policy. American politics is an especially dynamic people-oriented activity. There are countless avenues for connecting the people to their government, from public opinion polls to interest groups to campaigns for public office. In fact, the avenues for political participation in American politics seem to be growing at an enormous rate with recent developments such as local access cable television, electronic mail, and of course the Internet. Modern

37

communications and technology have changed the course of American politics by creating the opportunities for individualizing, if not customizing, participation in the process of public life. Where this stream of opportunities for political participation will end is anyone's guess.

But before getting into the ways in which Americans can participate in politics in the coming years, it is essential to define who these players are that will be shaping our democracy. Taking a quote from the baseball world, "you can't tell the players without a program." As a result this section will seek to describe the players in the American political drama. This is not an easy task or an exact science. America by definition is not only a nation of enormous diversity, it is also an ever changing nation with conditions and trends that rise to the surface and shift the direction of politics with little warning or explanation. Defining the players thus must be a snapshot, a temporary picture that tells a story at one specific time. So here is my snapshot of the American players who are the heart and soul of politics.

- As of 1998 there are 267 million Americans, up from 248 million in 1990.
- 134 million Americans are women, 128 million Americans are men.
- 115 million Americans are married, 30 million Americans are divorced or widowed. 71 percent of children under 18 live in two-parent families, 25 percent live in one-parent families.
- 73 percent of the 248 million are white, 12 percent are black and 10 percent are Hispanic, with the greatest increase occurring in the Hispanic population.
- There are currently 33 million Americans over 65; in the year 2010 there will be 40 million, and in 2030 there will be 70 million.
- 26 percent of Americans are below the age of 17.
- We remain a nation of immigrants, with almost 33 percent of our population growth attributed to immigration.
- 13.8 percent of Americans speak a language other than English at home.
- 61 million Americans are homeowners.
- 125 million Americans are employed.

- The fastest area of job creation is in white collar professional; the biggest decline is in agriculture.
- 75 percent of Americans live in urban areas.
- The fastest growing region in terms of population growth is the West; the slowest growing region is the Northeast.
- The number of Americans finishing a four year college has doubled to 24 percent in the last twenty years.
- Per capita income for Americans was $14,696 in 1995, nearly a $5,000 increase from 1970.
- The median household net worth (in real terms) has doubled to $48,887 since 1970.
- 65 percent of Americans are classified as middle class.
- 13.8 percent of Americans are living in poverty, an increase of almost 2 percent since 1970.
- In 1998 Americans worked till May 11th to pay off their federal, state, and local tax burden.
- An average American family's share of the $5.2 trillion national debt is nearly $80,000.
- The government spent an estimated $4,800 on each Medicare recipient in 1995; in the year 2002 that amount will rise to $8,400.
- The murder arrest rate for youths 10–17 has doubled since 1980.
- The number of Americans incarcerated in state and federal prisons has increased 200 percent since 1980.
- 31 percent of the children born in America are born out of wedlock, a 50 percent increase in the last twenty years.[1]

This brief statistical outline tells much about the key forces that are currently driving the political process in the United States—an aging population with its accompanying health and welfare needs, racial and ethnic tensions residing just below the surface of society, enormous prosperity amidst growing poverty, and disturbing societal problems,

---

[1]Sources: U.S. Census, U.S. Department of Commerce, U.S. Bureau of Labor Statistics.

particularly associated with the young. Because it is the political system that must ultimately deal with such dynamic forces, politicians are paying increased attention to the demographic, economic, and social time bombs that are ticking away. Politicians are looking at the retirement age of the baby boom generation to determine in what year the Social Security and Medicare systems will be most vulnerable to financial pressures. They are also debating how best to address the problems associated with the volatile mix of people who are changing the face of America.

Then there is the constant barrage of economic data that fills the airways with inflation rates, interest rates, tax rates, and mortgage rates, signaling whether we are becoming richer or poorer, more in debt and less secure or ultimately better off. What probably gets the most attention, however, are the data that tell us about the way our society is living on a day-to-day basis. Divorce rates, crime statistics, drug use figures, and teen pregnancy trends often paint a disturbing picture of how America is failing to cope with the demands of an increasingly complex and difficult society.

As America moves into the year 2000 and beyond, the political system and the politicians who shape that system will be forced to deal with some of the most confounding domestic problems that can face a nation. The question that immediately pops into mind as this demographic data runs across the page is whether the American people and the American government are ready and willing to face the challenges of the twenty-first century. Do we have the right stuff to respond to what we are and what we are likely to become?

To get to the heart of those questions we need also to develop a kind of political snapshot to go along with our demographic snapshot. We need to find out who we are as American citizens and what difference we are likely to make to the way our government responds to the challenges of the twenty-first century. In order to develop this political snapshot, a number of polls have been conducted over the years on American political culture. This data provides the basis for judging whether we have the right stuff as citizens to move forward with confidence into the next millennium. Here are some of the highlights from a 1996 survey of American political culture conducted by the Medias Res Educational Foundation:

- 80 percent of Americans stated that they "support our system of government," and 69 percent stated that "our system of government is the best possible system."
- 96 percent of Americans agreed that "with hard work and perseverance anyone can succeed in America."
- 91 percent of Americans describe themselves as "patriotic."
- 91 percent of Americans believe in providing equal opportunity to all.
- 90 percent of Americans believe strongly in civic responsibility.

But along with these encouraging responses come the following:

- 50 percent of the respondents felt that the United States is in a period of decline.
- 32 percent of the respondents expressed confidence in the federal government.
- 50 percent of the respondents stated that "they don't have much say about what the government does."
- 66 percent of the respondents stated that while the system of government is good, "the people running it are incompetent."
- 63 percent of the respondents felt that the federal government "controls too much of our daily lives."[2]

Although it is always difficult to take that giant leap from poll responses to generalizations, the above political snapshot of American citizens and their views toward government suggests that we continue to hold strong beliefs about our democratic system, but have grave doubts about how well that system functions today. Americans think that government doesn't work very well, that it is too intrusive in our lives, and that it doesn't listen to us. As a result, we do not have a large reservoir of faith that government will be able to tackle the

[2]Statistics taken from "The State of Disunion," 1996 Survey of American Political Culture, Medias Res Educational Foundation.

problems that beset us; in fact we think that government is likely to mess up those problems and even make them worse.

So what about the agenda for the twenty-first century? If meeting those challenges requires active citizens convinced that they can make a difference and confident that their government is in capable hands, then we may very well be in trouble. The premise that undergirds our system of politics is that the relationship between the American people and the government is critical for the health and welfare of our country. That premise is at this time going through a disturbing reevaluation. Americans, particularly the young, are growing increasingly disinterested in national politics and national politicians. What goes on in Washington, D.C., has attracted less and less interest in recent years. While the federal government still spends hundreds of billions of dollars and passes thousands of pieces of legislation and regulation each year, Washington and Washington politics has become an afterthought for most Americans. With the economy going strong, a foreign threat non-existent and people just sick and tired of the games played by politicians in our nation's capital, there is a distinct shift of attention away from national politics. Rather than getting agitated over the decisionmaking culture of Washington and the contentious partisanship of Washington politicians, Americans have begun to ignore what goes on at the federal level, expressing their disgust by making national politics increasingly irrelevant in their lives. An article in the *Washington Post* in 1997 described our nation's capital and the political establishment that resides there as "Dullsville": The real action is happening elsewhere.

This country is undergoing enormous change. The American people are far different from their predecessors—they are more wary of government, more suspicious of politicians, and more cynical about their chances of making politics work for them. Moreover, the needs of Americans are equally different—there is far less interest in national and global concerns and more focus on the human issues of everyday life such as family, job, and financial security. The political process and the political leaders who shape that process will be forced to make adjustments to respond to these new Americans and the new way that they look at America. The question is whether the political process and the politicians will make the adjustment to this new wave of change in a timely fashion before the interest and faith of the American people diminish even further.

Box 2.1   *How Well Do You Know Your Civics?*

Americans may love their country and believe in its vision, but they leave much to be desired when it comes to knowledge of government. Here is a ten-question exam that comes from the test given to those seeking U.S. citizenship. See how well you do.

1. What do the stripes of the flag mean?
2. Who elects the President of the United States?
3. How many changes or amendments are there to the Constitution?
4. For how long do we elect each U.S. Senator?
5. How many representatives are there in Congress?
6. What is the Bill of Rights?
7. Who becomes President of the United States if the President and the Vice President should die?
8. How many terms does a President serve?
9. Which President is called the "Father of our country"?
10. Who is commander in chief of the U.S. military?

Answers

1. They represent the original thirteen states.
2. The electoral college.
3. Twenty-seven.
4. Six years.
5. 435.
6. The first ten amendments of the Constitution.
7. The Speaker of the House of Representatives.
8. No more than two.
9. George Washington.
10. The president.

How Do I Know Whether I Am a Liberal or a Conservative?

We hear so much about liberals and conservatives that it is natural to ask ourselves who we are and what we are. Answers, unfortunately, are not easy to come by. The title of liberal or conservative has become lost in a kind of ideological war. The media, with its interest in short nuggets of information, and politicians, always anxious to cast an opponent in a negative light, have made liberalism, which supports government as the problem-solver of society, and conservatism, which supports less government involvement in societal problem-solving, simplistic labels. This is not very helpful to those Americans who are interested in political self-definition and serious about what political philosophies to embrace.

Labeling people is the easy way out, and yet we have succumbed to this practice. We do it most in politics. Rather than examining with precision what politicians say or do, we bunch them together and put a title to them. There is nothing inherently wrong with giving a politician a label, except that a label does not differentiate between politicians or take into account the subtle nuances of public policy positions. A label is the equivalent of one-stop shopping, promising to tell the voters all they need to know about their president, senator, or representative. It may not be fair or precise, but it is the American way.

As the discussion in the previous question indicated, Americans do believe in a basic creed of values, principles, and visions. But when it comes to defining specifically what we want from government and how we want our leaders to act on our behalf, we are shy or lost at sea. Americans are full of contradictions about their relationship with government. Americans don't like big government, and yet they keep demanding more from it; they are wary of governmental action but then scream to high heaven when a government program is cut; and they lambaste our institutions as slow and ineffective and then praise our Constitution for setting limits on our leaders. We are so conflicted about our relationship to government that the most popular label Americans are willing to admit to is that wishy-washy title of middle of the road. Americans love to be moderates and do not want to be cast as being left of center or right of center, just center of center.

But despite the problems we have in defining our political philosophies and the drawbacks to relying on glib labels, public opinion pollsters are forever trying to get a handle on where the American public fits into what is termed the political spectrum. Just as the light spectrum used to identify chemical compositions, Americans, whether they want to define themselves or not, are regularly placed on a range of ideology from far left (that is, in favor of more government intervention) to far right (that is, in favor of less government intervention). Every year questions are asked of sample Americans to find out whether they are liberal, conservative, or just plain middle of the road. The polls directed to defining America's ideological positions are one of our key measures for defining political behavior. A shift in one direction or the other on the political spectrum could signal a significant shift in philosophy and policy perspective in the country.

The most recent polling done by the Gallup organization on the liberal-moderate-conservative continuum show that for 1996 the breakdown is as follows—those identifying themselves as liberals, 17 percent; those identifying themselves as moderates, 45 percent; those identifying themselves as conservatives, 34 percent; those with no opinion, 4 percent. Comparing this data with that of 1990, the liberal point of view has declined from 20 percent to 17 percent, the moderate point of view has stayed steady at 45 percent, and the conservative position has increased from 28 percent to 34 percent. This shift toward the conservative point of view, which is generally associated with less taxes and regulation, more personal responsibility, and an accent on private solutions to public problems, matches the rise in Republican power in Congress and the general shift away from the liberal philosophy of big government.

Although there has been constant attention placed on the liberal-conservative dichotomy, some of the more recent research has concentrated on what those wishy-washy middle of the roaders are thinking. A recent book by sociologist Alan Wolfe entitled *One Nation, After All* seeks to find out what's on the mind of the so-called silent majority. What Wolfe found in his lengthy interviews with middle class Americans in Massachusetts, Georgia, Oklahoma, and California is that those Americans who are in the middle display a "mature patriotism." They exhibit considerable faith in government, albeit mixed with a healthy skepticism, and are willing to hear contrary and contending viewpoints. Moreover, they are opposed to the government trying to impose a specific vision on the country. But most of all the Americans Wolfe interviewed were pleased with their position in the middle. To quote the author, middle class Americans "believe themselves to be modest in their appetites, quiet in their beliefs, and restrained in their inclinations."

Although the liberal-conservative-moderate spectrum remains the most popular way of defining the political character of Americans, there are other ways to measure what Americans think about their political system. One way that is gaining increased interest is to compare what men and women are thinking. As a result of the 1996 election in which the female voter was critical in helping President Clinton carry the day (whereas a majority of men favored Republican challenger Bob Dole), there has been more focus on gender difference and what females want from their government in terms of public policy. Data from 1995 and 1996 show that women are inclined to support a range of domestic issues from abortion choice to affirmative action to programs that assist those on welfare. Men are more apt to be concerned with taxes, defense, and the overall strength of the economy. It would be simplistic and erroneous to suggest that there is a clear line of demarcation between women and men, but it is fair to state that women tend to believe that government should be a protector of those in need and are much more conscious of the barriers that exist to personal freedom and economic opportunity. Men, on the other hand, are more mistrustful of big government with its penchant for intervention and regulation.

As we try to explain this question of political philosophy and the American public, it is also important to talk about how we acquire our beliefs, attitudes, opinions, and prejudices. Our political philosophy and vision of government didn't just fall out of the sky, nor is it part of a complex DNA chain reaction. Rather what we are as political people is shaped through a process that political scientists call political socialization. Each of us evolves into a specific political person as a result of some key interventions starting in our youth.

The primary socialization agent is the family. What happens for the first eighteen or so years around the kitchen table or in the family room has a definite impact on what people believe about government and how they view politicians. A young person, in a family where mother and father vote regularly, are patriotic, participate in local or national politics, and see the value of government, is likely to be influenced by the thinking and behavior of their parents. On the other hand, if family life is marked by regular criticism of the government, apathy if not cynicism toward the political process, and constant complaints about elected officials, there is a good chance that a future mistrustful American is being produced. There of course is no guarantee that son and daughter will turn out to be the same as the parents, but the seeds of personal politics have been planted in the home, and as the old saying goes, "the acorn doesn't fall far from the tree."

After the family, the educational system has a profound effect on political socialization. Pledging allegiance to the flag, reciting the Preamble and the Gettysburg address, and learning about the great American political heroes are all designed to enhance support for the governing system. Teachers remain, after parents, the single most influential guides in a person's life. Teachers are in a powerful position to shape opinions and make impressions. Students first learn about American history and American government from teachers. Later on, in high school, teachers will likely discuss current events and inevitably put their personal views on the table. By the end of the twelfth grade a young man or woman will have been exposed to home and school socialization and be ready to make up their own minds about what approach to politics is right for them.

In the world of work and independence, political socialization is carried forward by interaction among friends, work colleagues, and neighbors. There is some truth to the observation that once young people get out of school and go into the work place they become more conservative, meaning that they see government as tax collector rather than benevolent protector, as intrusive regulator rather than patriotic symbol. This shift is certainly not universal, since circumstances can turn any individual into a proponent or critic of government, but it is one way the transition into adulthood can play a major role in shaping political philosophy.

Who you are politically can also be linked to factors such as race, ethnicity, religion and income. Growing up an African American is a very different experience from growing up white, particularly because of the legacy of discrimination and the powerlessness often felt by blacks. So too with many ethnic groups, especially those groups who are recent arrivals in this country, such as Asians and Latin Americans. The unique cultural heritage of these groups often influences the way in which they view the political world around them.

Then there is the religious influence. In the past the connection between religion and politics was close, as more Americans participated actively in their churches and synagogues. But with the increasing secularization of society and the downturn in church attendance, the impact of religion on political values has diminished somewhat. The big exception to this last statement is the significant influence of the Christian right on the political socialization of its members. The Christian Coalition, the loose umbrella group of the Christian right, has had a profound effect on the political values and political participation of its members.

Political socialization finally has a powerful set of tools in the world of television, the Internet, talk radio, and all the other elements that are part of our media-driven culture. American political views are constantly being shaped by what is shown on the evening news, what drive time radio says, what new Internet sites provide, and what movies, magazines, and pop heroes say or do about politics. The media may be slowly but surely replacing the home and the school as the key definers of political values and beliefs. Although media executives downplay the power of the tube, Americans spend over three hours a day watching television, and young people spend more, making it difficult to discount the influence of visual images on political points of view. For example, the nightly television footage of the Vietnam War and the protest on the homefront had a profound effect on people's attitudes toward the war and their government's handling of the war. Implementing the Vietnam policies of the Johnson and Nixon administrations was just that more difficult and contentious because of the constant barrage of television footage on the news.

What is most intriguing about political philosophy in the United States is that rather than choosing between supporting more government, more taxes, and more regulations and supporting less government, less taxes, and less regulation, many Americans choose a mix of both. Americans are fence-sitters, who reside in the center of the political spectrum and move oh so carefully to the left or to the right, based on their perception of whether the government is a help or a threat in any particular situation.

But being in the middle should not be disparaged as a cop-out. Because we are a people with a governing structure that requires us to cultivate the art of compromise and balance, it is natural that the predominant political philosophy and view of government should also reflect this condition of being in the middle. Aristotle, the great Greek political thinker, talked about the importance of government reflecting what he termed the "Golden Mean." What Aristotle preferred was a government that balanced democracy with aristocracy, a kind of middle of the road compromise that would create support and keep leaders from the extremes. Americans, it appears, may be Aristotelians without even knowing it, because even though some of us are liberals and some of us are conservatives, most of us are members of the silent majority, who sit in the middle and see equally the good and the not so good of government in our lives.

Box 2.2   *Are You Liberal or Conservative?*

You Might Be a Liberal If . . .

Franklin Delano Roosevelt is your hero.

You believe the Democratic party will best protect your health and welfare.

The Department of Education is your favorite government bureaucracy.

You can't stand tax loopholes and subsidies for big corporations.

Freedom of speech is the most important right you possess.

You believe Bill Clinton is a brilliant but flawed politician who is the victim of a Republican vendetta.

You see poverty and injustice as the key problems in this country.

(continues)

Box 2.2   *(continued)*

You are convinced that affirmative action is essential to achieve
   racial equality.
You value the importance of community and helping those who
   can't help themselves.
You are made uneasy by the enormous wealth in the hands of a
   few Americans.

You Might Be a Conservative If . . .

Ronald Reagan is your hero.
You believe the Republican Party will help you keep more of your
   money.
The Department of Defense is your favorite government bureau-
   cracy.
You can't stand the IRS.
The Right to Bear Arms is the most important right you possess.
You believe Bill Clinton is a slick liar who has brought disgrace to
   the Presidency.
You see high taxes and big government as the key problems in this
   country.
You embrace the principle of personal responsibility as the best
   means to achieve social equality.
You value individualism and private property rights.
You take pride in the accumulation of wealth as the American way.

Why Is There So Much Apathy and Cynicism About Politics in America?

One reason it is almost impossible to pinpoint why the American
public has soured on politics is that a negative attitude towards politics is nothing new. We have had frequent periods in our history
when the quality of politics was so poor that the citizenry turned
against the politicians and the political system. Usually the triggering

event that got the ire of the American public up had something to do with corruption. From Andrew Jackson's kitchen cabinet to U. S. Grant's corrupt entourage to the Teapot Dome scandal that rocked the Harding Administration, scandal in high office has been a recurrent theme, and has brought alienation in its wake.

As well as administrative scandals creating negative perceptions of government, there have been electoral scandals, such as the infamous Tilden-Hayes presidential race in 1876, a case study in vote fraud. One of the periods of greatest public cynicism was the era of the big city political machines, from Tammany Hall in New York to James Michael Curley in Boston to the Prendergast organization in Kansas City. An atmosphere of payoffs, corruption, nepotism, and bold-faced illegality in major cities convinced many that those in government were not public servants but self-serving criminals.

If one event has had a clear connection to the recent precipitous decline in support for politicians and the American political system, it is the Watergate scandal during the Nixon presidency in the 1970s. The investigation of the break-in at the Democratic National Committee headquarters in 1972 by men hired by the Committee to Reelect the President (CREEP) eventually reached the White House. The ensuing attempts by President Nixon to cover up his complicity in the break-in led to a nearly two-year constitutional crisis, which included the famous Watergate hearings, the initiation of impeachment proceedings in the House of Representatives, and the eventual resignation of the President, the first such occurrence in our history. As President Nixon left office with a bare 24 percent approval rating in the public opinion polls, the levels of trust in government and confidence in our governing institutions began to nosedive. Public trust of the government, for example, dropped 28 percent from 1972 to 1980, and confidence in Congress dropped to 13 percent during the same period. Despite the fact that Watergate was about one president and his administration, the damage from this scandal reached to the very core of popular beliefs about government.

Although popular opinion about government rebounded somewhat during the Reagan years, the Iran-Contra scandal at the end of the Reagan presidency sent the numbers on trust and confidence plummeting again. During the Bush and Clinton presidencies the

American public was erratic in their attitudes toward political leaders and government in general. The Clinton presidency, in particular, saw a combination of popular criticism of the president's personal life with general support for his presidency.

But the key to understanding the attitudes of Americans toward their government in the 1990s is not so much an analysis of their reactions to individual presidents as an understanding of the political malaise that has gripped American society. The American people have been more than just unwilling to give their trust to their leaders or to express confidence in their institutions; they have been out and out apathetic about participating in the political process and thoroughly cynical about their ability to change the system for the better. The American public has just not been interested in listening to their political leaders, and many have openly sneered at the democratic process and the possibilities for reform. Perhaps another word needs to be added to the title of this book, changing it from *Angry, Bored, and Confused* to *Angry, Bored, Confused, and Disinterested*.

This shift of attention away from politics is best seen in a recent Pew Research Center study which asked Americans whether they pay "very close" or "fairly close" attention to policy issues on the national scene such as health care, gun control, and congressional budget battles. In 1994 the number of Americans who answered that they paid "very close" or "fairly close" attention was 68 percent. In 1996 the response to the same question dropped to 51 percent. Add to this the woefully low number of Americans who do not have a clue about who their national leaders are in the three branches of government, and the only conclusion that can be reached is that the American people have turned their attention elsewhere.

Of course Americans have not shut their eyes to the problems that surround them. They still know that there is a crime problem, a drug problem, a welfare problem, and an environmental problem, but they are convinced that pleading with Washington for assistance on these problems is not going to do the trick. More and more Americans are coming to the view that if this country is going to be saved from itself it will be done house by house, block by block, town by town, and not because the federal government develops a new multi-billion dollar program with reams of implementation regulations.

Perhaps the best evidence of this anti-Washington shift is that since the mid-1980s over 160 members of Congress have left voluntarily to head back home to teach or practice law or enter the business world. Many of those legislators left the contentious culture of Washington to enter the real world beyond the Beltway. Most have little regret about their decision. Most have made significant contributions to their state or community. Former U.S. Senator from Illinois Paul Simon, who now heads a public policy center at the Southern Illinois University, has bemoaned the lack of interest on the part of his students in politics, but admitted that national politics is "a tougher sell now than it has been in some time. . . . The public rightly senses that too often we're playing political games."

But even though the shift in interest from a national perspective to a state and local one is happening, that does not automatically translate into a burning desire on the part of most Americans to pitch right in and solve those pressing home-based problems. There are certainly countless examples of citizens, either individually or in organized groups, addressing a local problem, but the norm in America in the 1990s is that most citizens are so overwhelmed by work and family issues that they cannot find time to get involved in their community. Moreover, Americans are increasingly so focused on other areas of our culture, whether sports, entertainment, technology, that they have little interest in public affairs. Politics just doesn't capture the interest of Americans like pro football, and politicians cannot compete effectively with the like of Michael Jordan or Michael Jackson.

So how did we get this way? In no real order of importance, here are the factors that have contributed to this sad state of affairs:

Negative Campaigning

Politicians running for election or reelection bought into the strategy that tearing down their opponent by playing to the prejudices and fears of the voters was the best way to win. Campaign consultants, always anxious to earn their keep by trying out new means of assuring victory, fashioned these negative campaign tactics and promoted them as a surefire ticket to victory. Television ads became the vehicles for these mudslinging campaigns. Dire statements criticizing the opposition filled the airwaves, pushing out issue spots designed to educate the public. After a few years of this stuff, most voters have become sick and tired of the sleazy barrage and demand a change, but in the meantime, negative campaigning has turned off a new group of citizens to politics. But unfortunately, politicians have been convinced that negative campaigning works, and so it continues. The 1998 congressional campaigns were chock full of negativity.

Money and Politics

The cost of statewide and national campaigns grew exponentially during the 1990s. Politicians seeking to stay in the race turned into money hustlers as they begged and groveled to get donors to raise their contributions. Democrats and Republicans were equally guilty of this begging and groveling and were unwilling to take steps that would make it unnecessary. Agreements to either move to some sort of public financing of elections or to accept a lower threshold of giving from individuals, corporations, and special interests were put on the backburner. For example, between January 1, 1997, and October 14, 1998, the Republicans and Democrats raised $292 million, another record. When Americans see that politicians are talking about reform while they still have their hands out, another nail is driven in the coffin of political participation.

Conspiracy Theories and Sex Scandals

Strangely, the '90s may be remembered as a time when our system was weakened by questions such as who shot JFK and whether Bill Clinton lied about having sex with Monica Lewinsky. American politics too often wandered from a serious discussion of the issues to a carnival sideshow, as tabloid magazines and sensational television programs captivated the country with conspiracy theories about secret government operations—the X-Filing of America—and the seedy sex exploits of public figures—Americans fighting over who would get to read the tawdry Starr report first. Even the mainstream press and media could not avoid taking this new road of shock journalism as they spent precious print space and air time recounting or rebutting charges of conspiracies and sexual misdeeds. With nearly daily doses of this stuff, Americans seemed still anxious for more, and in the process their attention turned away from what really mattered to them.

The Mishandling of the Militia Movement

In 1995, when the FBI and the Alcohol, Tobacco and Firearms (ATF) agents destroyed the compound of the followers of David Koresh in Waco, Texas, the American public came to see the oppressive side of the United States government. Although Koresh and his followers had clearly broken a number of federal gun laws, the sight of the burning buildings with children inside and the eventual death of over eighty people was enough to send the militia movement into the forefront of public consciousness. Although the militia movement has never been more than a fringe aspect of American politics, the American public, after Waco, began to express more and more doubts about the power and intrusiveness of their government. Heightened interest in and sympathy for the militia movement ended in Oklahoma City with the destruction of the Murrah Federal Building and the death of 167 Americans. Nevertheless, while Americans abhorred the terrorist act of Timothy McVeigh, they kept lingering doubts about their own government and its ability to do the wrong thing.

The Dark Side of the Evening News

Some of the more popular segments on the evening news these days are clones of NBC's long-running "The Fleecing of America." Networks love to show the viewing public how incompetent, corrupt, and wasteful the government is. Investigative reporters are sent out into the field to find examples of governmental malfeasance, and then they play up their findings on the nightly news to millions of Americans. Although the networks have every right to inform Americans when their government is abusing their public trust, they also have a responsibility to show when government is working. True, networks are beginning to air segments on solutions to problems, many times holding government up as the main problem solver. But this shift comes after years of going out of their way to find every possible bit of evidence of bad government, while neglecting the overwhelming good that government does every day. No wonder people think government is lousy.

More of the Same, More of the Same

Americans frequently say that they are turned off by government because the way politicians work is just so aggravating. The constant charges and countercharges of ambitious politicians, the failure of Democrats and Republicans to work together, the half-truths of Representatives and Senators designed to embarrass the other side, the countless examples of Congress doing nothing rather than doing something—all these have taken their toll on the body politic. Americans are certainly patient and reasonable people, but they know from their own experience at home and at work that their world is far removed from the governing culture. Their world is usually one in which people make sacrifices, pitch in and give a helping hand, work for the good of the company or the community, and treat others with dignity and respect. When the world of the average American meets up with the world of Washington, D.C., there is a gap as wide as the beltway surrounding our nation's capital. And when average Americans ask for a little civility and cooperation in government, their government gives them the same old Washington culture of conflict and partisanship.

Fortunately, amidst all this apathy and cynicism, there are some hopeful signs. The level of support for governing institutions and public officials is no longer mired in the basement. Public trust in government is moving ever so slowly up from the netherworld, but it is going up. And Americans are willing to admit that certain agencies of government are doing a good job (the IRS remains a pariah, but at least NASA gets high ratings). Insiders state that these upticks in pro-government opinion are the results of a vibrant economy, a view that makes sense. It is also important to stress that government's standing was so low, that the chances for some form of revival were high.

Certainly these promising developments, should not be interpreted as the beginning of a return to the days before Watergate, when

Americans were willing to give government and government officials the benefit of the doubt. Building back trust and confidence may take another generation of good government and good leadership, before the legacy of Watergate and the participation catastrophe that followed is overcome. This rise in pro-government opinion may turn out to be a blip when the economy sours and people begin to blame government for their problems.

How Do Americans Participate in Politics?

The United States is a country that prides itself on options—thirty-one varieties of ice cream, AM talk vs. FM rock; megamalls with three hundred stores and of course the ultimate option, five hundred cable channels. The consumer society that we live in is a breeding ground for endless opportunities to make money and feed our individual thirst for difference. Although politics is strictly speaking not a commodity that can be neatly packaged and sold on the open market, there is nonetheless a consumer-like quality to this public activity. We live at a time when the range of options available in the political arena is expanding dramatically. Voting certainly remains a critical expression of participation and a key gauge of citizen opinion. But it is important to stress that there is an ever widening range of options available to Americans who are interested in politics and seek involvement in the political process.

There are, of course, the traditional options for political participation that most of us are familiar with. There is the couch potato brand of participation which includes reading *Time Magazine* and yelling at the evening news, and the more sophisticated and time-consuming brand of participation which includes joining an interest group or a political party and working on an electoral campaign. For the adventurous participant there remains the ultimate option—running for public office (an option that is increasingly being shunned like the plague). For the rebel participant there is the '60s style demonstration, sign and all, with the added possibility of being handcuffed and fingerprinted and doing jail time for the cause. For most of us, however, participation means occasionally complaining about government and maybe going down to the town hall every two or four years and marking an X next to someone's name who's running for public office.

But remember this is the '90s, the go-go decade, where ideas are flying by at a mile a minute and new ways to link up with the political arena are beginning to crowd out the traditional options for participation. Many of the new participation options are associated with the technological revolution. Whereas participation in the past meant getting off the couch and actually doing something political, the computer and the cable wire have offered citizens a new brand of involvement with the political scene. This new style of participation might best be called "passive engagement." Citizens can now sit in the privacy of their own home with a mouse or a clicker and have the world of politics open up in front of their eyes. Internet homepages about politics and government abound, opportunities to e-mail members of Congress, the White House, and the bureaucracy are exploding at a dizzying pace, and live coverage of congressional hearings, interviews with government officials, and debates over controversial issues are ready for viewing twenty-four hours a day. There is just no excuse for pleading ignorance about public affairs, and no reason to criticize government for not offering opportunities to hear complaints.

Nevertheless, computer and cable participation remains passive engagement,—mere cyberspace involvement that remains impersonal. Americans may e-mail their representative or follow closely on television the Senate debate on a major piece of legislation, but that is a long way from attending a meeting to protect wetlands or licking envelopes for a candidate. Technological advances have made it so that we can participate without really participating. Cable television broadcasts local town meetings, computers conduct public opinion polls, and there is even talk that in the future citizens will be offered the option of voting from the comfort of their couch on not just who will occupy the White House, but key public policy issues. We may be headed for a time when participation is conducted from the comfort and the safety of our home bunker.

While passive engagement is becoming an increasingly popular form of political participation, the traditional options of arguing, joining, running, and demonstrating are all in varying states of decline. In particular, the joining part of participation has become the center of a debate on the state of political involvement in America. Robert Putnam, a Harvard political scientist, took the position in 1996 that the United States was in the grips of what he termed the "bowling alone" syndrome. By "bowling alone" Putnam meant that Americans were losing their interest in joining civic associations and choosing to become unconnected to the community they live in. This bunker mentality could, in the view of Putnam, eventually lead to a weakening of the social and political ties that hold our society together. By bowling alone, America was becoming a nation of nonparticipants, with little interest in working with others to improve their institutions, their community, and ultimately their own lives.

The publishing of the "bowling alone" thesis unleashed a flood of analysis and criticism from other experts on participation. The main criticism of "bowling alone" was that while so-called traditional civic associations, such as the PTA, the Girl Scouts, the Veterans of Foreign Wars, and bowling leagues, had seen a decline in membership, other organizations, such as soccer clubs, hobby groups, and self-help associations, had seen a substantial increase in their membership. Rather than showing a decline in civic associations, "bowling alone," according to its critics, failed to look at the new ways of participating and the new civic associations.

So are we participants or bunker-based couch potatoes? Although this debate on participation continues, there are some numbers out there in America that may bolster the view of a regeneration of involvement. Granted the numbers aren't overwhelming and are still scattered, but they at least do point to a new climate of civic participation. Here are a few examples of what may be a renewal of American participation in civic life:

- There is a distinct trend in America towards community organization and action. Grass-roots citizens groups, crime patrols, youth athletic associations, and non-profit foundations are being formed on a daily basis. While Americans may have soured on national politics, they are increasingly committed toward improving conditions in their home town.
- Talk radio has become a powerful voice for Americans. Over 1,000 talk shows are now on the air offering Americans

an opportunity to speak their mind. The Rush Limbaugh show alone has over 20 million listeners daily. Listeners who frequent these shows often use the airwaves to initiate grass roots campaigns that would not see the light of day using the traditional political processes.

- Volunteering is starting to make a comeback, with a steady increase in the number of Americans giving something back to the community, whether as literacy teachers, home builders, big brothers and big sisters, pro bono legal advocates, or community fund-raisers. President Bush's Thousand Points of Light program and President Clinton's National Service Proposal have increased interest in helping others. A recent international poll found that the United States had the highest rate of volunteerism in the industrial world. There is not yet a groundswell of support for volunteering, but the numbers are encouraging.

- Although male participation in national elections is down, female participation is on the increase. In fact, female support for President Clinton in 1996 was considered crucial to his victory. Also more and more women are running for public office with considerable success. There are now fifty-eight females in the United States Congress, up from seventeen in 1970.

- The use of the initiative and referendum remains a popular means of bypassing the traditional governmental institutions and providing the people with a voice in their political system, despite the fact that minorities face serious disadvantages when referendums are initiated. Although California leads the way in the use of these forms of direct democracy, many other states make important policy decisions based on the results of initiatives and referendums. This trend is expected to continue.

These examples of citizen participation don't receive as much attention as the numbers on declining voting turnout and confidence levels, but they do suggest that the American people are in the process of sorting out their role in the political process. There is a definite shift in this country towards participation in smaller groups with smaller objectives. There is also a shift in this country away from following the traditional path of participation—voting, calling up a congressman, demonstrating with a sign, joining an interest group or a political party. Today the problems of this country are being addressed at the state and even more commonly the local level, with government often bypassed because it is viewed as an obstacle to the solution. This of course is highly unusual in a nation that takes pride in its governing institutions and its democratic politics. But it is important to stress that much of this new brand of citizen involvement is political, and is aimed at improving the public life of American communities.

Box 2.3 Is the United States a Great Democracy?

How many times have you heard a politician say that the United States is "The World's Greatest Democracy?" Although this claim is usually greeted with a lot of nodding heads, the available data point to another conclusion. Let's take a look at what kind of democracy we are when we compare our performance with the rest of the world.

- In 1990 the United States ranked 139 out of 163 democracies in terms of turnout for national legislative elections.
- Out of twenty-one industrial democracies, the United States ranked second to last in overall turnout for national elections. Switzerland was last.
- The United States leads industrial democracies in terms of citizen willingness to sign a petition, write their legislators, and join an interest group.
- The United States leads the industrial democracies, and the less developed countries as well, in terms of citizen satisfaction with democracy—64 percent of Americans are satisfied, 27 percent are dissatisfied.
- Only 28 percent of Americans can name their congressman and 11 percent have no idea who the vice president is, responses that cause citizens in Europe and other advanced countries to express disbelief.

(continues)

Box 2.3   (continued)

If democracy means going to the local town hall and casting a ballot, then we are not the "world's greatest democracy." But if we mean by democracy, a willingness to get involved, a propensity to make our opinions known, and an appreciation of democratic values, then we certainly are at least in the category of near great. Supporters of the claim of greatness state that democracy means more than voting. Critics of our dismal level of ballot box participation say that our failure to vote is a national disgrace. Is the United States a great democracy? You be the judge.

SOURCE: International Social Justice Project

What Is the Outlook for Participation in the Future?

The answer may lie in examining the next generation of Americans and the numbers that are associated with them. Such an examination unfortunately reveals a frightening lack of interest in politics and public affairs on the part of young people. A poll commissioned by the *Christian Science Monitor* found that the vast majority of college students in the Class of 1998 viewed politics as "boring." Other studies show that America's young people are not only disinterested in politics, they are resigned to a kind of political impotence—they believe that they cannot make a difference. Along the same lines, many surveys of college students have found that this new generation has little sense of civic duty and little hope that politics will change in some way that might stimulate their future involvement.

Although there is no one clear cause of this massive youth turnoff to politics, studies such as the one done by the Harwood Group for the Kettering Foundation in the early 1990s found that young people between the ages of eighteen and thirty are products of the entitlement generation who view government as a source of benefits, rather than a place where citizens act out their civic responsibilities for the greater good. The study also found that scant political education goes on in the secondary schools and colleges that might help young people to appreciate the unique character of their political system. Finally, the youth of America have been brought up in a culture of individualism, in which concepts such as civic duty and popular participation for the common good have been overshadowed by the constant cry of "what's in it for me." As a result, this cohort of young Americans has been dubbed by one observer the "watcher generation," standing on the sidelines, waiting to see what happens in politics, but not terribly willing to get involved.

From my own experience as a college instructor it has become clear that the members of generation X feel a sense of helplessness about their ability to work in the world of politics and bring about constructive solutions to a range of problems. Moreover, they harbor some animosity toward previous generations, especially the post–World War II baby boom generation. Xers feel Baby Boomers are responsible for many of the ills that beset modern society. They are not impressed with the idealism of their predecessors, with the Civil Rights marches, the Vietnam War protests, and the feminist movement. They feel that these activities have little to do with the problems they face today. When asked what they are going to do about solving the problems that do affect them, these watchers quickly slip into blank stares and shrugs, promising that they will do something, but not necessarily right away. They have, after all, careers to build and money to make.

What the views of the "watcher generation" and a disturbing number of Americans from earlier generations mean for the future of American politics and American democracy is not encouraging. If the future voters, interest group members, party leaders, campaign workers, and members of Congress have been brought up to be against politics or worse yet to see politics as irrelevant for their lives, then there certainly is cause for concern. America in the twenty-first century may well be a place where public affairs and public solutions stir up little interest.

There are some serious institutional consequences of this growing irrelevancy of politics. If the diminution of politics and political participation is indeed on the horizon, then certain results follow close behind. The growing power of special interest groups, while political parties decline, is one of those consequences. Historically political parties were mass-based institutions open to a wide spectrum of citizens. They were organized from the grass roots upward and afforded many citizens an opportunity to choose candidates and define public policy positions. Today, however, American politics is dominated by a complex collage of special interest groups that participate in a feeding frenzy to get their cut of the public pie, often times at the expense of other groups and more importantly the common good. Interest groups remain a valuable part of our democratic experience, but increasingly groups represent ever narrower segments of American society and are headed by leadership teams that are beholden to a board of directors and not to the nation as a whole.

Another disturbing consequence is that key public decisions will likely be placed in the hands of a smaller and smaller bureaucratic elite. When the people freely give up their right to participate and influence the direction of government policymaking, there is a natural vacuum that begs to be filled. What usually fills that vacuum are the bureaucrats, appointed or career civil servants, who take on the burden of making government run, but do so with little accountability or popular input. Already in most industrial democracies the bureaucratic elite, the technocrats as the Europeans call them, have pushed aside the elected segment of the government and now make the key decisions about public policy and national direction. Under this model efficiency and specialization replace the uncertainties associated with democratic politics. What is more distressing is that there don't appear to be that many complaints about government run by the bureaucrats rather than by the politicians.

This kind of neo-Orwellian version of American democracy in the coming millennium may merely be an exercise in unwarranted pessimism. Each generation of participants in this country usually finds its own way of making democracy work. The future of participation may be more technological than personal, more informal than institutional, but if it is participation geared toward strengthening the country and improving the lives of the citizenry, then it is participation well spent. But if it is participation by a limited number of players that leads to catering to special interests, then it will be a disturbing form of democracy. We'll just have to wait and see what the watcher generation does about making this democracy work for the common good.

Box 2.4   John F. Kennedy on Politics as a Profession

The selection is from a speech delivered by John F. Kennedy at Syracuse University on June 3, 1957. It presents a powerful argument for the life of politics and public service.

The high regard in which your education at Syracuse is held is evidenced by the intensive competition which rages between those hoping to benefit from it. Your campus is visited by prospective employers ranging from corporation vice-presidents to professional football coaches. Great newspaper advertisements offer inducements to chemists, engineers, and electronic specialists. High public officials plead for more college graduates to follow scientific pursuits. And many of you will be particularly persuaded by the urgent summons to duty and travel which comes from your local draft board.

But in the midst of all these pleas, plans, and pressures, few, I dare say, if any, will be urging upon you a career in the field of politics. Some will point out the advantages of civil service positions. Others will talk in high terms of public service, or statesmanship, or community leadership. But few, if any, will urge you to become politicians.

Mothers may still want their favorite sons to grow up to be President, but, according to a famous Gallup poll of some years ago, they do not want them to become politicians in the process. They may be statesmen, they may be leaders of their community, they may be distinguished lawmakers—but they must never be politicians. Successful politicians, according to Walter Lippmann, are "insecure and intimidated men," who "advance politically only as they placate, appease, bribe, seduce, bamboozle, or otherwise manage to manipulate" the views and votes of the people who elect them. It was considered a great joke years ago when the humorist Artemas Ward declared: "I am not a politician, and my other habits are good also." And, in more recent times, even the President of the United States, when asked at a news conference early in his first term how he liked "the game of politics," replied with a frown that his questioner was using a derogatory phrase. Being President, he said, is a "very

(continues)

Box 2.4   (continued)

fascinating experience, . . . but the word 'politics,' . . . I have no great liking for that."

Politics, in short, has become one of our most neglected, our most abused and our most ignored professions. It ranks low on the occupational list of a large share of the population; and its chief practitioners are rarely well or favorably known. No education, except finding your way around a smoke-filled room, is considered necessary for political success. "Don't teach my boy poetry," a mother recently wrote the headmaster of Eton; "Don't teach my boy poetry, he's going to stand for parliament." The worlds of politics and scholarship have indeed drifted apart.

I would urge therefore that each of you, regardless of your chosen occupation, consider entering the field of politics at some stage in your career. It is not necessary that you be famous, that you effect radical changes in the government or that you be acclaimed by the public for your efforts. It is not even necessary that you be successful. I ask only that you offer to the political arena, and to the critical problems of our society which are decided therein, the benefit of the talents which society has helped to develop in you. I ask you to decide, as Goethe put it, whether you will be an anvil—or a hammer. The formal phases of the "anvil" state are now completed for many of you, though hopefully you will continue to absorb still more in the years ahead. The question now is whether you are to be a hammer—whether you are to give to the world in which you were reared and educated the broadest possible benefits of that education.

A Few Books You Should Read

Delli Carpini, Michael X., and Scott Keeter. *What Americans Know About Politics and Why It Matters*. New Haven: Yale University Press, 1996. A contemporary look at the key issue of political knowledge, in particular the lack of political knowledge in America.

Dionne, E. J. *Why Americans Hate Politics*. New York: Simon and Schuster, 1991. A detailed account of why Americans are turned off by politics and politicians. Written by one of America's most gifted observers of the political arena.

Elshstain, Jean Bethke. *Democracy on Trial*. New York: Basic Books, 1995. A serious examination of the current state of American democracy, its strengths and weaknesses.

Greider, William. *Who Will Tell the People?* New York: Simon and Schuster, 1992. A devastating account of the ills and evils of American politics. Not for the fainthearted.

Grossman, Lawrence K. *The Electronic Republic: Reshaping Democracy in the Information Age.* New York: Viking Press, 1995. An important discussion of the impact that technology is having on the American political process.

Rimmerman, Craig A. *The New Citizenship.* Boulder, Colo.: Westview Press, 1997. A solid guide to the current state of citizen participation in America.

Fishkin, James S. *The Voice of the People.* New Haven: Yale University Press, 1995. The author takes on talk radio; he calls for a more serious discussion of national issues. A thorough discussion of the deliberative poll.

Stanley, Harold W., and Richard Niemi. *Vital Statistics on American Politics.* Washington, D.C.: Congressional Quarterly Press, 1995. All the data you need on American politics.

3

THE INGREDIENTS OF POLITICAL POWER

I Tell You Folks, All Politics Is Applesauce.
—*Will Rogers, American humorist*

Why Are There So Many Public Opinion Polls?

Exit polls, tracking polls, telephone polls, deliberative polls; focus groups, stratified sampling, margin of error, survey research—this is the lingo of public opinion polling, the fastest growing segment of American politics. What was once a cottage industry controlled by a few giants—Gallup, Roper, Harris—is now a multi-billion dollar enterprise employing thousands of number crunchers, telephone interviewers, and data analyzers. At last glance, there were over two hundred polling organizations active in the United States.

Public opinion polling has become an absolute necessity for campaigns. Public opinion pollsters have risen to the level of gurus whose advice on how to properly divine the message from polls is sought after by an ever growing number of politicians anxious to get that critical edge over their opponents. It is not an exaggeration to state that polls and pollsters have transformed the American political scene. During the period from the infamous Gallup poll of 1948, which wrongly predicted a victory by Thomas Dewey over President

Harry Truman, to the highly accurate polls done in connection with the 1996 election, public opinion polling has become more sophisticated in terms of data generated and more precise in terms calling the outcome.

The rise of public opinion polling should come as no surprise; it is a mere extension of scientific methods into the political arena. In the past, gauging the public mood was a mix of old-fashioned pressing the flesh and a little bit of political savvy. Today, however, finding out what's on people's minds about candidates and issues is the domain of complex mathematical models based on census data, random telephone numbers, and current voting lists. Public opinion polling has risen from the casual phone call the day of the election to a highly competitive profession, always conscious of its reputation for accuracy and wary of making a misstep in judging the mood of the voters. Since millions of dollars in fees are at stake from politicians, newspapers, and television networks, pollsters are forever honing their techniques (many of which are closely guarded secrets) to ensure that the predictions they make will always fall within that prestigious margin of error of plus or minus three.

Because public opinion polling has become such a central part of the American political process, there is increasing attention placed on polling organizations and pollsters. Concerns have been raised in recent years that polls are driving elections and election results. Polling organizations have been criticized for shoddy questioning practices and outright deceit in their attempts to get quick snapshots of the electorate. The way a question is phrased or the way key information is absent from the question can go a long way toward achieving a predetermined response. For example, one can ask citizens whether they support "welfare," or one can ask them whether they support "assistance for the poor." The two questions are guaranteed to provide different conclusions and of course different perceptions of public opinion on the policy debate surrounding poverty.

Politicians as well have been taken to task for utilizing questionable polling results to energize their campaign. When candidates broadcast the results of an overnight poll, usually termed a "push poll," with a narrow sampling of respondents designed to be favorable to them, and then use the results (undoubtedly positive toward the candidate) to create a bandwagon effect, there are serious ethical questions that must be raised. Also candidates hungry for victory at the ballot box have been too apt to follow polls rather than clearly define an issue and inform the electorate of the ramifications of a particular policy course. Convinced by consultants, who accent the marketing of the candidate rather than substantive political debate, too many politicians have become followers of polls rather than leaders of people.

The questionable use of polling has made the public more suspicious of polls, more reluctant to give pollsters information, and more willing to provide answers that do not represent their true feelings. The argument from critics of polls is that polls often measure the opinions of citizens who are uninformed about the issues and the candidates, and therefore the responses they provide do little to gauge true public opinion. Furthermore, citizens are increasingly aware that politicians are using polls to claim they are listening to the people, when in fact polls rarely provide a true measure of what's on the voters' minds. We have reached a stage in American politics where politicians feel an obligation to do polling, not in any real effort to connect with the people, but rather to "test the waters," to track the voters and anticipate the next wave of opinion.

Despite the questions that are being posed concerning the accuracy and ethics of polling, politicians running for office, from the president of the United States to the mayors of small town America, are spending scarce campaign resources to conduct polls to define the electorate. Bill Clinton, in both his campaigns for the White House, placed heavy emphasis on polls and polling data to chart his strategy and define his issues. Stratified sampling gave the Clinton campaign a picture of how the race was progressing in four geographic regions. Clinton was able to use the polling data to make critical decisions on where to make appearances and where to funnel television advertising money.

The Clinton campaign also used small focus groups to determine what was on the mind of the average voter. These informal conversations with voters, in which a series of issues are raised, were convened regularly as a means of defining more precisely the policy agenda that would put Mr. Clinton in the best light. It was

TABLE 3.1   How Groups Voted in 1996

	Clinton	Dole	Perot
All (100%)	49%	41%	8%
Men (48%)	43%	44%	10%
Women (52%)	54%	38%	7%
Whites (83%)	43%	46%	9%
Blacks (10%)	84%	12%	4%
Hispanics (5%)	72%	21%	6%
Didn't complete high school (6%)	59%	28%	11%
High school graduate (23%)	51%	35%	13%
Some college (27%)	48%	40%	10%
College graduate (26%)	44%	46%	7%
Postgraduate (17%)	52%	40%	5%
Age:			
18–29 (17%)	53%	34%	10%
30–44 (33%)	48%	41%	9%
45–59 (26%)	48%	41%	9%
60 and up (23%)	48%	44%	7%
Family income:			
Less than $15,000 (11%)	59%	28%	11%
$15,000–29,999 (23%)	53%	36%	9%
$30,000–49,999 (27%)	48%	40%	10%
$50,000–74,999 (21%)	47%	45%	7%
$75,000 or more (18%)	42%	50%	7%
Protestants (55%)	43%	47%	9%
Catholics (29%)	53%	37%	9%
Jews (3%)	78%	16%	3%
Family financial situation compared with 1992:			
Better (33%)	66%	26%	6%
Worse (20%)	27%	57%	13%
About the same (44%)	46%	44%	8%
Democrats (40%)	84%	10%	5%
Republicans (34%)	13%	80%	6%
Independents (26%)	43%	35%	17%
Liberals (20%)	78%	11%	7%
Moderates (47%)	57%	32%	9%
Conservatives (33%)	20%	71%	8%
1992 votes:			
Clinton (44%)	85%	9%	4%
Bush (34%)	13%	82%	4%
Perot (12%)	22%	44%	32%
First-time voters (9%)	54%	34%	11%
Union households (24%)	59%	30%	9%
Nonunion households (76%)	46%	44%	8%
Religious Right (16%)	26%	65%	8%

SOURCE: Voter News Service exit polls for 1996 in *National Journal,* with permission from Voters News Service.

through such focus groups that the Clinton campaign recognized the strength of Clinton's support among women and the importance of moving to the center of the political spectrum. Finally, tracking polls, which most news organizations sponsor, were used by the Clinton campaign as a daily method of charting the status of the candidate and developing responses to the hills and valleys of popular support.

Outside of specific campaigns for public office, the most useful polling tool, which is primarily directed at explaining the results of an election, is the exit poll. Employed mostly by news organizations, the exit poll, in which voters are queried about their vote immediately after they leave the voting booth, has become essential for those experts seeking to make sense of the election and for campaign officials anxious to find out why they won and why they lost. The value of the exit poll is that it is a face to face interaction between the voter and the polling agent. Questions are asked while the voter still has a fresh remembrance of the decisions made and the reasons for those decisions. Also the exit poll is free of the embellishments and gratuitous explanations (commonly called spin) that come from supporters of a candidate, when they use their commissioned polls to present their view of the election and the vote. Although some voters are annoyed that they are approached as they leave the voting booth, exit poll data has become the most helpful resource for accurately analyzing voting behavior.

A section on polling would be incomplete without presenting some hard data on how America voted in the last election. Table 3.1 presents the results of exit polls from the 1996 presidential election conducted by *Voters News Service*.

How Groups Voted in 1996

At first glance the poll results provide a broad overview of what America is thinking. Every demographic category, every nook and cranny of America life is targeted to achieve a definitive answer to the question: How did America vote? As a whole the poll found some important tidbits of information about the American people and their presidential preferences in 1996. Women certainly were a significant source of President Clinton's reelection victory, as were blacks and

Hispanics. If you were rich, you likely voted for Dole, if you were poor, you likely voted for Clinton. Bob Dole got the conservatives and the religious right, Bill Clinton got the liberals and the union households. Perhaps most importantly, if you felt that your economic situation had been better during the last four years, then Clinton was your man. As a tool of analysis the *Voters News Service* poll makes an important contribution to the study of American politics and the American voter. It is this kind of postelection polling that tells us much about ourselves and our nation.

Despite the annoyances that are associated with polling and the questionable use of polls by politicians, they are useful. Fortunately, a new method of polling called deliberative polling may provide the bridge uniting the needs of the politician to get a quick and accurate reading of the voting public and the mission of a democratic society to create a political environment where citizens can participate meaningfully in their own governance. In 1996 the National Opinion Research Center conducted a polling experience in Texas, in which six hundred citizens were first asked their views on a range of issues and then given the opportunity to listen to experts debate the merits of the issues. They then expressed their opinions a second time.

The participants in the deliberative poll did actually change their views on some of the issues, from the value of foreign aid to state control of welfare policy. Although the Texas deliberative poll was costly ($4.5 million) and time-consuming (three days of intensive discussions), many observers were impressed with the attempt to link polling with serious conversations about national issues and problems. Unfortunately, the deliberative poll was a one-shot experiment, whereas the number of quickie telephone polls and push polls remains high, reflecting the continued reliance on instantaneous opinion-gathering. Serious discussions about serious matters just aren't that popular in American politics.

And therein lies the answer to the question of why public opinion polling has become such a critical ingredient in American politics. Politicians, driven in their desire for victory and anxious to find out how best to utilize their financial resources, want to find out quickly what the voters are thinking and what the voters want from a political leader. The unrelenting desire is to find out, "Am I up or down?"

"Why am I up or down?" and "What do I have to do to stay up and not go down?" Nowhere in this litany do politicians ask, "How can I best educate the public about the issues and problems of day?" or "How can I develop a more personal relationship with the voters?" Granted a few politicians do sometimes call town meetings real citizen dialogue, but such examples of public discourse rarely happen in American politics today. Politicians don't seem to have the time for such a dialogue, and citizens have just gotten used to giving their offhanded opinions to nameless questioners over the phone.

How Much Does Money Drive American Politics?

It may be best to answer this question with a question: Who is influencing the political process more effectively, the citizen who votes regularly in national elections or the citizen who gives $1,000 to a candidate for federal office? By voting, average American citizens fulfill their responsibility to participate in the democratic process and help the candidate running for office get that precious additional ballot cast on election day. But by contributing $1,000 (actually the legal limit is a total of $25,000 per year), the American citizens will likely get their picture taken with the candidate, a personal thank you, time to discuss the issues, and most importantly an unstated understanding that if the candidate wins, the contributor should be granted access to the governing process. Access is part of the unwritten rules of politics in which office holders, feeling beholden to financial contributors to their election, open their doors and their decisionmaking processes to those who have handed over money to them.

If America had a political system that was pure as the driven snow, in which voting was the sole arbiter of power, then the answer to the above question would be easy—casting a ballot has great significance in choosing leaders and influencing public policy. But as we all know, American politics is far from pure, and voting is not the only method of choosing leaders and influencing public policy. Today being elected president, for example, carries a $600 million price tag, while the cost of all national elections in 1996 was $4 billion, up from $540 million just twenty years ago. That $600 million price tag for the presidency and $4 billion for all other national offices comes from personal, interest group, and corporate contributions, moneys not necessarily given out of patriotism or commitment to the democratic process. Access to power by financial contributors has become the real mode of participation in contemporary American politics. Cast a ballot and express your preference, write out a campaign check and have a politician for a friend: So runs the current mantra of national politics.

Running for public office at the national level is no longer a quaint exercise in seeking popular support. Rather it is an unrelenting search for money; money to pay for television, money to pay for consultants, money to pay for bumper stickers and buttons, money to pay for hotels and transportation, and money to pay for office space and printing. The search for money has led to the creation of one of the most important positions in electoral politics—the fund-raiser, the person who shmoozes with rich "fat cats" to convince them to make a tax deductible contribution to their candidate. Needless to say, this is big business with huge stakes and little margin for error. Failure to raise enough cash could spell the end of the campaign. More than one campaign has crashed and burned because there wasn't enough money available to buy television time or to pay for airline tickets.

Although it may seem from the headlines and the talk shows that the influence of money on politics is completely out of control, rules have been set to bring some order to the practice of making campaign contributions. In the wake of the Watergate scandal, Congress passed the Federal Campaign Election Acts of 1972 and 1974. These two pieces of legislation sought to control the abuses that had led to the downfall of the Nixon presidency. The two acts created the Federal Election Commission, a regulatory body designed to monitor campaigns and campaign expenditures. Also the legislation instituted partial public financing of elections by providing federal funds for presidential primaries and elections and set the ground rules for the amounts that individuals may contribute to campaigns.

The impact of reform was lessened in an important way in 1976, when the legislation was modified so as to permit corporations, unions, and special interest groups to create Political Action Committees (PACs) to funnel campaign contributions to candidates. PACs have become the key players in the drive for more money to feed the election machine. Financing campaigns was also modified by a Supreme Court decision (*Buckley v. Valeo*) that declared unconstitutional the provision of the 1972 act limiting how much an individual could spend on his or her own campaign. Citing the First Amendment right to freedom of expression, the Court stated that limiting personal expenses in a campaign was a violation of the right of the candidate "to engage in the discussion of public issues and vigorously and tirelessly to advocate his own election." Although campaign finance may seem to have little to do with freedom of speech, as we will see, reform of this giant machine continues to be made much more difficult by First Amendment guarantees.

The history of campaign finance reform since 1972 has been marked by frequent efforts to find creative methods of legally avoiding compliance and raising more cash. The end run that has become a superhighway of campaign contribution goes by the name of "soft money." Soft money has nothing to do with the quality of the currency, but refers to the channeling of contributions to the political party, rather than to the candidate. The political parties use the money to run the conventions, help get-out-the-vote drives and provide state and local organizations with badly needed resources.

What soft money has meant to campaigns is that candidates for public office are regular attendees of the ten thousand dollars a plate dinner. Contributors—individuals, corporations, unions, and other groups—sit down to a fish or chicken dinner (usually worth about fifty dollars in the real world) and listen to a series of political speeches. When it is all over, the party has a couple of million dollars, which they can use to further the cause of their candidates, and the donors have had an exclusive face-to-face discussion with a political mover and shaker. As for the candidates, they go home pleased with themselves for building up that all important campaign war chest. And soft money is not a minor element in the overall campaign finance picture. In 1996 it is estimated that soft money accounted for as much as $150 million in the presidential election race.

Not surprisingly, all of this search for money has led to illegalities and irregularities. The Clinton campaign in 1996 was targeted by the Republican majority in Congress as a major offender against existing campaign rules. Allegations of foreign contributions to the campaign, questionable policy discussions with campaign contributors, coffee klatches with the President, and sleazy access arrangements, such as the opportunity to sleep in the Lincoln bedroom in exchange for a large contribution, suggested that maybe the president of the United States could be up for sale. The Republicans had their own campaign finance problems, as Speaker Newt Gingrich was reprimanded by the House of Representatives for fund-raising violations.

Campaign finance reform is a phrase that comes out of the mouths of many politicians. In New Hampshire, after the 1996 election, President Clinton and Speaker Newt Gingrich shook hands and pledged to work for a comprehensive campaign finance reform law. Nothing happened. In fact both men became further embroiled in controversies associated with their drive to raise more funds.

But even as both Democrats and Republicans engage in campaign finance overkill, there are those who are taking seriously the impact of these scandals and irregularities on the democratic culture in this country. The best chance of reform of the campaign finances laws has come from the bipartisan effort of Senators John McCain of Arizona and Russell Feingold of Wisconsin, two maverick senators who recognize the toll taken by the drive for money on the level of trust Americans have in their government. The McCain and Feingold Bill would close the soft money loophole, move further along with public financing by including Congressional races, and make the Federal Election Commission a regulatory body with real power to enforce the existing laws and any new laws that might be passed.

The task of campaign reform, however, is a difficult one. Despite all the disapproval of money grubbing by politicians, it is extremely difficult to change past practices, especially since the cost of campaigns continues to move into the stratosphere, and the American people do not seem to have the interest and the will to demand change from their public officials. The system may be broken, but it still works, so why fix it, particularly when the public has not expressed strong opinions on the need for reform.

And so McCain-Feingold went down to defeat in 1998. A bipartisan group of reformers was unable to get the sixty votes necessary to break a filibuster. In the words of Senator Olympia Snowe of Maine, a moderate Republican, "The Senate has once again proven that the

American people's cynicism about Congress's ability to pass meaningful reform is well-founded." Leading the victors in staging the filibuster was Senator Mitch McConnell of Kentucky, who cast his opposition in First Amendment terms: "Spending is speech."

For now the issue of campaign finance reform is on the back burner, but it is by no means dead. There continue to be outspoken proponents of reform in both the House and the Senate. So what is the answer? Some reformers say that we should move to a comprehensive system of public financing of elections of the kind many European nations have implemented. This route certainly seems prudent in light of the constant abuses and excesses of campaign finance. There is of course the First Amendment problem raised by *Buckley v. Valeo* and reflected in Senator McConnell's statement that "spending is speech." Denying Americans the right to use their own money to get their message across sounds un-American until the question of resources and a level playing field is introduced. Not every American is a Ross Perot billionaire who can pump millions of dollars into a campaign to get his/her message on the television screen. Public financing of election campaigns means that citizens with limited resources would have access to the dollars to get their message out and compete with the Ross Perots of the world.

Public financing as practiced in Europe would also mean that there would likely be a much smaller pot of money to pay for all the stuff that has become part and parcel of American campaigns. Television executives would bemoan the loss of advertising revenue, political consultancy firms might fold, and the endless peripherals of the campaign, from planes to hotels to those silly hats, would have to be limited. The Europeans run short, inexpensive campaigns that are no nonsense discussions of the issues, not the two-year multi-billion-dollar extravaganzas that put Americans to sleep. To move to public financing would require additional public funds and would radically change the face of campaigning in the United States, but it would avoid a president selling a night in the Lincoln bedroom and politicians groveling for cash from people they don't know.

More importantly, money politics is having a corrosive effect on democracy. As Ronald Dworkin said in an article in the *New York Review of Books* in 1996, "Money is the biggest threat to the democratic process. The time politicians must spend raising money in endless party functions and in personal ways—not only during an election campaign but while in office, preparing for the next election—has become an increasingly large drain on their attention." Stated quite simply, if our legislators are out there raising money and being compromised by contributors in the process, how can they do the people's work. The answer is becoming shockingly clear—they can't.

Box 3.1   The Fund-Raising Circuit

From October to December of 1997, President Clinton attended twenty-seven Democratic fund raisers and brought in ten million dollars to the party coffers. Here is his exhausting but highly lucrative itinerary:

October 31	Palm Beach, Florida: Democratic National Committee Lunch—$180,000
November 1	Boca Raton, Florida: Democratic Congressional Campaign Committee Dinner—$600,000
November 1	Jacksonville, Florida: Democratic National Committee Retreat—$25,000,000
November 4	Washington, D.C.: Dinner for Senator John Kerry—$600,000
November 12	Washington, D.C.: Reception for Vermont Governor Howard Ream, Democratic National Committee Dinner—$300,000
November 14	Las Vegas, Nevada: Democratic National Committee and Women's Leadership Forum—$350,000
November 15	Sacramento, California: Democratic Business Council Lunch—$300,000
November 16	Los Angeles, California: Democratic Business Council Dinner—$700,000
November 17	St. Louis, Missouri: Dinner and Reception for Senate candidate Jay Nixon—$400,000
November 18	Washington, D.C.: Events related to Democratic National Committee—$650,000

(continues)

Box 3.1 (continued)

November 22	Denver, Colorado, and Seattle, Washington: Democratic National Committee and Democratic Senate Campaign Committee—$1.1 million
December 1	Washington, D.C.: Events Related to Democratic National Committee—$800,000
December 3	Chicago, Illinois: Events Related to Democratic Congressional Committee and Illinois Democratic Party—$900,000
December 10	New York, New York: Democratic National Committee Dinner—$1 million

SOURCE: White House and Democratic National Committee

Why Are There So Many Interest Groups in American Politics?

One of the ongoing myths about how American politics works is the image of the dedicated and persistent citizen single-handedly fighting politicians and government bureaucrats to bring about a policy change. But in this era of political cynicism and apathy, Americans are increasingly coming to the conclusion that making government respond to their specific needs is an outdated concept. Today American politics is interest group politics, special interest politics to use the current nomenclature. The lone citizen fighting for change has been replaced by well tailored, highly paid lobbyists who represent corporations, trade groups, professional associations, unions, and an ever expanding list of consumer, environmental, economic, and social organizations. The earnest pleadings of wide-eyed citizens urging their elected public officials to make needed changes has been transformed into well organized, well financed information and public relations campaigns designed to convince anyone who will listen (especially those in government) that special interest X, Y, or Z is worthy of a tax break, a contract, an appropriation, or a legislative maneuver.

With some 30,000 special interest groups active in American politics employing hundreds of thousands of lobbyists and support staff and spending billions to get their message out, the average citizen faces a highly organized and well financed political machine. There is of course nothing stopping any citizen or group of citizens from following the same game plan and participating in interest group politics. In fact there are a number of groups that were started through the sheer power of one individual who wanted to make a difference. Candy Lightner's Mothers Against Drunk Driving and Ralph Nader's Public Citizen, Inc., are examples of well recognized interest groups organized by ordinary citizens that have become players in the Washington game of politics. MADD has become a national voice to change laws regarding drunk driving and the punishment of drunk drivers, while Public Citizen, Inc., is an eclectic organization which advocates for governmental reform, citizen rights, and business responsibility.

Although it is true that ordinary citizens can get aboard the special interest group bandwagon and become players in Washington politics, the world of lobbying public officials is dominated by the megagroups such as the American Association of Retired Persons (AARP), the U.S. Chamber of Commerce, the National Rifle Association (NRA), the National Organization of Women (NOW), the National Association of Manufacturers (NAM), the American Federation of Labor/Congress of Industrial Organizations (AFL-CIO), the American Medical Association, the National Education Association, and the National Association for the Advancement of Colored People (NAACP). These interest organizations have huge memberships (the AARP has 33 million members), large staffs (the Chamber of Commerce has a staff of over 1,700 people), and substantial operating budgets (NAM has an annual budget of over $15 million).

At the core of the power of the megagroups as they seek to influence the course of public policy is their use of campaign contributions. The special interests in Washington all have ancillary groups, the aforementioned political action committees, that have been established to distribute money to members of Congress, candidates for federal and state office, and of course those seeking the presidency.

PACs are often the chief persuasive tool in the arsenal of the lobbyist and the organization he or she represents. In 1995 there were 4,000 PACs registered with the government, with the largest number of PACs associated with the corporate sector, followed closely by labor, trade associations, and the health industry. In 1996 PAC contributions to congressional candidates topped $200 million. Some of the more generous PACs are those associated with the American Medical Association, the National Education Association, the United Auto Workers, the National Rifle Association, and the American Federation of State, County, and Municipal Employees.

With the cost of running for state and national office so exorbitant, politicians have come to depend on the contributions from PACs. Special interests may proudly state that their lobbying strategy includes testifying before Congress, contacting public officials, presenting research conclusions, and developing grassroots support from its members, but the fact that PAC money given to members of Congress increased from $12.5 million in 1974 (when PAC formation was made legal) to over $200 million in 1996 attests to the significance of financial contributions to political campaigns. In the 1994 midterm elections over 3,000 out of 4,000 PACs made campaign contributions, with of course the megagroups leading the way: The Political Action Committee of the American Medical Association gave $2.39 million, and the National Education Association PAC gave $2.26 million.

What is most disturbing about PAC contributions from special interest groups is that often moneys are targeted at members of Congress who are involved with a particular area of legislation. Major legislative initiatives, such as the extension of the Clean Air Act in 1990, the North American Free Trade Agreement in 1993, the Telecommunications Act in 1995, and the budget and tax bill of 1997, brought the special interests out of the woodwork as they not only conducted multipronged lobbying campaigns designed to convince members of Congress, but also joined this traditional approach with cold hard cash to key committee chairs and undecided Representatives and Senators. Anyone looking at this sudden financial interest in members of Congress by groups with a major piece of legislation up for consideration could only come to the conclusion that there is a suspicious connection between votes on bills and cash contributions.

Of course members of Congress, presidential candidates, and state officials vehemently deny that there is any connection between voting decisions and PAC contributions. The argument is that interest groups have the right to use legal tactics to convince office holders and office seekers of the merits of their cause. As the logic goes, PAC contributions are permitted by law as valid means of showing support for officials who have aligned themselves with a particular special interest group and as a strategy for building new support from officials who might be undecided. But as is obvious from the numbers, average Americans do not have the financial capacity to provide public officials with millions of dollars of campaign support.

The role of special interests in the public policy process at the national level was made clear during the recent negotiations leading up to the compromise budget and tax bills that were agreed to by President Clinton and the Republican Congress in 1997. Although most of the attention was focused on balancing the budget by 2002 and providing a range of tax cuts and credits for Americans, a mini-controversy arose over a number of special tax breaks to narrow interests that became part of the legislation. For the first time in U.S. history, President Clinton exercised his newly acquired line-item veto to strip the legislation of three special tax breaks that would save $600 million over a five year period.

The three items—extra funding for New York State's Medicaid health care program, a measure deferring taxes on overseas income by U.S. financial services firms, and a tax break for some food-processing companies that sell assets to farmer cooperatives—were just the most recent examples of how special interests have been able to convince Congress to load a comprehensive piece of legislation with special benefits for the few at the expense of the many. Nevertheless, although President Clinton spoke forcefully about the use of the line-item veto to strip the tax bill of special interest breaks, he was not telling the American people about the seventy-nine other special interest tax breaks in the legislation, some that were necessary in order to implement the legislation, some that had been agreed upon by both the Congress and the White House, and some that were just pure and simple additions to the legislation to satisfy a particular constituency.

One such special interest tax break that did not meet with the President's line-item veto was the hard cider tax. Cider manufacturers in Vermont (less than 100 people) had worked for three years to reduce the tax on hard cider from $1.07 a gallon to 22.6 cents, equivalent to the rate wine is taxed at. The hard cider special interest had worked closely with Vermont's two senators, Patrick Leahy, a Democrat and James Jeffords, a Republican, to bring about this change in the tax laws. Hard cider manufacturers were ecstatic over the President's decision not to go after this special interest, and Republican Senator Jeffords made the bold claim that this decision by the President was "good news for apple growers and the hard cider industry not only in Vermont, but across the nation." The good news about the victory of the hard cider manufacturers is that there still is room in our interest group politics for the small player who represents a narrow interest that benefits but a few people. The bad news is that the tax cut bill could have been a little bit more generous to the vast majority of the Americans, but instead gave away a tax benefit to an organized group. Democracy, yes, interest group politics, yes, public policy made in the national interest, maybe not.

Periodically Congress has passed legislation to monitor interest groups and regulate their activities. As recently as 1995, legislation was passed to further put the clamps on interest group activity. Besides requiring registration of groups and lobbyists and semiannual expenditure reports, the legislation seeks to monitor U.S. owned subsidiaries of foreign-owned companies and lawyers representing foreign entities. The legislation also encourages grassroots groups and tax-exempt organizations to enter the lobbying arena. Linked with this legislation are the efforts of Congress to avoid the appearance of impropriety in dealings with special interests. Both the House and Senate have strict rules on receiving gifts and those all-expense-paid golf trips, vacations, and other freebies.

Madison, in his famous *Federalist no. 10*, anguished over what he termed the "mischief of factions"; in particular, he was concerned that a majority faction would oppress the weaker minority. His solution, as stated earlier, was to increase the number of factions so that the potential for influence would be dispersed. Madison, however, never anticipated that interest group power would be linked so closely to money and that the "mischief" would come not from the number of groups but their ability to transform the democratic process into a huge money pit.

Box 3.2   Where Is the Money Coming From?

One of the benefits of living in a democratic society is that citizens occasionally get to know how the governing system works. As a result of laws requiring interest groups to disclose their spending for lobbying efforts, the American public in 1998 got an eye-opening glimpse of the extent to which powerful and wealthy groups spend money to advance their causes. According to data compiled by the Associated Press from federal disclosure files, interest groups spent $633 million in the first six months of 1997 on lobbying; that's $100 million a month. Here are the top ten spenders:

American Medical Association	$8,560,000
Chamber of Commerce of the United States	$7,000,000
Phillip Morris	$5,900,000
General Motors	$5,200,000
Edison Electric Inst.	$5,000,000
Pfizer	$4,600,000
United Technologies	$4,160,000
General Electric	$4,120,000
AT&T	$4,120,000
Citicorp	$4,100,000

Are Political Parties Still Important in American Politics?

The proper response to this question is no and yes with a little bit of a maybe thrown in for good measure. The reason for this academic sleight of hand is that American political parties are moving through a long and arduous period of transformation in which their role as the premier agents of democratic politics is being called into question. Using the word transformation to describe the current state of political party activity in this country carries a sort of positive spin. It suggests that the old standbys, the Democrats and the Republicans, are somehow in the process of making themselves over in order to enter the twenty-first century with new ideas and an organizational vigor that will ensure their vitality for years to come.

As most textbooks in American politics show, political parties are made up of like-minded individuals whose objective is to work for the election of candidates who share similar policy positions. In order to achieve electoral victory for its candidates, political parties must build broad-based coalitions of voters, provide a range of resources to assist candidates in their quest for office, articulate a common policy platform that can attract voters, and once in office, structure government around its elected officials and its policy platform. This is no small task, since political parties are in essence both the catalyst of democratic participation and the glue that keeps the political system together. What has happened in the last twenty years or so is that American political parties have become neither democratic catalysts nor the political glue.

At one time, political parties in this country controlled the electoral and the governmental process. Political parties not only recruited and directed the campaigns of local, state, and national politicians, but in towns, counties, and cities throughout this country parties actually served as employment agencies, charitable organizations, and social clubs. Parties in a real sense were the center of the political universe. The image of the smoke-filled back room where deals were made on the future of aspiring politicians seemed to capture the essence of party politics, with its powerful bosses from the fictional Frank O'Hara in the classic *The Last Hurrah* to the realities of New York's Boss Tweed and Tammany Hall, Boston's Rascal King, James Michael Curley, and Chicago's Mayor Daley. These political bosses made certain that they set the rules, named the leaders, and on numerous occasions personally ensured that the vote outcome was as they desired.

But that was long ago and never more. Today, political parties are the shell of their former selves. An ever growing number of Americans (now around 40 percent) choose to identify themselves politically as independents rather than become associated with the Democrats and the Republicans. Voters are increasingly shying away from straight ticket voting, further weakening the party's ability to attract loyal supporters. The once vaunted party machine is in shambles, replaced by paid consultants, political action committees, and interest groups who raise money, develop strategy, and steer the candidates toward their own issue agenda. The days of back-room deals by party pols are mere memories, as sterile but democratic primaries, where voters, in a kind of pre-election, choose their party's nominees and control the choice of national leaders. And the nominating convention for president every four years, which once was the premier event of the summertime television doldrums in the fifties and sixties, has all but disappeared from the screen due to lack of interest.

The decline of political party influence is masked, however, by the names Democrat and Republican. As a nation we still define our politics as a tussle between the two major parties. Elections are analyzed in terms of the strength or weakness of the Dems or the GOP, and government remains organized around which party gains the majority and the control of power and perks that accompanies that majority. But while the two major parties continue to play in the political arena, they are sharing the space with new and more powerful players who are clearly gaining the edge in deciding how candidates are chosen, how campaigns are run, and how issues are defined.

Perhaps the most important challenge to the traditional dominance of the political party in American politics is the rising influence of the paid consultant. One of the first decisions that a candidate for public office will make is which election consulting firm will be hired to manage the campaign. The election consulting firms have become one-stop shopping enterprises that provide the candidate with everything necessary for victory, from polling to speechwriting to fundraising to media relations. The political parties in turn are becoming more like second-stringers, who provide helpful support to the team but are not on the playing field at crunch time. The parties continue to offer candidates an organizational network of activists ready to make phone calls, stand with signs, and lick envelopes. More importantly, the parties are the source of the soft money that is absolutely essential for sustaining long and costly campaigns. But this is where the influence of parties comes to an end.

The actual running of the campaign and all the ancillary activities associated with winning public office have been taken over by hard-driving hired guns who charge large fees to guide the candidate through the minefields of electoral politics. The consultants are the political bosses of the 1990s. Consultants such as James Carville (President Clinton's 1992 campaign chief), Dick Morris (Clinton's 1996 guru), the late Lee Atwater (President Bush's 1988 strategist), and Mary Maitlin (President Bush's 1992 campaign consultant and Carville's wife) have become famous and wealthy because of their expertise at managing the intricacies of the campaign. These individuals are not part of the party organization; they report directly to the candidate, and they often oversee the operation of the party to ensure compliance with the electoral strategy that has been developed, a strategy that they most likely have fashioned and sold to the candidate.

The American political system is definitely paying a price for this turn away from party organization and toward political consultancy. Political parties in this country have in the past been one of the prime connections between government and the people. But by sharing the political playing field with interest groups, political actions committees, and now paid campaign consultants, parties have become less able to achieve this connecting role. As a result the grassroots quality of American politics, in which voters were joined together, at least for a time, around the banners of the Democrats and the Republicans, has faded into the background.

It is worth pointing out that even though political parties are in trouble these days, this does not mean that the Democrats and the Republicans are inconsequential participants in the electoral process. Parties have become the most important source of dollars for campaigns. Some experts on American political party activity believe that the fund-raising capabilities of the parties may be a means to resuscitate these institutions by transforming them into the key conduits of the essential electoral resources. Also, party organizations in most states remain solid. Membership may be down, but those running state organizations exert considerable influence on the political landscape. On the national level, political parties remain visible, as they nominate candidates, run elections, organize governmental power, and engage in old-fashioned patronage by employing supporters.

There is thus still life in the political parties; it is just that their dominance of the political scene has been diminished and their prospects for regaining their importance have dimmed.

The difficulties faced by American political parties in this era of increased competition for dominance of the electoral and governmental scene have spurred a call for change. In recent years there has been heightened clamor for a reform party that would challenge the Democrats and the Republicans by offering new answers to the problems facing the country. The campaign of Ross Perot in 1992, when the straight-talking Texan gained 19 percent of the popular vote, reinforced the view that America may be ready for an alternative to the Dems and the GOP. Public opinion data also confirmed this trend when over 50 percent of Americans polled agreed that they would prefer to see a new party come on the political scene.

There is a great deal of high and mighty discussion concerning political party rejuvenation, but those who are honest about turning the Democratic and Republican organizations into major players again return to the issue of campaign finance. There has been some talk of allowing taxpayers to designate on their tax returns a contribution to the political party of their choice. With a new pool of public moneys directed to the parties, it is anticipated that these organizations would be able to regain their influence in the electoral and governmental process. Public officials, so the argument goes, would not have to look solely to special interests for campaign support. Another idea is to permit parties to distribute even larger amounts of cash to campaigns than the current laws permit. The argument here is that it is far better to have rich and powerful political parties that speak for a broad band of American citizens than to have the political process controlled by the Balkanizing character of thousands of special interests. But with already weakened parties, special interest groups will not be easily pushed out of the political arena.

At the core of the need for stronger political parties are the advantages that would accrue to public officials. As currently constituted, a weak party system in the United States does not permit politicians to stand together as a cohesive voting unit. Weak parties means that congressmen, senators, governors, and even presidents are often out there

Box 3.3 Who Are the Democrats?
Who Are the Republicans?

During the 1996 Democratic and Republican conventions, polling of the delegates helped develop a picture of party activists and define the positions of the party rank and file. Here are the results:

Democrats

47 percent defined themselves as moderate.

31 percent defined themselves as liberal.

46 percent reported household income of more than $75,000.

31 percent were between 40 and 49.

29 percent were between 50 and 59.

45 percent had postgraduate degrees.

39 percent were union members.

5 percent were part of the religious right.

82 percent were in favor of affirmative action.

65 percent were in favor of reducing military spending.

72 percent opposed reducing spending on social programs.

52 percent felt abortion should be legal in most cases.

Republicans

52 percent defined themselves as conservative.

22 percent defined themselves as very conservative.

56 percent reported household income of more than $75,000.

31 percent were over 60 years of age.

2 percent were between 18 and 29.

36 percent had postgraduate degrees.

2 percent were union members.

21 percent were part of the religious right.

83 percent were opposed to affirmative action.

85 percent opposed reducing spending on defense.

84 percent supported reducing spending on social programs.

59 percent felt that abortion should be illegal in most cases.

SOURCES: Democratic National Committee and Republican National Committee

in the political fray alone without any backup. At present, with party loyalty, party discipline, and party influence at all time lows, there are scant few instances where politicians can feel confident telling anxious voters and pushy interest groups that their position was dictated by party requirements or a unified party leadership. The age-old axiom, there is strength in numbers, applies to the advantage of having powerful political parties that can allow politicians to make tough decisions and ward off the constant pressure of special interests.

The fact that political parties are in some degree of trouble these days should not diminish the contribution that these institutions of democracy have made to American politics. Parties historically have expanded voter participation, informed the public on important local, state, and national issues, and served as a testing laboratory for up and coming political leaders. Perhaps most importantly, parties have brought order and predictability to the process of decisionmaking in government. These are no minor contributions to advancing our way of life and form of government.

It is true that times change, people's preferences change, and politics change. But if political parties have fallen behind the curve and experienced a downturn in their fortunes, that does not mean that they are permanently out of the picture. As stated above, there are ways of rejuvenating party politics in this country. And since parties are democratic institutions, their revival can only mean a strengthening of our democracy.

Does Television Exert Too Much Influence on American Politics?

In order to answer that question, a few vignettes from American electoral history are necessary. In the 1960 presidential debates the Republican, Richard Nixon, miscalculated the importance of a fresh appearance on television. Nixon did not bother to shave off the five o'clock shadow, refused pancake makeup to contain his sweating, and was not briefed on how to use the camera to his advantage. His Democratic challenger, John Kennedy, sensed that he had entered a new arena of politics and came onto the podium looking fresh, confident, and savvy about the proper uses of the unforgiving camera. Kennedy won the televised debate hands down and went on to electoral victory. Nixon, who won the debate among those who listened on radio, became the textbook case of how not to prepare for politics in the age of television.

In 1964 Lyndon Johnson was seeking to win his first presidential race after the tragic assassination of John Kennedy. Barry Goldwater, the conservative Republican Senator from Arizona, was his challenger. Johnson and his electoral advisors recognized that in order to win they had to paint Goldwater as an extremist whose anti-Communist positions would jeopardize the security of the United States. In order to create this image of extremism, Johnson's team developed a television ad that showed a little girl pulling flower petals off in front of a picture perfect sky. Suddenly a nuclear mushroom cloud exploded, and the screen turned black, except for the message to vote for Lyndon Johnson. Forever painted in the minds of the voters as a nuclear extremist, Goldwater was defeated in one of the biggest landslides in the history of modern presidential elections.

In 1988 Michael Dukakis, a successful governor from Massachusetts, sought to end the Republican control of the White House by challenging Ronald Reagan's vice-president, George Bush. Dukakis, a solid debater with a wealth of knowledge on public policy issues, was giving Bush a run for his money, despite the fact that the vice-president was viewed as the heir to the Reagan presidency. And then came Willie Horton. Bush advisers ran a television ad that showed the Dukakis administration as apparently lax in its parole system, since it let convicted criminals like Willie Horton out of jail early. (Horton had brutally beaten a Maryland couple after leaving prison.) The ad showed stern-looking African American men walking through a prison turnstile on their way to freedom. The ad was criticized as racist in tone and inaccurate in portraying the Dukakis administration as overly lenient on crime. Nevertheless, the ad was a powerful message to voters, and it worked.

These are just three of the most famous examples of how the images that come through the television screen influence our perceptions of politics and politicians. Since that fateful day in 1960 when television crowned the next president of the United States, those seeking elected office in this country have had to become ever more adept at using the pictures that come through on the screen to their advantage. Politicians who have failed to recognize the power of those images have usually lost. Campaigns for public office are now driven by rules set by television and those who control television. Candidates are concerned about how they look, what they say, and how their policy positions are packaged. If they are fortunate enough to survive the test of television popularity and be elected, the preoccupation with image and sound bite does not end there. Government officials are now required to use television effectively or see their ratings plunge.

Television can be a powerful weapon in the arsenal of a politician. Used properly, television can make candidates and officials into leaders, heroes, and statesmen. Former President Ronald Reagan, the Great Communicator as he came to be called, had an innate understanding of the camera and knew instinctively how to deliver a speech or story to Congress and the American people. Reagan also had brilliant advisers like PR man Michael Deaver, who knew how to present his boss on television, usually in front of American flags or with admiring war veterans. The 1984 Republican convention will likely go down in history as one of the most effective political commercials in the annals of campaigning. Timed to the second, ever conscious of proper image, heavy on pageantry and patriotism, the convention was a prime time coronation of a Republican hero orchestrated by a team of public relations and television experts who knew how to win the hearts and minds of the American voters.

But television has an unforgiving side as well; it can quickly turn on a politician and be a source of embarrassment and declining support in the polls. President Gerald Ford will forever be remembered for his pratfalls caught on camera and on the comedy skits of *Saturday Night Live,* as much as for his cool and competent guidance of the country during the post-Watergate years. And President Jimmy Carter's inability to win a second term in office had much to do with the evening news and its nightly counting of the days that Americans were held hostage in Iran. Television made Gerald Ford into an uncoordinated bumbler and Jimmy Carter into a vacillating weakling, both images far from the truth. With both Ford and Carter, their presidency was defined by the image portrayed on the television screen.

Most people know instinctively that television has a controlling influence on their lives and that their understanding of the world, and particularly the world of politics, is filtered through that 27-inch Sony in the family room. Politicians have become proficient in knowing how best to present themselves and their message, and voters too often are like lambs to the slaughter as they passively sit in front of the tube and take in the image-making and self-promotion.

Of course one answer is to shut off the television and read the newspaper, *Time*, *Newsweek*, or even the tons of available campaign literature and government documents that explain in far better detail what is happening in the world of politics. Unfortunately, this is an unrealistic option, since most busy, stressed-out Americans are hooked on television and rely on getting their news and their knowledge of politicians from television. A recent study by the Pew Center, for example, found that 69 percent of Americans rely on television for their political news, as opposed to 43 percent who rely on newspapers, 16 percent on magazines and other written sources of information, and 10 percent on the Internet.

Moreover, the news we get from television about our politicians and their proposals and policies is not sufficient to expand our knowledge or make sound judgments. Harvard University's Center for Media and Public Affairs study of presidential campaigns found that the average sound bite—that kernel of information that television editors glean from the stump speeches of candidates—has decreased from 42.3 seconds in the Nixon-Humphrey campaign of 1968 to 7.3 seconds in the Clinton-Bush campaign of 1992. That's 7.3 seconds to find out about what our candidates for the highest office in the land are saying about important issues.

Even more troubling is the growing gulf between the American citizenry and the media. Americans mistrust newspaper and electronic journalists, not only because of the numerous recent instances of reporters fudging the facts and doing character assassinations on political figures, but also because the media do not seem to accurately represent what Americans are thinking and what Americans are interested in. James Fallows, in a recent *Atlantic Monthly* article entitled "Why Americans Hate the Media," says this: "When ordinary citizens have a chance to pose questions to political leaders, they rarely ask about the game of politics. They want to know how the reality of politics will affect them—through taxes, programs, scholarship funds, war. Journalists justify their intrusiveness and excesses by claiming that they are the public's representatives, asking the questions their fellow citizens would ask if they had the privilege of meeting with Presidents and senators. In fact they ask questions that only their fellow political professionals care about."

Because of the glaring deficiencies of media politics, numerous reforms have already been proposed that could change the campaign environment. Putting an end to negative ads on television that seek only to tear down a candidate rather than explain public policy positions would elevate the debate and add a tone of seriousness to the electoral process. More town meeting formats where candidates and public officials interact with citizens (instead of television anchors), and citizens get to ask the questions that are really on their minds would create a stronger tie between the people and their leaders. Increasing issue oriented news broadcasts that take the time to explain public policy issues rather than relying on juicy sound bites would force candidates to better inform the people. And finally, free air time for candidates, even the fringe candidates, would level the playing field, so that politicians would not have to grovel for money to get on the air and incumbents would not have an unfair advantage in getting their positions across to the voters.

There is, of course, a major problem with all these suggestions. Are the American people really interested in getting television politics to become more serious, more open to new ideas and less reliant on image rather than substance? We live in the age of tabloid journalism, in which a public official's private life or the hint of corruption is more eye-catching than C-SPAN running congressional hearings or CNN televising call-in shows with politicians. Unfortunately, the television colossus may have already won the battle about defining what is news and how the news should be reported. Politicians tend to like stability and predictability and are not about to go out on a limb and clamor for television to clean up its act when the current brand of political television helped them get where they are today. Furthermore, network executives are not about to jeopardize their hold on the viewing public by extending the evening news or putting corporate resources toward programming that people would probably not watch. Television networks are out to make money and the way to make money is to give the people what they want, which at this time is image rather than substance.

As with much of what happens in the way of political reform in this country, television networks will have to be pushed and pulled by those out there who want more from political television than a pretty face or a catchy phrase. There are some signs of hope. Negative campaign ads, which flourished in the 1988 and 1992 campaign season, have dropped somewhat because of citizen uproar. Networks are talking more about free air time for candidates, in order to stop the endless quest for money and permit a more serious discussion of the issues. And political debates are gradually becoming a conversation between candidates and the citizen rather than an opportunity for a journalist to score points. Change will not happen overnight, but change is definitely in the air.

Still, changing television politics will only succeed if enough citizens demand to be treated as intelligent voters rather than consumers who are buying a product. The television colossus does not budge easily, and the politicians who feed the colossus are not easily convinced that Americans deserve more than sound bites and beautiful pictures.

Box 3.4   *Some Guidelines for Watching the Evening News*

The nightly news remains a staple of television watching in America and the primary source of information about government and politics. Since television is a visual medium and a powerful shaper of public attitudes, it is important for Americans to be keen observers of what comes on the screen during the dinner hour. Here are some guidelines for watching the nightly news and for forming opinions about the world of government and politics:

(continues)

Box 3.4 (continued)

- If possible watch more than one news program. They're not all alike, and the definition of what is news on any given day can vary enormously from station to station.
- Beware of reporters who use terms like "I think" or "an unnamed source said." Remember the news is about presenting facts and is not a speculative exercise.
- Politicians and government officials are increasingly using television to create a favorable image of themselves rather than using television to talk straight or expand upon the issues. Watch out for those news segments that are clearly puff pieces designed to make the viewers feel good.
- Politics is about give and take, two sides to a story. Be conscious of balance in news reporting, and watch out for slanted news stories.
- Remember that without the commercials, the nightly news is only about twenty-six minutes. Ask yourself, what are the news items that never make it to the screen and why did the editor choose these stories that did get on the screen?
- As a corollary to the above, remember also that the choice of what goes on the air is not a terribly democratic process, but is usually the decision of Dan Rather, Tom Brokaw, and Peter Jennings. They may be wonderful journalists, but determining what's news is still their decision.
- Again, if possible, watch one of those extended news shows or panel debates to get beyond the two-minute compressed segment. Most issues cannot be fully understood or appreciated without time, the most precious commodity in the twenty-six minute nightly news.
- Be ever mindful that news shows have ratings and sponsors like all the other television programs. That means that news programming is not pure journalism, but is influenced by network competition for viewers and dollars. You are seen by the networks as a consumer just as much as a concerned and inter-

(continues)

Box 3.4   (continued)

ested citizen. The result of the consumerization of news is that the "boring" stuff of policy can be easily supplanted by the "exciting" stuff of disaster, crime, and sex.

- The nature of news in this country is that stories about the world at peace and people getting along are often pushed off the screen. News is about the 4 C's—controversy, conflict, criticism, and confrontation. Networks are getting better about showing the good news, but don't get the impression that the nightly news is a picture of America; it often is not.

- Do at least stick with the nightly news. It still is our window to the world and a valuable restraint on excessive power in the hands of government. The Founding Fathers got it right when they included freedom of the press in the First Amendment.

A Few Books You Should Read

Alexander, Herbert E. *Financing Politics: Money, Elections and Political Reform,* 4th ed. Washington, D.C.: Congressional Quarterly Press, 1992. Alexander's book remains the authoritative account of the role money plays in American politics.

Asher, Herbert. *Polling and the Public: What Every Citizen Should Know.* Washington, D.C.: Congressional Quarterly Press, 1988. The title says it all in this classic study of polling.

Bibby, John and L. Sandy Maisal. *Two Parties—or More? The American Party System.* Boulder, Colo.: Westview Press, 1998. A timely discussion of the American political party system with additional commentary on the prospects of new parties emerging in the future.

Birnbaum, Jeffrey. *The Lobbyists: How Influence Peddlers Get Their Way in Washington.* New York: Random House, 1997. All you ever wanted to know (and perhaps more than you want to know) about how interest groups influence the policy process in Washington.

Jamieson, Kathleen Hall. *Dirty Politics: Deception, Distraction and Democracy,* New York: Oxford University Press, 1992. An important discussion of the seamier side of American politics and the toll it takes on democratic values and democratic practice.

Kurtz, Howard. *Spin Cycle: How the White House and the Media Manipulate the News.* New York: Simon and Schuster, 1998. A rousing, no-holds-barred discussion of the ways in which the media manipulates the news and in the process the American people.

Miller, Warren E. and J. Merril Shanks. *The New American Voter.* Cambridge: Harvard University Press, 1997. Miller builds on his classic, *The American Voter,* with new insights on voter turnout, party identification, and an interesting discussion of generational differences and voting choice.

Mitchell, Michele. *A New Kind of Party Animal: How the Young are Tearing Up the American Political Landscape.* New York: Simon and Schuster, 1998. A Generation X look at the American political process. Full of insights into where we may be going as a democracy.

4

THE ROAD TO POWER IN AMERICAN POLITICS

All candidates should be subjected to a rigorous physical and psychological examination before the nominating convention. Anybody with minor psychological hang-ups should be accepted in order to assure that somebody is available, but congenital liars, twisters and obvious nuts should be rejected before the primary elections begin.

—James Reston of the New York Times

Why Would Anyone Want to Become President of the United States? (Or Senator or Representative or Governor, for That Matter?)

Remember when you were young and some adoring aunt or uncle asked you what you wanted to become when you grew up. One choice (after policeman and fireman) usually was president of the United States. The dream of becoming this famous man of politics was rooted in our egalitarian heritage—anyone could rise to the highest office in the land. The office of presidency was a cherished one that garnered respect and admiration in large part because it symbolized the greatness of the country and the value of politics as a central activity in society.

These days young boys and girls do not readily dream of being the president of the United States, maybe the president of Microsoft or Disney Studios or the Green Bay Packers, but not the president of the United States. Offices where political and governmental power are exercised now compete with corporate, media, or sports power for the attention and admiration of the nation. For many the simplicity of just making money in the private sector is far more appealing than the mundane reform of Social Security or the endless quest for a balanced budget.

Many Americans, even though they still grudgingly accept that public officials from presidents to governors are a necessity, now refuse to look upon these officials with awe or make them the stuff of youthful dreams. In a yearly *Newsweek* exercise that names the most powerful people in the United States, only three public officials made the list with regularity in the late '90s—President Clinton (he's still number one), the Chairman of the Federal Reserve, Alan Greenspan (he influences interest rates and the general direction of the economy), and the former Speaker of the House, Newt Gingrich (last on the top ten list). The majority of the people on the list were captains of industry, media moguls, and computer giants, attesting to the growing dominance of nonpolitical leaders in our country and the continued decline of politics and politicians. No Supreme Court justice, no senator, no vice president, no governor, no adviser to the President, no general, no shadowy intelligence head, but plenty of CEOs.

And yet despite the declining fortunes of political leadership, every two or four years there is never a shortage of men and women who put their names up for consideration for high public office. There always seems to be that allure that goes with the political life. Where corporate CEOs bask in the knowledge that they will earn seven figure salaries, stock options, and all the lovely perks from golf memberships to chauffeur-driven limos, those seeking public leadership cannot count on a lucrative package of goodies. They can, however, count on controlling the power of government, on managing billions in taxpayer moneys, on saying yes and no to crucial policy questions, and on remaining on center stage, taking the credit for all the good that happens in the public sector, if they're lucky.

But even though substantial power still resides with public officials, the job of conducting the people's business is becoming increasingly difficult. Besides the ceaseless quest for campaign finances, public officials must pass muster on vigorous ethics rules that pry into their personal finances. Then there are the compromises that politicians must make with marriage and family responsibilities, compromises that too often lead to divorce and estrangement. And one also cannot forget that public officials are the targets of all the kooks, nuts, and self-righteous patriots who now think nothing of threatening, if not doing bodily injury to their leaders. All this grief and turmoil for $250,000 for the president of the United States, $133,600 for members of Congress, and anywhere from $0 to $100,000 for governors. Certainly nowhere near the hundreds of millions Michael Eisner makes at Disney.

Popular culture does little to make political leadership attractive. Hollywood movies have for years portrayed presidents as ineffective PR guys, members of Congress as duplicitous blowhards, and governors as low-intelligence masters of backwoods fiefdoms. The 1997 movie season, for example, had the following offerings: "Murder at 1600" (a weak president surrounded by scheming advisers), "Absolute Power" (a kinky, abusive president), "The American President"(a decent but horny widower), and "Primary Colors" (a thinly veiled portrayal of Bill Clinton—a southern governor with an overactive libido seeking the presidency). Thankfully for American presidents, along came "Air Force One" with Harrison Ford, in which the chief executive is a war hero who single-handedly saves his plane and family from terrorists—not exactly plausible, but at least a positive image of public leadership.

What all this denigration of presidents and other elected officials means is that the concept of public service in our country is in big trouble. When Americans view their political leaders with cynicism and disdain, what they are really saying is that running for public office and managing the affairs of the people has little worth. These are clearly not the days of wide-eyed college students joining the Peace

Corps because their president (in the tradition of John Kennedy) has asked them to give something back to their country.

If citizens want to help their fellows or solve a community problem, they are more likely to do it as volunteers associated with a nonprofit organization rather than by running for office or working for a candidate. Political leaders, both at the national and state level, are thus increasingly talking about partnerships with business and community groups as they work cooperatively to address the needs before them. In many respects this arrangement is beneficial, for it sends out the message that the public and private sectors are on the same page. But it also reveals how political leaders have been forced to share the center stage of problem-solving and conflict resolution with other nongovernmental leaders, a major departure from the way this country responded to problems and conflicts in the past.

While we are on the matter of shifting leadership and power in America, there is also another discernible movement afoot that cannot be ignored. Washington, D.C., has seen its prominence take a series of hits in the last few years, as more of the direction and control of public policy has been bestowed on the states, and in particular on the governors of the states. For example, the shift in welfare policy implementation to the states along with the money for the various programs has shaken up the policy process and reinvigorated governors, who now have taken the reins of leadership in one of the most visible and expensive areas of government responsibility. Moreover, with the ascendancy of the Republicans in Congress, there is a new resolve to shift power to the states and the governors, thirty of whom are Republicans. The position of the Republicans, that power should reside where it is closest to the people, has also begun to weaken the influence of Washington policy-makers. If there is a promising star among the political leadership in the country, he or she will most likely now be found in the state capitals and not within the Beltway.

The shift in leadership from Washington to the state capitals may bring hope for at least some politicians, but there is a more disturbing trend in leadership at the local level. Former Speaker of the House Thomas Tip O'Neill said that "all politics is local," but the local residents of the thousands of small towns and cities in America appear to be moving away from accepting responsibility for local politics. Electoral races for school committees, finance committees, regional planning boards, county commissioners, and yes, even dog catchers and tree wardens are going uncontested. In some cases, the offices are even remaining vacant.

Many citizens at the local level seem wary of running for public office and assuming the mantle of community leadership. Too often local politicians encounter hostility from their neighbors and friends and decide that public service is just not worth the time and the aggravation. The reluctance of Americans to become local officials has not reached crisis proportions yet, but the number of uncontested seats in town and city elections means that democracy is not vigorous and certainly not competitive.

So what does this all mean? If the dreams of young boys and girls accurately predict the future of politics and politicians, then America is destined to become a nation where elected officials are not special and managing government is just another function of a complex society. Members of Congress will continue to reside near the bottom of the rankings of socially acceptable occupations, and presidents will be permanently off the pedestal of hero worship. Yet respect has served as the foundation of public officialdom.

Respect, after all, is one of the main perks of the political life. If the money is only adequate and the pressure is ceaseless, at least, so the argument goes, being a political leader means that the public respects the political process and ultimately respects those who make the political process work. Take away respect and being a politician holds no great appeal. There may be power, and there may be personal satisfaction, but when respect is absent, then being a politician is just another job.

What Does It Take to Become President of the United States? (Warning—It's No Walk in the Park)

Just in case the above discussion didn't completely turn you off, let me sketch a road map for anyone who still wants to serve the public by running the government. The basic requirement for an aspirant to the highest office in the land and the de facto title of most powerful person in the world is enormous endurance. Getting to the White House is one of the most time-consuming, costly, and physically demanding processes known to humanity. Many who have traveled this road to the White House agree that running for president is like a marathon, in which the candidate with the best race plan and staying power gets the golden ring.

Perhaps the most important step in running for the presidency of the United States is making the actual decision to run. Those who have campaigned for high office in the past have anguished over whether to put themselves, their families, and their staff through what is certain to be two years of constant travel, fund-raising, speech making, media attention, and intense scrutiny of past performance. Add to this the torture of staying in strange hotels, getting your hand disfigured as you shake hands with everyone in sight on the campaign trail, and giving the same speech ten times a day, and the job search looks less attractive.

Once the candidate accepts the personal challenges of the run for the White House, the next step involves building an organization, which means getting people in place who know what they are doing. Needless to say, this is no minor task. It is not enough to merely announce a run for the presidency and expect that voters will either like you or reject you. Campaign professionals, party activists, and volunteers by the boatload have to be brought on board to handle every detail involved in running a national election. The most crucial consideration is how to raise millions of dollars to pay for all the basic necessities required to run a successful campaign. Then there is the hiring of a consulting firm to formulate a strategy that will make the candidate attractive to potential voters. Finally, it is vitally important to formulate positions on key national issues and prepare responses to challenges on these issues from competing candidates.

With these essential building blocks of the campaign in place, the candidate can begin moving out among the voters and preparing for the next stop on the road to the White House—the primaries. The primaries are much like the game of King of the Hill that most of us played as a kid. Primaries are the political system's survival of the fittest process of selection. Candidates with the capacity to withstand a series of challenges from opponents from their own party over a five month period accumulate support from delegates who will be attending the party's nominating convention. The candidate accumulates this delegate support by winning primaries throughout the winter and spring months of the election year. Starting in New Hampshire in the dead of winter and ending in New Mexico in late spring, the primaries afford the voters an opportunity to participate in a series of pre-elections designed to see who can stay standing the longest, thereby earning the right to represent the party in the regular election.

The primaries eat up a great deal of the campaign money and help feed the insatiable appetite of the media for news about the candidates. The primaries also permit the paid consultants to earn their keep and charge enormous bills for polling, speech writing, strategizing, and general management of the campaign. In short, the primaries are good for business. But what the primaries are not good for is democracy, because they divide and weaken parties, create a long and boring road to the party nomination, and most importantly compartmentalize the selection process state by state, region by region, in order to offer the people a chance to participate in the King of the Hill game.

Once the primary season is over, the two candidates with the largest bloc of delegates pledged to them proudly stride across the stage at the national party conventions and receive the thundering applause of the faithful assembled to coronate their choice for president. Much of the convention these days is fluff; the competition for the nomination is really over, and the canned speeches and ceremonies are just designed to convince the viewers at home that the Dems or the GOP have the best person for the job at the White House.

This lack of real tension and competition is one of the main reasons that Americans have decided to tune out the conventions in favor of enjoying the wonders of summertime. The speeches given by the two nominees do give important signals of what the candidates are about and what might happen if the candidates get into the White

House, but most Americans are not listening, preferring rather to wait a few more months for the debates, or for a visit from the candidates to their state.

Come Labor Day the campaign gets into high gear. Summer is over, and people are back to work and back to paying some attention to politics. Candidates begin crisscrossing the country making scores of speeches and trying to avoid any noticeable gaffes that could prompt the media to zero in for the kill. Public endorsements from key interest groups become important to candidates as they seek to shore up their support. Television takes its place as the central focus of the campaign, as precious resources are used to buy prime time to get the image and the message across to the voters. Tailoring the message from the candidate to the particular concerns and problems of individual states is essential. And as always, damage control is forever on the minds of the campaign staff, in case the candidate or someone connected to the campaign says something or does something that could prove disastrous.

Midway through the final stretch of the campaign the debates are held. Debates can be critical to those undecided voters. The television camera does not lie, and candidates and their advisors prepare religiously for the give and take of the verbal contest. Those candidates who relish debate and the interaction with media types will thrive in the debate atmosphere. Those candidates who do not possess the talent to speak off the cuff, or worse yet, who put the audience to sleep, are in for trouble. The attention span of the American electorate is getting shorter and shorter, and those candidates who know how to drive home their point and have the gift for the sound bite are at a distinct advantage.

As the campaign heads down the homestretch, financial resources are thrown into those states where polling data show a chance to win. This is the time of media blitzes, more and more speeches, and little sleep. Since our electoral system is based on a winner-take-all proposition for the available electoral college votes in each state, candidates approach the campaign in near military terms as they chart their strategy to take California or make incursions into the Solid South. Modern campaigns have become something of a Big State proposition, since victory in the largest eight or ten states can get the candidate close to the magic number of 270 electoral votes and victory.

On election night, with no time left to change the minds of the voters, candidates settle in and watch as Rather, Jennings, and Brokaw tally the votes, score the state victories, and tell the American people who the next president of the United States is. Because this is a media-driven exercise, Americans have the rather strange experience of having a newsman tell them who has won the highest public office in the country. For the victor there is the triumphant appearance before the American people; for the loser there is the conciliatory concession speech.

Technically the election is not over on the first Tuesday after the first Monday in November. Because of the quirkiness of the electoral college, electors in each of the states and the District of Columbia must meet in early December and officially cast their ballots for the president. These electors, who represent the victorious political party in each state, come to state houses dressed to kill and simply sit down at a desk and mark an X next to the presidential and vice-presidential candidates who got the most votes in the state. Those ballots are then carried to Washington and counted out in Congress in January. It is only in January that the president of the United States is legally certified as the victor.

That completes the long journey to the White House—two years of a life, hundreds of millions of dollars, thousands of campaign workers, hours and hours of advertising, and countless words and promises. All that is left is Inauguration Day, with its pomp and circumstance, the hand on the bible and the parade of the states along Pennsylvania Avenue.

The American people have a president. This is no small feat, since the transfer of power in an election is not as common as it appears to Americans. Many countries still sit on needles and pins, hoping that this time democratic succession will run smoothly. In our system democratic succession runs so smoothly that we take it for granted. The process may be tortuous, expensive, and too often cosmetic, but somehow it works.

Box 4.1   Tip's Rules

Former Speaker of the House of Representatives Thomas "Tip" O'Neill wrote a book in his retirement called *All Politics Is Local*. The book was both a remembrance of his political life and sage wisdom on achieving success in the world of politics. Here is Tip's Political Checklist for budding politicians:

1. Vote your conscience, your country, your district, the leadership, in that order.
2. Never question the honesty or integrity of a colleague.
3. It's a round world—what goes around, comes around.
4. You can accomplish anything if you're willing to let someone else take the credit.
5. Never lose your idealism.
6. Lead by consent, not demand.
7. The bigger the crowd, the lower the vote.
8. Learn to say, "I don't know but I will find out."
9. K.I.S.S.—Keep it simple, stupid.
10. Don't stay mad—there's always tomorrow. Today's enemy is tomorrow's ally.
11. Never speak of yourself in the third person.
12. Tell the truth the first time and you don't have to remember what you said.
13. The horse that runs fast early fades in the stretch.

SOURCE: *All Politics Is Local*, with permission Random House Publishers.

Why Do Some People Win and Others Lose When They Run for Public Office?

This is one of those questions with a thousand answers. Elections, whether they end in a victory or a defeat, are stand-alone events that reflect the political, economic, social, and cultural times in which they occur. Everything from the way the candidate looks and speaks to the positions that are taken on controversial issues can sway the voters and seal the final result. Historians and journalists have made their careers and a lot of money examining the minute details of campaigns to determine the causes of winning and losing, and still there are lasting debates over what really happened to the campaign of candidate X or incumbent Y.

Nevertheless, the analysis of victory and defeat in American elections is not some dark puzzle with no answer. Some reasons for why politicians win and lose come up again and again, and can even be expressed as campaign rules, commandments that candidates must remember if they are to have any hope of gaining public office. Here are the five commandments of electoral victory in the American political system.

Thou Shalt Find and Hold the Center

If there is a fundamental commandment of electoral politics in this country, it is that successful politicians never permit themselves to be portrayed as either of the extreme right or the extreme left. Being smack dab in the center may not be terribly exciting or controversial, but it wins elections. Americans have traditionally been centrists, wishing not to be associated with the fringes, whether in political philosophy or political dialogue. Being in the center, or at least creating the perception of being in the center, allows politicians more room to maneuver. Candidates schooled in the art of the center can finesse their way around issues by taking positions that do not offend or scare a majority of the voters.

Finding and holding the center has been unattractive to those candidates who are drawn to controversy. Occasionally, those who take risks on the issues get away with it and make what was once viewed as an extreme position the norm. But for every politician who leaves the bland center for the thrill of the extreme and emerges victorious, there are scores of winners who got there by the safe road of becoming centrist. One thing that most successful politicians have learned is never to be caught out on a limb promoting a position that only a minority finds attractive.

One of the most difficult challenges for the candidate in American politics is to sense where that center lies and maintain the campaign on that center course. American public opinion and behavior is forever shifting and in need of stability. The astute politician knows just how to gauge public opinion and tune the campaign properly. It is far more difficult to find the center than to hold the center. But if the candidate has found what the majority of the voters want, then the only remaining challenge is not to blow the election by going off course.

Being a centrist politician may be smart politics, but it has its drawbacks. The need to find and hold the center means that when candidates speak they are always afraid of offending anyone and can never propose bold new initiatives. The center is no place for risk takers or proponents of major reform. The center instead is occupied by the advocates of slow, piecemeal reform that is designed to appease as many constituencies as possible.

Thou Shalt Appeal to the Middle

A corollary to finding and holding the center is to get out the vote of the middle. By middle is meant middle class, middle aged, middle America. Successful politicians have learned early in the campaign that voters in some demographic categories have a track record for greater participation in the electoral process than others. Those categories can be bunched under the heading of the middle. If a picture were to be drawn of the average American voter it would look something like this—a white suburban male or female in their forties and fifties with some college education, kids in public schools, and a combined income range of $40,000–60,000. This is a shorthand picture of the American middle, but it accurately presents the constituency that votes most heavily, the constituency that politicians must talk to if they hope to win elective office. America may be a melting pot of different colors, religions, and cultures, but when it comes to election time, it is this white suburban middle class that will carry the day.

The middle class has in recent years gained even more attention from politicians. Because of consumer debt associated with corporate restructuring, rising costs for education, and uncertainties in the area of medical coverage and retirement, the middle class has told politicians in no uncertain terms to make their life more secure and predictable. In order to get the vote of this stressed-out class of voters, politicians have had to respond to their concerns by showing themselves as the champions of middle America. It should come as no surprise that the agreement to balance the budget and cut taxes between the Republicans and the Democrats in 1997 was chock full of benefits for middle America, from college tuition incentives to retirement savings plans. Politicians know that if they want to stay in office, they will have to bring about some semblance of reform for the middle class or face the consequences with their constituents.

Appealing to the middle, though, usually means that politicians do not pay extraordinary attention to those Americans who are not in the middle. Certainly some public officials advance the cause of minorities, urban dwellers, or young people, especially if one of these groups is important in their voting constituency. But most politicians, particularly those who run for statewide or national office, know that they cannot hope to win if they are defined as the voice of a particular group unaffiliated with the great middle.

Most important, as I suggested before, election data clearly confirms that certain demographic groups, such as urban minorities and young people between the ages of eighteen and twenty-five are not likely to come out to the polls in great numbers, unless they are actively courted, as African Americans were by President Clinton and the Democratic Party in the 1998 congressional elections. Politicians know how to count, and the numbers they see are most apt to remind them of the importance of that white suburban family. Many Americans say that their vote doesn't count, but the reality of the voting process is that the votes of certain people do matter a great deal, simply because politicians know who puts them in office and who takes their jobs away. It's all in the middle.

Thou Shalt Talk Pocketbook Issues

Americans have always been practical, bottom-line kind of people. So when they cast their votes for a candidate, the strength of the economy, often characterized as the pocketbook issue, tends to be the deciding factor. Those who run for public office at the national and state level are forever perusing the data on economic growth, inflation, and interest rates, on unemployment data and trade balances. They know that although voters may not have a working knowledge of these standard indicators, the economic environment created when these indicators are all on the positive side can translate into votes for the incumbent, who will undoubtedly take credit for deeper pockets and fatter pocketbooks. Many an electoral victory for the incumbent has come when times are good; many a defeat has been endured when times are not so good.

Perhaps the best example of the pocketbook issue at work is the 1980 presidential election between incumbent Jimmy Carter and Republican challenger Ronald Reagan. Carter was seeking reelection with an economy in a funk. Inflation rates were in double digits, interest rates were skyrocketing, national growth was stagnant, the trade imbalance with Japan was astronomical, and employment figures were nothing to write home about.

In short, Carter was faced with justifying his reelection at a time when many Americans were not pleased with the overall status and direction of the economy. Reagan, for his part, played upon the economic downturn and laid the blame for it at Carter's feet. He pledged to the American people that he would get the economy moving again. Defeating an incumbent president is not an easy task, but Reagan had the ultimate electoral weapon, an economy begging for change and voters distressed over their financial circumstances. Carter was roundly defeated.

Fast forward to 1984 and the reelection of Ronald Reagan. Despite a mild recession in 1981 and 1982, the economy was definitely in overdrive by 1984. Jobs were being created along with personal fortunes. Businesses were seeing orders increase, and money was more available as interest rates plummeted. President Reagan was seen as a friend of corporate America, with his emphasis on deregulation of the economy, his tough stance against unions, and his vigorous promotion of the capitalist system. When the President asked the American people at the Republican National Convention, "Are you better off now than you were four years ago?" it was possible to see Americans nod their heads in unison. To make matters worse for the Democrats, challenger Walter Mondale had boldly stated that he would not stand in the way of a tax increase in order to pay for a range of social programs. Taxes are the death knell for any candidate, and even though Mondale was viewed as courageous by his supporters, the American people saw him as just another politician who wanted to take money from their pocketbooks. Reagan won in a landslide.

There are countless other stories about politicians, elections, and the pocketbook issue, and all of them center around how the voters perceive the state of the economy and their place in that economy. An incumbent may try to finesse this issue by accenting favorable economic data—after all, there is usually some bright spot. But the American people are not easily fooled. They know when times are good and when times are bad, simply because they live through it. Politicians are in a real sense prisoners to the pocketbook issue. Politicians may learn to manage finding the center and appealing to the middle, but they cannot manage the pocketbook issue; it manages them.

Thou Shalt See the Big Picture

Voters like to keep it simple. No matter how academics bemoan the soundbite character of American politics, come Election Day the decision about who gets into office often turns on a phrase, a symbol, or a slogan. Voters know the broad outlines of the issues, and they certainly have a sense of what shape the pocketbook is in, but the image that is placed in their mind about the candidates can still make a difference. Voters want their leaders to have an understanding of where America is and where it should go, or in other words, the Big Picture. Sometimes the Big Picture involves peace; other times it's change; sometimes it's prosperity, and other times it's security. The ability of candidates for office to portray themselves as in touch with that Big Picture can lead to a victory celebration.

The sign in Clinton campaign headquarters in 1992 stated simply—"It's the Economy, Stupid." James Carville, Clinton's campaign manager, had the ability to recognize the Big Picture; he constantly reminded staff members to emphasize the theme that a Clinton presidency would mean a revitalized economy. Even more importantly, Carville linked Clinton with the word *change*. Clinton was new, Bush was from the past; Clinton represented the future, Bush was tied to the old ways; Clinton would take the country into the twenty-first century, Bush was still back in World War II.

As the campaign progressed, Carville and Co. hammered home the message, endlessly repeating that economic revitalization would be brought about by a vigorous young politician who would change the country. By constantly emphasizing economic change, the campaign ensured that the American people would begin to think of the candidates in an easy shorthand—Bush would follow the same road, Clinton would take a new road.

The final touch in this creation of a Big Picture was to present the president as a symbol of generational change. That goal was accomplished on the Arsenio Hall show: Mr. Clinton put on dark glasses, picked up the saxophone, and played "You Ain't Nuthin But A Hound Dog" in front of millions of youthful Americans and an equal number of surprised middle Americans. Never before had a presidential candidate been so hip, so relaxed, so like the rest of us—instantly, Clinton became the candidate of the future, a man in tune with the times and able to connect with the new generation.

Creating a campaign around the Big Picture is not as simple as it would appear. Defining a candidate in such narrow terms creates serious risks. The voters may see the candidate as without substance or as a mere figment of a publicist's imagination. Candidates can't just ride into office with slogans or symbols, they have to take positions and explain their beliefs. The American voter might want to take the easy route in deciding on a leader, but that same American voter doesn't want to be taken for a fool. Nevertheless, candidates who find the right image for the times have a definite leg up on their opponents. It certainly worked for Bill Clinton.

Thou Shalt Persuade the People

Lest we forget, running for public office still requires that politicians convince the voters of their worthiness for the job. Therefore, politicians with good persuasive skills and a savvy public relations organization have the basic ingredients to secure that all-important check mark next to their name on election day. No doubt American voters have a short attention span, but do listen, especially in the closing days of the campaign, as they begin to realize that they have a decision to make.

As a result, the debate has come to play a critical role in persuading the people. On the national level, the Kennedy-Nixon debate initiated the custom of a series of a verbal contests between the two major-party nominees every four years. At the state level, debates in contests for U.S. senator and representative and governor are also now firmly entrenched in the electoral process. The debates have become a key step in moving the large number of undecided voters off the dime and toward commitment. Debates get high viewer ratings, in part because of the prospect of verbal fireworks between the candidates, in part because they mean the first focused discussion of the issues. Unlike the stump speeches, debates are unpredictable; candidates do not control the question agenda or the questioners, which makes for some real drama. Ronald Reagan's poor showing in the first debate with Walter Mondale in 1984 almost sealed his defeat (he rebounded in debate two); George Bush's casual, bored look at his watch during the 1992 debate with Clinton and Perot sent the wrong message to the viewers; and in 1996, Bill Clinton's easygoing style in answering questions compared to Bob Dole's stiff responses strengthened the President's popularity.

Studies indicate that those who watch the debates are more apt to confirm their earlier decisions than change their minds. Seeing their candidate answer questions as they expected them to be answered serves as a powerful means of voter solidification. But for undecided voters, the debates can be the final step in choosing their candidate. No candidate enters the debates without hours of preparation. Stand-in opponents, hours of rehearsals, foot-thick position papers, and endless strategizing by aides over possible questions, all show the extent to which candidates take this persuasive event to heart. In the end, whether it is speaking on the stump to a group of supporters or before millions in debates, candidates for public office must be able to touch the voters with their message and their personality.

Although the five commandments of electoral victory may not have the importance of the ten commandments that Moses brought down from his encounter with God, they nevertheless require strict adherence. Failure to follow the five political commandments does not lead to the wrath of God and eternal damnation, but there is a price to pay. Too many politicians have turned away from the five commandments and have found themselves in electoral oblivion.

Box 4.2   Why Americans Don't Vote

While poor voter turnout of Americans gets the lion's share of the attention by analysts of American democracy, the more interesting story is the list of reasons and excuses given by nonvoters for their failure to cast a ballot. Below are the more common reasons and excuses given by Americans:

> They were not registered.
> They did not like the candidates.
> They were too busy, usually a work-related reason.
> They made a choice not to vote.
> They were uninterested.
> They did not meet the local or state residency requirement.
> They were sick or a family member was sick.
> They believed their vote did not matter.
> They had never voted before.
> They felt the voting process was too complicated.
> They had no way of getting to the polls.
> They were out of town.

What Does the Most Recent Presidential Election Tell Us About American Politics?

The most striking thing about the election is that Bill Clinton won a second term in office, the first time since Franklin Delano Roosevelt that a Democrat has won reelection to the presidency. Furthermore, Bill Clinton achieved reelection with a comfortable margin of 45.6 million votes (49.2 percent) to Bob Dole's 37.8 million votes (40.8 percent) to Ross Perot's 7.8 million votes (8.5 percent). The electoral vote total was even more impressive. Clinton garnered 379 electoral votes to 159 for Dole to 0 for Perot. The electoral vote total means that the president scored victories in a vast majority of states and thus gained the electoral votes that accompany victory. Since 270 electoral votes trigger victory, Clinton's total further confirmed that his election was no nail-biter.

The raw numbers of the 1996 presidential election do not tell much of a story, other than that the Democratic incumbent defeated his Republican challenger and a weak third party alternative. The real story about the 1996 election can be found elsewhere, in the level of voter turnout, the influence of women on the election, the impact of a favorable economy on Clinton's victory, the ideological and generational conflicts within the Republican Party, the differing regional strengths of the Democrats and the GOP, and the continuation of divided government in Washington. The 1996 presidential election may not go down in history as a terribly memorable or significant exercise in democracy, but it did point to some disturbing trends in electoral politics in the United States.

First the voter turnout. 95.8 million Americans went to the polls on that Tuesday after the first Monday in November. Although that may seem an impressive number, the turnout was actually down by over 8 million voters from the 1992 figure. The overall turnout was 48.8 percent of the electorate, the lowest turnout since the election of Calvin Coolidge in 1924. To put this voter turnout data in perspective, Bill Clinton, who received 49 percent of the votes cast, was really only elected by about 23 percent of the eligible voters. Presidents often look for a mandate, a clear and convincing victory that gives them the confidence to go out and fight for their policy agenda. Clinton could publicly claim a mandate with his solid victory over Dole and Perot, but the numbers belie that claim—Clinton was the choice of only a quarter of Americans, with nearly 50 percent of the voters as no-shows.

Although the election numbers are further validation of the decline of voter interest, the real importance of the 1996 presidential election may be found in the increasing influence of women on issue definition and candidate selection. Terms like gender gap, soccer moms, and women's concerns were heard with great frequency during the election. Polling data showed that not only had more women voted in 1996 than in past elections, but that women were instrumental in Bill Clinton's victory. While Clinton and Dole received predictable support from men (Clinton received 43 percent of the male vote, Dole 44 percent), the president scored a key victory with the female vote (Clinton received 54 percent, Dole 38 percent).

Clinton's support for social issues such as education, health care, Social Security, and Medicare, and to a lesser extent his championing of a woman's right to choose an abortion and equal treatment for women in the military and in the workplace, convinced many women that the President's policy positions and future agenda were right for the country. Dole, on the other hand, stressed traditional male issues such as taxes, the economy, and defense, issues that were certainly legitimate, but did not resonate with women.

While the election of 1996 may have ushered in the era of the female voter, the Clinton victory was perhaps above all determined by a strong and growing economy. Survey responses found a third of Americans stating that their financial circumstances had improved since the last election. Postelection polling found that these same people, who were experiencing good times, voted overwhelmingly for the President. The emergence of the pocketbook as the critical ingredient in the Clinton victory was certainly no surprise. The Republicans had been hoping that the American voters would be distracted by the Whitewater scandal and the character issue associated with the president's personal life. What the Republicans found out to their dismay was that despite having Bob Dole, a war hero and a decent man, they could not overcome low inflation, low unemployment, and low interest rates. These positive economic standards meant more to the American people than allegations about a seedy land deal and steamy private matters.

The Republicans also caused themselves problems; they seemed intent on weakening their own prospects, as they engaged in ideological and cultural warfare among themselves. As the campaign developed, it became clear that the Republican Party was divided among hard-line conservatives and the more moderate wing. The hard-liners favored an uncompromising social and economic agenda, which featured opposition to abortion and gay rights, support for deep cuts in many domestic programs, and an unrelenting drive for capital gains tax reduction. The moderate elements in the party, on the other hand, were willing to find a middle ground on these policy issues so as not to alienate key constituencies such as women, seniors, and the working class.

Once Senator Dole defeated the conservative Pat Buchanan, the Party felt relief, believing that Republicans would band together to defeat the President. But during the campaign the right wing of the GOP continued to harp on these divisive issues and called into question Dole's credentials as a champion of conservatism. All this political controversy did little to unite the party and sent a message to the voters that the Republicans were not all on the same policy page. Senator Dole was beaten by Bill Clinton, but he wasn't helped a great deal by his own party.

The Republicans may not have given Bob Dole the support he needed to unseat an incumbent president, but they did score some important victories. The GOP further strengthened its hold on the South, the Mountain States, and the wheat belt, from Kansas to North Dakota. The Democrats, on the other hand, held their traditional base in the Northeast and the industrial corridor in the Midwest, except for Indiana. California, which had been a Republican stronghold since 1968, remained in the Democratic camp for the second election in a row. With fifty-four electoral votes, California is the crown jewel of the electoral college tally. The electoral college map for 1996 thus looked fragmented, with Democratic control ranging from Maine to Minnesota, then interrupted by Republican dominance in the center of the country and in the South, only to return back to the Democrats on the "left" coast. This pattern mirrors closely the map of the 1992 election, prompting election observers to speculate that this geographic fragmentation should hold true for sometime to come.

The substantial victory that Bill Clinton attained in 1996 was not a complete victory. The American voters were in no mood to throw the Republicans out of their newfound control of Congress. The Democrats did close the gap a bit, particularly in the House of Representatives, but not enough to regain a majority even there. The return of the Republicans to control of Congress thus left American politics with divided government once again, a state of conflict and occasional stalemate that may be inefficient but remains a popular way of limiting the power of both the executive and legislative branches. There is no firm evidence that American voters went into the ballot booth with the intention of maintaining divided government, but there is enough wariness of power and concern over abuse of office in the electorate that deliberate ticket-splitting cannot be discounted.

When Bill Clinton went before the American people to declare victory, there was great elation among his campaign supporters and in the Democratic Party as a whole. The Dems had kept the White House, made some inroads in the House of Representatives, and solidified their electoral bases in the East, the Midwest, and the West. But most observers of the 1996 election took a much dimmer view of the Clinton victory. CNN analyst William Schneider said the following about the reelection of Bill Clinton:

> It was a status quo election. The voters weren't angry. There was no frenzy for change, comparable to 1992. Incumbents did extremely well. And not much changed. . . . In the end President Clinton won an unimpressive victory. Voters rewarded him for his economic performance. But they didn't come to trust him, and they didn't give him much of a mandate.

Fred Wertheimer, the former president of Common Cause, a reform-minded interest group, was not so matter-of-fact about the Clinton victory and the election of 1996. Wertheimer stated:

> I say without hesitation that this election will go down as the worst in modern times, if not in our history. In important ways, the abuses involving hundreds of millions of dollars are worse even than the illegal contributions gathered by Richard Nixon's men during the Watergate era. . . . When you add it all up—the illegality, the cheating, the evasion, as well as the arrogance and cynicism—what we have is a collapse of the system on a scale we haven't seen before.

Certainly these are not glowing endorsements for the American electoral process or the 1996 election. The nation got through another exercise in democracy, but it was not an uplifting experience. What the

American people saw unfortunately in 1996 was a bland, corrupt, and self-serving political process that had little connection to the people.

Box 4.3   1996 Election Trivia

- There were 525,000 elective offices available to run for.
- The voter turnout was 95.8 million people, the lowest since 1924.
- South Dakota led the way with the largest voter turnout—63.9 percent of registered voters.
- "None of the above" received 5,608 votes for President.
- President Clinton's campaign for reelection cost $222 million.
- The average cost of a U.S. Representative campaign was $525,000, a Senate campaign was $4.5 million.
- Bill Clinton received 379 electoral votes, 179 more than necessary to win.
- Bill Clinton was one of only three presidents to win two terms while receiving less than 50 percent of the vote each time (the others were Cleveland and Wilson).
- As a group, college graduates voted the most, Hispanics the least.
- 38 percent of voters identified themselves as Democrats, 29 percent as Republicans, 33 percent as Independents.

SOURCE: Federal Election Commission

Is There a Better Way to Elect Our Political Leaders?

No shortage of answers here. Just about anyone connected to the world of national politics can tell you that something needs to be done to improve the way we elect our governmental leaders. There is general consensus in this country that campaign and electoral reform is long overdue. With voters turning off from the process in droves and polls showing ever growing levels of distrust, it is clear that changes designed to improve the quantity and quality of participation are in order. To do nothing, certainly, is an option. But standing still and avoiding reform would only further narrow the playing field of politics and hand over popular rule to fewer and fewer Americans. The consequences of a standpat attitude would only deepen apathy and heighten mistrust.

In recent years those close to American politics have brainstormed extensively on how best to jump-start the democratic process and bring it out of its current decline. In the early '90s much of the attention on campaign and electoral reform centered on term limits for public officials. The position taken by the advocates of term limits was that the best way to clean up the system was to have politicians not stay in power long enough to do serious damage to our governing institutions. After a number of successes at the state level, the term limits bandwagon stalled as a result of court challenges. Also legislators at both the national and state level were either leaving office on their own or being defeated. No use pushing ahead with a solution when the problem was being solved without it.

In any case, throwing the rascals out is a rather narrow and vindictive reform effort. Reform needs to make our campaign and electoral systems less focused on special interests and more responsive to the public. Most urgently, reform initiatives must address the issue of citizen participation in the political process. But as with most change in this country, reform will likely come in small increments over a period of time. Lawmakers will have to be pushed and cajoled into moving away from past practices and citizens will need to have their confidence restored that reform is indeed real. The problem of course is how to reach a consensus on ways to get back on track. Let's take a brief look at the areas of change that will get the greatest attention in the coming years and may hold the key to further democratizing the American political system and increasing voter participation.

Primary Election Reform

As currently constituted, the road to the White House has to go through a mind-boggling maze of primary elections and state caucuses designed to separate the fringe candidates from those who have the greatest chance of winning the nomination and the presidency.

Starting with the first caucus in Iowa and the first primary in New Hampshire in February, this preelection season extends through June, when the voters in Alabama, Montana, New Jersey, and New Mexico get to cast their votes for the Democratic and Republican candidates for their party's nomination.

This process of giving voters a chance to influence the party nominee wouldn't be so bad if it weren't for the myriad of state laws governing this process. The primary/caucus process is so complicated that lawyers have opened up new specialties in election law. But the real problem with this pre-election process is that it lengthens the campaign and makes the elective process a traveling road show, as candidates travel from state to state begging for votes, and in the process wearing down not only the competition but the voters as well.

The solution that has been bounced around for years is to have a short primary/caucus season with a few regional primaries (much like the Super Tuesday primary grouping of southern states that exists currently) or perhaps even a national primary day in which this pre-election nominating ritual is conducted simultaneously around the country. If the party leaders want to increase voter interest and cut down the cost of campaigning, the six-month "Long March" from the snows of New Hampshire to the nominating conventions should be condensed and organized in a more rational manner. Of course since television stations, hotels, restaurants, airlines, car rental agencies, polling organizations, and campaign consultants see the "Long March" as an opportunity to make money, don't look for change coming soon.

Political Party Convention Reform

After the 1968 Democratic Convention in Chicago, which was marked by protests and violence associated with the Vietnam policy of the Johnson administration, changes were made to delegate selection procedures to ensure wider representation. Greater emphasis was placed on the primary as the key means of determining the nominee of the party. Rather than the backroom deals of yesteryear, delegate selection in open primaries throughout the country was viewed as an essential electoral reform. This democratization of the convention has generally met with wide support, although there has been criticism that the input and judgment of party leaders has been ignored. The Democrats, in particular, have been struggling with the democratization of the delegate selection process and its impact on candidate selection at the convention. Democratic officials complain that the primary process has led to weaker candidates being elevated to the position of nominee and leader of the party.

What is being talked about now is the staging of preprimary national conventions, where party leaders would participate in a selection process and present to the party faithful the candidate they feel has the best chance of succeeding in the race for the White House. Those candidates who were not selected in this preprimary selection process would still be permitted to travel the long primary road, but without the endorsement of the party. The advantage of the preprimary convention would be that it would eliminate candidates who do well in the early primaries but are in fact unrepresentative of national opinion. Most importantly, a preprimary would strengthen the party, at least according to the party activists who want a little less democracy and more opportunity for savvy political judgment when it comes to choosing a presidential nominee.

Voter Registration Reform

Every election in this country usually ends with the wringing of hands by political scientists, journalists, the League of Women voters, and reform groups like Common Cause. The reason, poor voter turnout. Poor voter turnout is one of those political problems that has been overexplained and overanalyzed. We have plenty of data on why people do not vote and plenty of schemes to get people out of their homes and over to the town hall to cast their ballot. The problem is that either the remedies are difficult to implement or fraught with dangers to the integrity of the vote. Nevertheless, state governments, which have the authority to change the way voting is conducted, have begun to implement more attractive methods of getting out the vote.

Some states have begun to institute a mail-in registration process to allow voters to avoid the trip to the town hall to register. All citizens would have to do is mail the postcard back to the election officials and show up to vote on Election Day. The mail-in registration effort comes on the heels of the motor voter legislation passed during the first Clinton administration, which allows people to register to vote when they register their car. This change has not been completely embraced by state political leaders, who have failed to provide financial resources or advertising money to alert citizens to this easy way of getting on the voting lists.

There are also proposals that voting in the future should be permitted from home using available computer and cable technology. Citizens would be given a personal PIN code allowing them to access the voting center and cast their ballot from their favorite easy chair. The proponents of the traditional method of leaving the house and casting a vote at the town hall feel this kind of voting procedure would destroy the sense of community and create serious fraud problems, as PIN numbers could be shared and voting would become less serious, voters less responsible. The battle over how to get Americans to vote is beginning to heat up as it is clear that new ways have to be developed to entice people to participate in public decisionmaking.

Popular Election Reform

Changing the Constitution is no easy task, but many Americans agree that something should be done about that relic we call the electoral college. Because of the Founding Fathers' desire to limit the ability of the voters to choose their president, we engage in a form of indirect democracy in which the majority vote of the states elects presidents rather than the majority vote of the citizens. Candidates for the presidency scurry around from state to state trying to win those precious electoral votes. What this translates into is that the vote of the American people is less important than the vote total of each state.

It may be splitting electoral hairs to say that the states rather than the people elect presidents, but the current arrangement does deprive voters of that ultimate power—the ability to elect their leader directly. At the present time voters only influence that decision and share it with those electors who also get to cast a ballot one month after the election. Few instances exist where the electors have gone against the wishes of the people, but there is still that indirectness, denying voters the ultimate power to name their president.

There is a simple resolution of this dilemma—get rid of the Twelfth Amendment, which contains this constitutional relic, and move to a system where the people directly elect their president with no strings attached. It seems like a simple change that reinforces democratic practice and allows the people the right to make the key governing decision. Changing the Constitution to achieve this reform has been talked about for years. But as with most changes to this hallowed document, it may take a crisis or at least a major foul-up in some future election to precipitate a move to a more democratic way of choosing our president. Just because direct national elections sound good, that does not mean that the old system is headed for the graveyard. States like the ability to be important players in the national election, campaign strategies have been developed over the years based on state electoral vote counts, and political parties see the electoral college as a way to reward party activists by giving them a chance to make history with their vote.

All of the above areas of political reform require substantial backing from key elites both in and out of government. There is a long road to travel before any of these changes comes to pass. But while fundamental political and electoral reform is difficult, it is possible to attain some qualitative reforms that depend only on the good will and common sense of those involved.

- Candidates should pledge themselves to conduct positive campaigns that do not stoop to character assassination and false advertising.
- Political parties should not wait for legislative campaign finance reform but should engage in their own cleanup.
- All participants in the races for elective office should pledge to shorten their campaigns.
- Candidates should remember that educating the public about the issues not image-making should be the primary objective of campaigns.
- Public officials and all concerned citizens should keep up their efforts to encourage voting, targeting their campaigns at America's young people.

It is important to remember that reform of politics is not without precedent in this country. The Progressive Era in the early 1900s brought many changes to the way we choose our public officials and manage our politics. The Vietnam War period and particularly the 1968 Democratic convention debacle intensified the movement toward opening up popular selection of presidential nominees. The post-Watergate era brought significant changes to governmental ethics and campaign finance. As we approach the millennium, there is a new opportunity to shake up the system in the name of democracy. It is possible to change the system and to create new opportunities for people to have their voice heard. Of course because the reform movement inevitably runs up against powerful and entrenched interests, the going will not be easy. But as with past reform initiatives, eventually democracy wins the day.

Box 4.4   *What Is Good Leadership?*

James MacGregor Burns is perhaps the most noted authority on political leadership in America. In his book *Leadership,* he presents his vision of the essential qualities of effective leadership:

> The function of leadership is to *engage* followers, not merely to activate them, to commingle needs and aspirations and goals in a common enterprise, and in the process to make better citizens of both leaders and followers. To move from manipulation to power-wielding is to move from the arithmetic of everyday contacts and collisions to the geometry of the structure and dynamics of interaction. It is to move from checkers to chess, for in the "game of kings" we estimate the powers of our chessmen and the intentions and calculations and indeed the motives of our adversary. But democratic leadership moves far beyond chess because, as we play the game, the chessmen come alive, the bishops and knights and pawns take part on their own terms and with their own motivations, values, and goals, and the game moves ahead with new momentum, direction, and possibilities. In real life the most practical advice for leaders is not to treat pawns like pawns, nor princes like princes, but all persons like *persons.*

A Few Books You Should Read

Goddard, Teagan D., and Christopher Riback. *You Won Now What? How Americans Can Make Democracy Work from City Hall to the White House.* New York: Simon and Schuster, 1998. A nice handbook for those Americans interested in using the electoral process to make a difference.

Ehrenhalt, Alan. *The United States of Ambition: Politicians, Power and the Pursuit of Office.* New York: Times Books, 1991. A critical look at the people who seek public office in this country and their motivations for going through the rigors of campaigning.

Euchner, Charles C., and John A. Maltese. *Selecting the President: From Washington to Bush.* Washington, D.C.: Congressional Quarterly Press, 1992. A good historical examination of how presidents have run for office and why they won.

Jamieson, Kathleen Hall. *Dirty Politics: Deception, Distraction and Democracy.* New York: Oxford University Press, 1992. One of many books on what is wrong with American electoral politics, but certainly one of the best.

Morris, Dick. *Behind the Oval Office: Winning the Presidency in the Nineties.* New York: Random House, 1997. Although discredited in his own sex scandal, Morris, Clinton's campaign consultant in 1996, remains perhaps one of the most savvy political consultants around today.

Sabato, Larry. *Millennium: The Elections of 1996.* Boston: Allyn and Bacon, 1997. One of the best commentaries on the national and state elections in 1996, written by one of the most knowledgeable analysts of the American political system.

Scammon, Richard, and Ben Wattenberg. *The Real Majority.* New York: Coward-McCann, 1970. One of my favorite books about American politics. The authors present a clear and concise explanation of what it takes to win the presidency and what the American voter responds to in a campaign.

Wayne, Stephen. *The Road to the White House, 1996: The Politics of Presidential Elections,* 5th ed. New York: St. Martin's Press, 1996. Part of an ongoing series that documents the strategies, the personalities, the issues, and the key events in the 1996 election. An essential guide.

5

POLITICIANS AND PUBLIC SERVANTS

He pays too high a price
For knowledge and for fame
Who sells his sinews to be wise,
His teeth and bones to buy a name,
And crawls through life a paralytic
To earn the praise of bard and critic.
Were it not better done
To dine and sleep through forty years;
Be loved by few; be feared by none;
Laugh life away, have wine for tears;
And take the mortal leap undaunted,
Content that all we asked was granted?
But Fate will not permit
The seed of gods to die
Nor suffer sense to win from wit
Its guerdon in the sky,
Nor let us hide, whate'er our pleasure,
The world's light underneath a measure.
Go then, sad youth, and shine,
Go, sacrifice to Fame;
Put youth, joy, health upon the shrine,
And life to fan the flame;
Being for Seeming bravely barter
And die to Fame a happy martyr.

—*Ralph Waldo Emerson, "Fame"*

Who Runs the Government of the United States?

The immediate answer to "who runs the government of the United States?" is that there are 2.8 million federal workers employed in fourteen cabinet level bureaucracies and scores of independent executive agencies, regulatory commissions, boards and government corporations. But this response does little to help us get to the heart of who really wields power in our national government. Another avenue toward answering this question is to pull out all those complicated organizational charts which describe in rather sterile fashion the chain of command and hierarchy of responsibility in the various government bureaucracies. Again, this would be helpful in narrowing our focus, but line drawings do little to reveal whether the person at the top of the chain of command is indeed a major player in government or just another bureaucrat with a job to do.

A less traditional method of finding out who runs the government of the United States is the "visibility test." Simply stated, who has power and responsibility in Washington can be determined by sitting in front of the television during the evening news or reading the newspaper and counting up the times a government official appears announcing a program, offering an opinion, or criticizing the way the country is being run. If indeed media sources are the primary filtering agent of fame and influence, then it follows that those who get their faces and their words in front of the American public on a regular basis must be placed somewhere high on the list of major players in our governmental system. If you were to follow the visibility test approach to assessing who controls the levers of power and responsibility in American government, the holders of the following positions would likely rise to the surface:

President of the United States
Vice President of the United States
Secretary of State
Secretary of Defense
Secretary of the Treasury
Speaker of the House of Representatives
Majority Leader of the Senate

Majority Leader of the House of Representatives
Minority Leader of the House of Representatives
Minority Leader of the Senate

The individuals who occupy these ten positions are constantly being interviewed by the print and electronic media; they are the subject of ceaseless analysis and criticism; and they often are at the table when key policy decisions or national initiatives are being discussed. Just for the record (and subject to change), the Big Ten are as follows:

President of the United States—William Clinton
Vice President of the United States—Albert Gore
Secretary of State—Madeline Albright
Secretary of Defense—William Cohen
Secretary of the Treasury—Robert Rubin
Speaker of the House of Representatives—Dennis Hastert
Majority Leader of the Senate—Trent Lott of Mississippi
Majority Leader of the House of Representatives—Richard
     Armey of Texas
Minority Leader of the Senate—Thomas Daschle of South Dakota
Minority Leader of the House of Representatives—Richard
     Gephardt of Missouri

Noticeably absent from this list, but at the same time worthy of a high score on our visibility test is the president's press secretary, who is on television almost every night answering questions from the media about the day's events. In this case, however, visibility does not reflect power, since the press secretary articulates a response that is agreed upon at a higher level. Also not on the list is the First Lady, neither an elected or appointed governmental official, but nevertheless someone who is constantly in the news, whether at the side of the president or as an unofficial representative of the White House. Lastly, the Chairman of the Federal Reserve Bank, who is nominated by the president and approved by Congress, has become a media star, in large part because of his influence on interest rates and the general health of the nation's economy. Although he is enormously important in terms of fiscal and monetary policy, it would be a stretch to state that the Chairman of the Federal Reserve helps to run the government—maybe the economy, but not the government.

It is not enough to merely list the Big Ten of government and conclude that they wield power. The next step is to outline how they go about the business of operating U.S.A., Inc. Notoriety is one thing, the manner in which power is used is another. For example, everyone knows that the president of the United States is a powerful government leader with enormous responsibilities both on the domestic front and in matters outside this country. But the American people are usually short on details when pressed to define the job description of the chief executive.

The president of the United States is a powerful governmental leader because the Constitution gives him control over foreign policy, the armed forces, and millions of government bureaucrats; it also stipulates that he shall work closely with the legislative branch on "measures as he shall judge necessary." Beyond these specific constitutional powers, the president of the United States is at the center of the decisionmaking process in our government. As chief executive, he is the point man for many of the policy initiatives taken in this country. As chief executive, he is usually in the thick of the partisan battles that accompany the lawmaking process, lobbying for his proposals and making deals in order to ensure their passage. And as chief executive, he takes the credit and the blame for the policies that emerge during his time in office.

In a discussion of the power of the president, it is easy to concentrate on his control of our nuclear arsenal or his ability to send troops to a foreign land, but these powers are held in reserve, hopefully never to be used. The core of the president's power is related to his position as governmental leader. The president has the opportunity to set the agenda for the country and then shape public opinion in order to advance that agenda. If a president adroitly develops his agenda, directs it through the snares and pitfalls of the governing system and effectively develops popular and institutional support for the agenda, then he will be a force to be reckoned with. This is how the American government works, and the American government works best when the president works best.

As for the vice president, his role may best be summed up by the familiar comment of John Nance Garner, one of Franklin Delano

Roosevelt's VPs, who said that being the second in command "wasn't worth a bucket of spit." John Adams, the first vice president, was a little more diplomatic but in unison with Garner's comments when he said that the office of the vice president was "the most insignificant office that was the invention of man." Fortunately for the current VP, Al Gore, his boss has given him a number of key policy responsibilities dealing with the environment, legislative relations, and technology. Moreover, Gore meets regularly with the president and is a key member of the inner circle of advisers.

Clinton's use of Gore in a more substantive policy formulation role, however, is not the norm; VP's such as Dan Quayle (Bush's vice president) and Spiro Agnew (Nixon's vice president) reflect the more usual reality of a second in command who is an election ticket balancer and a stand-in for the chief executive at state events. Most Americans will continue to see the vice president, no matter how influential he may be in government, primarily as someone who is there should the unthinkable happen—the death or incapacitation of the president of the United States. Maybe not a warm bucket of spit, but mostly someone who is there in case of an emergency.

The vice president may usually be a highly paid reserve player in government, but some key cabinet secretaries are often at the center of decisionmaking in Washington. In particular, the secretaries of state, defense, and the treasury are mentioned frequently as members of an small elite circle of advisers to the president. Despite the fact that the focus of politics in the late 1990s is on domestic matters, the secretary of state, Madeline Albright, remains the voice of the United States to the 190 nations that exist in the world today. Presidents have historically counted on their secretaries of state to provide them with wise counsel on a range of international issues and the proper means of addressing national security crises.

Joined with the secretary of state in the higher levels of governing responsibility is the secretary of defense, William Cohen. Secretary Cohen is responsible not only for the million men and women in uniform but for a budget that is one of the largest in government. Providing national defense remains the core responsibility of government, but national defense also means jobs for soldiers, defense contractors, and the millions of Americans who depend on the presence of the military in their town or state. Finally, secretary of the treasury Robert Rubin has been called by some the American prime minister because of his responsibility for guiding the economic ship of state and for ensuring financial stability in this increasingly interconnected world.

What remains of the Big Ten of national government are the key leaders in the Congress. Congress is a natural setting for adversarial relationships—Republicans vs. Democrats, majority vs. minority, leadership vs. loyal opposition. Therefore any discussion of governmental power must focus on those individuals who occupy the Republican majority leadership positions and their counterparts, the Democratic minority leadership.

The Speaker of the House of Representatives, Dennis Hastert of Illinois, is positioned at the top of the power pyramid. The Speaker has traditionally been at the center of Congressional power; his position allows him to set the legislative agenda and direct the flow of legislation through the House. When Hastert's predecessor, Newt Gingrich, assumed the mantle of power in 1994 he became the center of a whirlwind of controversy as he presented his legislative agenda, the Contract With America, and spoke often about the need to move the country away from its liberal moorings.

Because our legislature is bicameral, the Republicans also have another leader almost as powerful in the other chamber. The Senate majority leader, currently Senator Trent Lott of Mississippi, is the dominant voice in the Senate; he uses his power to control the agenda and the process of lawmaking in the smaller legislative body. In the House, the Republican Speaker is aided by a majority leader, who often is responsible for the day-to-day management of the legislative agenda and often also acts as a kind of bad cop to the good cop of the Speaker. Representative Dick Armey of Texas is an unabashed conservative who speaks forcefully about Republican policies. The Republican majority leaders in both the Senate and House must also be good at counting heads and twisting arms, as they seek to control the vote and maintain the cohesiveness of their party in the legislature.

Although the Democrats are currently in the minority, our legislative system is organized in a way that permits the weaker party to exercise influence over the legislative process. The minority leaders in the House and Senate, Senator Tom Daschle and Representative Dick

Gephardt, can be influential thorns in the side of the Republican majority. They can use their debating and amending powers to win the
day; they can employ a range of parliamentary procedures to delay a
vote or kill a bill; and they can drum up public opinion to force the
majority to reconsider their agenda or end their quest for a particular
change in the law. Since much of Congress is a great compromise factory where deals are made constantly, the minority leadership can
never be counted out of the game, especially since their support is
often needed for success and their opposition can mean defeat.

My choices for the Big Ten of American Government may not be
shared by every observer of the Washington scene; other choices for
most powerful are also "on the bubble." No president works alone
or makes solitary decisions. Presidential power therefore is shared
with an effective advisory system in the White House. At the top of
the advisory ladder is the president's chief of staff.

The chief of staff, currently John Podesta, is one of those advisers
who wears many hats—confidant, gatekeeper, sounding board, protector, and alter ego. The chief of staff is the one person in the White
House the president will see on a daily, if not hourly basis. No one
gets through to the president except through the chief of staff, no important policy initiative is undertaken without the O.K. of the chief
of staff, and no crisis response is formulated or delivered unless the
chief of staff has granted his approval. In short, the chief of staff is
not just the president's right hand man, he is a quasi president who
controls the operations of the White House.

Also "on the bubble" are the president's national security adviser,
Sandy Berger, who manages foreign policy from the White House,
and the chairman of the Joint Chiefs of Staff, General Henry Shelton,
who is the top military man in the country. In the Congress, the
chairs of key Congressional committees such as Bill Archer, chair of
the House Ways and Means Committee (responsible for writing tax
legislation), and Pete Domenici, chair of the Senate Budget Committee (which sets budget goals for the nation), also wield considerable
power. Finally, it is difficult to ignore the chief justice of the Supreme
Court, William Rehnquist, and indeed all the justices, who, with life-
time employment and the power to interpret laws and declare them
unconstitutional, are collectively a mighty force to be reckoned with.

Probably the best way to conclude this little exercise is to state that there is a great deal of power in Washington. When an organization spends over a trillion of dollars a year, passes hundreds of pieces of legislation in a two-year session, and sets the direction of the country, it is not difficult to conclude that Washington oozes with power. So if you want to keep an eye on power in Washington, keep in mind the visibility factor and the Big Ten of government.

Box 5.1   All the President's Men and Women

The president of the United States may be the most powerful man in this country, if not the world, but he needs a lot of help running the White House. Below are the job categories for President Clinton's White House staff. The image of the lonely decisionmaker setting policy and responding to crisis is not quite accurate. The White House, with all its staff, is clearly a growth industry.

1.	THE PRESIDENT
1-a	The President's Personal Office
1-b	The Physician to the President
2.	THE VICE PRESIDENT
2-a	Personal Assistant
2-b	Chief of Staff
2-c	Deputy Chief of Staff
2-d	Advance
2-e	Scheduling
2-f	Legislative Affairs
2-g	Counsel
2-h	Military Assistant
2-i	Press Secretary
2-j	Assistant for National Security Affairs
2-k	Speechwriting
3.	THE FIRST LADY
3-a	Chief of Staff
3-b	Personal Assistant
3-c	Press Secretary

(continues)

Box 5.1 (continued)

3-d	Correspondence
3-e	Scheduling and Advance
3-f	Social Secretary
3-g	Graphics and Calligraphy
4.	THE CHIEF OF STAFF
5.	THE DEPUTY CHIEF OF STAFF
6.	THE STAFF SECRETARY
7.	THE CABINET SECRETARY
8.	EXECUTIVE SECRETARIES OF CABINET COUNCILS
9.	THE ASSISTANT FOR NATIONAL SECURITY AFFAIRS
9-a	The Situation Room
9-b	The Situation Room Support Staff
10.	THE ASSISTANT FOR DOMESTIC POLICY
11.	THE COUNSEL
12.	THE ASSISTANT FOR LEGISLATIVE AFFAIRS
12-a	House Legislative Affairs
12-b	Senate Legislative Affairs
13.	THE ASSISTANT FOR POLITICAL AFFAIRS
14.	THE ASSISTANT FOR INTERGOVERNMENTAL AFFAIRS
15.	THE DIRECTOR OF COMMUNICATIONS
16.	THE PRESS SECRETARY
16-a	The News Summary
17.	PUBLIC LIAISON
18.	SPEECHWRITING AND RESEARCH
19.	SCHEDULING
19-a	The President's Diarist
20.	PRESIDENTIAL PERSONNEL
21.	ADVANCE
22.	AD HOC SPECIAL ASSISTANTS
23.	THE WHITE HOUSE MILITARY OFFICE
23-a	Air Force One

(continues)

Box 5.1 (continued)

23-b	Marine Helicopter Squadron One
23-c	The Staff Mess and the Presidential Watch
23-d	Camp David
23-e	The Medical Unit
23-f	Emergency Planning Group
23-g	Naval Imaging Command
23-h	White House Garage
23-i	White House Social Aides
23-j	The Sequoia (if required)
23-k	White House Communications Agency
24.	THE WHITE HOUSE UNITS OF THE U.S. SECRET SERVICE
24-a	The Presidential Protective Division
24-b	The Vice-Presidential Protective Division
24-c	Protective Research
24-d	Technical Security
24-e	The Uniformed Division (White House Police)
25.	THE CHIEF USHER
25-a	The Curator
25-b	The Family Theater
26.	WHITE HOUSE OPERATIONS
26-a	Correspondence
26-a-i	Mail Room
26-a-ii	Volunteer and Comment Office
26-a-iii	Letters and Messages
26-a-iv	Agency Liaison Office
26-a-v	Gifts Unit
26-b	The Executive Clerk
26-c	Civilian Telephone Operators
26-d	The Photo Office
26-e	The Visitor's Office
26-f	Records
26-g	White House Administrative Office

What Makes a President Great?

The answer to this question could look something like a want ad for Mr. or Ms. Perfect—a great president would be a person of integrity, sound judgment, honesty, vision, energy, intelligence, and concern for the common good. Over the years Americans have expressed this kind of vision of the qualities they want in the person who occupies 1600 Pennsylvania Avenue. When it comes to the chief executive of the United States, the bar has been set quite high in terms of the essential ingredients of a great president.

Because this bar is set so high, it has been fairly easy in recent years to kick presidents off the pedestal because they have not measured up to the standard. Americans also want a President who gets things done and makes the country strong and prosperous. When life is good in the United States and the president keeps his affairs in order, public support soars and that place on the pedestal becomes more secure. But when that same president engages in the stuff of politics— bargaining, compromising, making controversial decisions, or saying no to Congress, the American people have been known to turn their backs in an instant, and what was once adulation becomes condemnation.

If we as a people ever give our presidents the benefit of the doubt, it usually is when they are faced with a particularly thorny crisis, whether a war, an economic downturn, or a domestic problem with far-reaching impact. Polls over the years have ranked the great and abysmal presidents from Washington to the contemporary chief executives, and most of those at the top of the list are men who led the country through difficult times or took the initiative to address a crying national need. Those at the bottom of the list are usually those who disgraced the office, either by doing very little or by using the office for personal or financial gain.

Abraham Lincoln, for example, is often viewed as our greatest president, in large part because of his steely determination to keep the Union together in the face of Southern secession. Historians remain impressed with Lincoln because of his decisiveness, his commitment to building a nation on the foundation of equality, and his ability to move the nation with his words and his presence. Lincoln fitted the profile of presidential greatness in many respects, but it was his performance during a time of crisis that has secured his place at the top of the list of our best presidents.

For a deeper understanding of what makes a president great, it helps to examine more closely the more recent occupants of the White House. It turns out to be possible to arrive at a reasonable consensus on which presidents over the last fifty years will likely survive the test of time and join the pantheon of greatness and which will forever be given the title of "mediocre" or "the worst."

The Great

At the top of the list of contemporary presidents is Franklin Delano Roosevelt. Roosevelt is challenging Lincoln these days for the top of the hill in presidential greatness. FDR was president longer than any other president, he took the nation through the Great Depression and World War II, and he was responsible for initiating some of the most popular and long-lasting social programs in our history. But Roosevelt is considered great not just because he was president during times of crisis or because he started new programs. Roosevelt is great because he was a leader who took charge during the worst of times, calmed the fears of a desperate nation, and tried new ideas rather than relying on old methods. Roosevelt certainly had his enemies and detractors, and many times his policies fell flat on their face. But he never wavered from his mission to get America back on its feet and win the war. His greatness is thus not only based on his success in achieving his mission, but also on the way he went about that mission.

When Roosevelt died in 1945, he left the office of the presidency to a virtual unknown, Harry Truman. With little experience at the national and international level, Truman was viewed by most insiders as a recipe for presidential disaster. Truman proved the insiders wrong. What Harry Truman did in office was to grow with the job and bring some common sense and common talk to the White House. He will be most remembered for deciding to use the atomic bomb on Hiroshima and Nagasaki, still a controversial decision. But Truman also integrated the armed forces, developed the strategy to contain communism, and moved the country from a wartime economy to peacetime prosperity.

Truman had his shortcomings and his missteps, such as his failed attempt to nationalize the steel industry and his unwillingness to get Congressional approval to enter the Korean conflict. Yet Truman is considered a president who took this country through some dangerous times after World War II. He was decisive, honest, and fairminded, a combination of qualities often sadly missing with national leaders.

Presidential greatness can come from someone who rises to the challenge like Truman, but it can also come from someone who takes the reins of power at a time of significant national change and leads the country forward. Such a president was John F. Kennedy. JFK was the second youngest president in our nation's history. But he entered office at a time when America was changing and Americans demanded more. The quiet fifties had exploded into the tumult of the sixties, with racial tensions, nuclear confrontations, sharp generational differences, and critical domestic needs. Kennedy's greatness resided in his ability to recognize the changes afoot in America and to speak to those changes.

Although little in the way of legislation came out of the shortened presidency of Kennedy, his legacy is in the realm of ideas, words, and promises. His emphasis on civil rights and action against poverty and his founding of the Peace Corps invigorated a new generation of Americans. When Kennedy was cut down by an assassin's bullet in 1963, America was crushed; the hope for change that the young president represented was crushed as well. The idealism was gone, the words were silent, the promises were missing. In Kennedy's case greatness was measured by the impact a president had on the soul of the American people.

The Not So Great

In the last fifty years the greatness associated with the likes of Roosevelt, Truman, and Kennedy is unfortunately balanced by the failures of Presidents Johnson, Nixon, and Carter. In the case of Lyndon

Baines Johnson, the record of legislative accomplishment would suggest that the successor to John Kennedy should be viewed as approaching greatness. But legislative output and billion dollar government programs to help the old, the sick, and the needy do not automatically translate into great leadership. Johnson will forever be remembered and judged for getting the country more deeply involved in the unpopular war in Southeast Asia.

An old school politician who could persuade anyone to vote his way, Johnson failed to convince the American public that sending young men to Vietnam was in our national interest. Johnson certainly struggled with the decision to expand American involvement in the war, but he nevertheless followed a decision path that most now agree was the wrong one. Johnson created the circumstances that divided the country, weakened our economy, and tarnished our reputation abroad. Johnson's refusal to follow what his heart told him to do in Vietnam will forever overshadow his domestic accomplishments.

When Johnson refused to run for reelection in 1968, he opened the gates to a Republican resurgence under Richard Nixon. Nixon, who had lost to Kennedy in 1960, was a politician with a remarkable talent for survival. Despite the 1960 defeat and an unsuccessful run for the governorship of California, Nixon returned to victory in 1968. But Nixon's survival skills were balanced by his sense of isolation, sometimes amounting to paranoia. At the same time that there were foreign policy victories in terms of better relations with the Soviet Union and China, there was also Watergate with its break-ins, coverups, enemies lists, stonewalling, and indictments. There was also a near impeachment of a sitting president and the first resignation of a president in the history of the republic. Scandal in office usually is enough to send a president far down the list of greatness, but in Nixon's case it was his behavior in office that ruined him in public opinion. This was a president who was out of touch with the American people and the constitution. This was also a president who surrounded himself with advisers who knowingly broke the law in order to protect their boss. The failure to respect the laws is the main reason Richard Nixon is far down the list of presidents.

This account of the Not So Great ends with Jimmy Carter, who unlike Richard Nixon was not a lawbreaker or a man contemptuous of the constitutional system of government. Carter was a president who just did not know how to make government work or how to connect with the American people. Being a decent, religious president may seem to be a solid foundation for greatness, but in Carter's case decency and religion could not overcome his inability to be decisive, to communicate his values to the American people, and to persuade Congress to follow his lead. In his four years in office the American economy took a slide, revolution erupted in Central America, hostages were taken in Iran, the Japanese began killing us in the trading markets, and Americans froze during an oil crisis. Jimmy Carter got through his four years with nary a scandal, but he will be remembered for little else but his outsider approach to Washington. In the case of Jimmy Carter, the failures in office had nothing to do with energy and initiative, but rather with follow-through. The great presidents were the communicators and the crisis managers, the not so great presidents just couldn't get the country moving.

The obvious next question is, what about Reagan, Bush, and Clinton? Where will they be placed in this list of greatness? How do they match up to our want ad? Most historians want to let some time pass before they go out on a limb and make an assessment about the greatness of recent presidents. Although this caution is sensible, let me go out on a limb and take a stab at evaluating the potential each of these recent presidents has for greatness.

Ronald Reagan just might make it into the halls of greatness, even though the very idea sends liberals into fits of fury. Ronald Reagan was a president who kept things simple and knew what he wanted to accomplish. He wasn't a workaholic, he had a short attention span, and he wasn't the brightest president we have ever had. Nevertheless, Reagan got things done his way in Washington, despite a Democratic Congress and a powerful liberal culture. Reagan had solid advisers, a keen talent for selling his message, and a fatherly way about him that endeared him to even his harshest critics. Under Reagan, the economy soared, the Soviet empire collapsed, the role of government changed. But also under Reagan, the debt skyrocketed, the poor began to lose some of their safety net, and the Iran-contra scandal took its toll. Some good things, some not so good things. Nevertheless, Reagan may go to the top of the list over time largely because,

through actions such as tax cuts, deregulation, and pro-business initiatives, he was successful in putting his conservative message into the
heart of the governing process. No small feat.

George Bush, Reagan's successor, won the Gulf War but lost the
domestic war and will probably reside somewhere in the middle of
the pack of American presidents. If there is a lesson in Bush's failure
to win a second term, it is never rest on your laurels, especially if the
economy is experiencing uncertainty. After the soldiers came march-
ing home to ticker tape parades, the American people were still in a
funk over the massive corporate restructuring that had displaced
hundreds of thousands of workers. Although the American economy
was by no means in serious trouble, rising health care and education
costs, concerns over the solvency of Social Security, and a national
debt that continued to push skyward convinced many Americans that
Reagan's Republican protégé was just not focusing on the plight of
the angst-ridden suburbanites.

When 1992 came around, the American people looked at the four
years of the Bush presidency and forgot about the bravery and skill of
their armed forces. They focused instead on their health plans, their
college tuition costs, their retirement income, and they said it was
time for a change. George Bush, the jack-of-all-trades president, with
a resume that was the envy of Washington, failed to see that Americans were hurting because a changed world had damaged their financial security. And so Americans opted for a change in leaders, making
it unlikely that Bush will be remembered for the greatness found in
his handling of the Gulf War.

And change is indeed what challenger Bill Clinton said was needed
in America. The young governor from Arkansas recognized that
Americans were in favor of their government taking new directions in
those areas that affected not just their pocketbooks but their future.
Gifted with a command of public policy and at ease in front of the
cameras, Bill Clinton told the American people what they wanted to
hear about health care, education, retirement, and the debt. With third
party candidate Ross Perot making inroads in Bush's electoral base,
Clinton won the presidency and began reshaping the domestic agenda.

The Clinton presidency may be remembered less for its successes in
debt reduction, welfare reform, and tax cuts and its enormous eco-

nomic advances and more for the constant ring of scandal and scandal-mongering. In that case, The Clinton years will be seen as a time when the character issue moved to the center of the political stage, as Whitewater land deals, campaign finance abuses, sexual harassment charges, and the White House intern episode made the American presidency into a tabloid circus. And yet despite the scandals, the American people have appeared desensitized to the charges made against their president, and Mr. Clinton has seemed immune to all the mud that has been slung his way. President Clinton has remained popular not because he has been viewed as a great leader, but because he served at a time when many Americans were enjoying the fruits of a

---

Box 5.2   The Worst Presidents

The greatest presidents? We all have some idea of what the answer to that question is. Lincoln, Washington, FDR, Jefferson are names that automatically come to mind. But historians have named not only the great and the near great but those who occupy the bottom of the ladder. Here is the list they generally agree on of the worst presidents:

Richard Nixon: The Watergate scandal; said "I am not a crook."
Warren G. Harding: The Teapot Dome and other scandals, including fathering an illegitimate child while in the White House.
James Buchanan: Weak leadership in the face of slavery and southern secession.
Franklin Pierce: ditto.
Andrew Johnson: Got caught up in the Reconstruction debate after the Civil War. Impeached, and escaped removal from office by one vote.
Ulysses S. Grant: Great general; poor president.
Calvin Coolidge: Took a three-hour nap every day.
Benjamin Harrison: Won the presidency in one of the most questionable elections.
William Howard Taft: Largest president (350 pounds), and that's about all.
Millard Fillmore: Four years in office and nothing to show for it.

global boom. Still, President Clinton may be remembered as a politician who was able to tough out the bad times and build on the opportunities of the good times.

Great leadership among our presidents is thus a huge mosaic of personal qualities, political skills, good advice, efficient management, and a whole lot of luck. Great leadership certainly does not depend only on decency, honesty, and integrity—they help but cannot stand alone. Greatness comes from the ability to seize the moment, to change the national landscape, to move the country forward. But greatness also means the knack for calming public fears, making people feel good, and getting the country to do things that it really doesn't want to do. Because presidents are human beings, they rarely possess all of the parts of the mosaic, and as a result they fall down in the polls or run into a hornet's nest of partisan opposition. The weaker presidents never regain the initiative and spend their time making excuses or fighting enemies. The great presidents recognize their limitations and build on their strengths; they rise from adversity and do what they are supposed to do, lead us onward.

Why Can't the President and Congress Get Along?

This may be one of the questions John and Jane Q. American ask most. The constant bickering between the executive and legislative branches of our government may be part of the way our system works, but outside the beltway in Main Street America, citizens just scratch their heads and ask, "Why can't they just get along?"

What Americans see on a regular basis is usually a president of one political party and a Congress dominated by another duking it out on the evening news as they promote their solutions to a particular national problem. Invariably, the president's solution is miles apart from that of the congressional leadership. As tempers flare and charges and countercharges fill the air, each branch ends up accusing the other of ruining the chances of passing legislation that will address the problem. This display of dueling policy positions may make for good theater, but it does little to make public decisions that benefit the common good. Instead, what John and Jane Q. American are treated to is governmental gridlock.

The tension between the president and the Congress is not some unintended quirk of our political system; rather it is the direct result of the separation of powers model of governance that the Founding Fathers championed as an essential check on excessive power in the hands of either the executive or the legislature. The original intent was to create a governing environment marked by frequent checks and balances as legislation moved through the policymaking process.

By giving Congress the control of the country's purse strings and the power to approve executive appointments and treaties, and then allowing the president to set the policy agenda and utilize the veto power over legislation, the constitution-makers knew that they were constructing a system of decisionmaking that was far from stream-lined. By vesting substantial policymaking powers in both branches, the Founding Fathers intended to create this tension between the branches and make lawmaking a process that would require compromise. Apparently, the objective was to create the circumstances where the two most visible parts of the government would be forced to fashion policies that endured an obstacle-strewn course and survived this course only as a result of hard fought and time-consuming coalition building and consensus. Certainly not a process designed to please ambitious and aggressive politicians with quick solutions to national problems.

Even though restraining the power of politicians makes sense in a democratic republic, the tug of war that has become the defining characteristic of lawmaking in recent years seems to be making the process more difficult than the Founding Fathers intended. Certainly it creates endless episodes of partisan posturing as Democratic (or Republican) presidents blame Republican (or Democratic) Congresses for failure to act on key legislative proposals. Why has the situation gotten worse? Increasingly, Congress and the presidency have become engulfed in ideological warfare that crosses over party labels. Conservatives and liberals in both parties have drawn further apart, with middle-of-the-road consensus-making losing out. It may seem admirable to hold firmly to one's beliefs, but the political system works best when rigidity gives way to practical compromise. Add to this ideological mix the realities of electioneering every two or four or six years, and the consequent need to play to the voting public, and the result is an atmosphere of contentiousness that is unrelenting and unforgiving.

This intersection between the constitutional framework and the influence of partisanship and electoral politics can be seen by examining a series of key legislative battles that occurred during the Clinton administration. In Clinton's first term, national health care policy, the balancing of the budget, and the North American Free Trade Agreement were held captive to this tug of war. Later in the second Clinton term it was welfare and tax policy. The conflict between the two branches over these critical policy initiatives became at times so intense and partisan that the governing process was literally consumed by the maneuverings of the White House and the Congress. On other occasions, however, the relationship between Congress and the president resembled a policy love feast. Here are some examples of the Jekyll-and-Hyde nature of the relationship between Congress and the president.

Establishing a national health-care system much like the European model with heavy government involvement and a huge bureaucratic machine was presented by the Clinton administration as the best way to guarantee health care for all Americans. Republicans saw the bill as another example of the Democrats using government to address a problem, at the expense of more bureaucracy and more taxes. President Clinton fought feverishly to keep national health care afloat, despite a massive media campaign from hospitals, doctors, and insurers. The Republicans were relentless in hammering away at the complexity of the program, while the White House gave example after example of how lack of secure health care can destroy the finances of the middle class.

Eventually, health care reform died a slow and painful death, as a combination of Republican opposition and interest group pressure destroyed the crown jewel of the Clinton policy agenda. Many who viewed the partisan struggle between the White House and the Republicans in Congress said that the president's plan was too ambitious and too complicated, involving too high a cost and too much expansion of bureaucratic responsibility. Others said that the Clinton team just failed to make the necessary compromises to ensure passage. However one sees it, score one for the Republicans.

The second key issue, balancing the budget and relieving the nation of the skyrocketing deficit load, became so contentious at both ends of Pennsylvania Avenue that Republicans opted to shut government down in 1996 rather than give in to the president's plan for balancing the books at the end of the fiscal year. Conservatives within the ranks of the Republican Congress were intent on cutting many areas of government that had been supported by Democrats for decades, especially in the areas of social welfare, Medicaid, and children's issues. President Clinton remained adamant that he was not going to stand for a decimation of these programs, which benefited those Americans at the lower end of the economic ladder.

As the Republican majority in Congress held up appropriations bills that would fund various agencies of government, federal workers were forced to take unpaid leaves and march with signs in front of television cameras bemoaning the shutdown of essential government services. This stalemate became one of those policy events in which the Republicans won the battle but lost the war. Their ideological zeal in sticking it to the president by closing down government created a hailstorm of protest from Americans, who did not want to see the most powerful nation in the world shut down. Eventually, the federal government reopened, the Republicans gave up on their mission to cut back on social programs, and the president emerged as the voice of reason and compassion in this encounter. Score one for the White House.

To give the impression that the president and Congress are usually at each other's throats and fail to deliver public policy is incorrect. The passage of the North American Free Trade Agreement (NAFTA) by the Congress in 1994 was a clear example where the executive and legislative branches did find common ground in a timely fashion to carve out an important piece of legislation. There was a catch though. President Clinton was able to forge an alliance with House and Senate Republicans to get the votes needed to pass NAFTA, which created a free trade zone from Canada to Mexico. But because Mr. Clinton's position on trade matched that of the Republican majority, opposition to NAFTA came from Democrats, particularly Democrats from labor union districts who feared that free trade meant a loss of jobs and economic uncertainty.

Mr. Clinton, a firm advocate of free trade and the globalization of the American economy, was forced to align with Republicans who represented business and financial interests. NAFTA passed the House (barely) and the Senate in large part because there was a strange kind of cooperation at work as the president broke ranks with his own party and worked with the opposition on something he believed in. Score one for bipartisanship.

In the second Clinton term it was welfare reform, and tax cuts that set the White House and Congress at loggerheads. The fight over welfare reform became a classic liberal vs. conservative confrontation. Ever since the Reagan years, conservative Republicans had made a concerted effort to tear down the system built by the Democrats in the heyday of Johnson's Great Society. Now the Republicans, sensing that the time was right to overhaul welfare, pushed for limits on the time spent collecting welfare benefits and stressed the importance of encouraging welfare recipients to get back to work rather than continue collecting a check. The Democrats, sensing that the Republicans had the votes to bring about the first major shift in welfare policy, turned to the president for support and leadership to save this classic liberal cause.

They were disappointed. The president again, as in the NAFTA vote, found himself more in agreement with the Republicans (and also with public opinion) than with the liberal Democratic wing in Congress. With the 1996 election fast approaching, the president chose to present his administration as behind the welfare reform, although he did express reservations about the impact of aid cutbacks on children and legal immigrants. Despite those reservations, the president did not want to appear as willing to accept the status quo, especially since polls showed clearly that Americans wanted a change in the philosophy of government assistance to the poor. Score one for smart election year policymaking on the part of the president.

Nothing is more likely to bring out a confrontation between a Democratic president and a Republican Congress than tax policy and tax cuts. But with the economy going full tilt and the treasury collections at an all-time high, both the White House and the Congress agreed that it would be possible to provide tax cuts to a wide range of constituencies without jeopardizing the battle to lessen the deficit in 1997. Under these conditions the president and Congress were remarkably efficient in agreeing to a major budget and tax bill that gave the middle class some needed tax breaks, business a capital gains reduction, and the nation a balanced budget.

Liberals, as usual, criticized the bill for giving too much in the way of tax breaks for the rich and meager benefits to the middle class, but in this case liberals did not seriously oppose the bill. The real story was that both sides were anxious to strike a deal, thereby resolving a budget issue that for years had been the equivalent of the 800 pound gorilla of government. Even though fashioning tax policy has the potential for ideological warfare, both conservative and liberal firebrands were noticeably quiet during the debate and followed closely the directions of the party leaders, who recognized the benefits that both parties would accrue with a compromise tax package. Score a victory for the American people and the American economy.

What is most interesting about presidential-congressional relations in recent years is that there is growing criticism of the "let's just get along" politics that accents bipartisanship. Increasingly, both liberal and conservative pundits call for a brand of politics where both parties hold identifiable positions on issues and fight openly to advance those positions. Whereas many Americans appear interested in a governing process based on finding the common ground and avoiding much of the nastiness that goes with partisan posturing, Republicans and Democrats just can't seem to give up their penchant for the good ideological and partisan battle. The Clinton impeachment process is perhaps the best example. A cooperative approach does have its downside—it is harder to see who stands for principle and who is willing to fight for that principle—but that approach may be more efficient and attractive to a citizenry used to gridlock. Fortunately, what is clear is that the more the American people make known their demands, the more the president and Congress will recognize the need to get along.

Box 5.3 *The Power to Persuade*

One of the classic studies of the American presidency is Richard Neustadt's *Presidential Power*. In his book, Neustadt lays out his argument that the key power of the modern presidency is the power to

(continues)

Box 5.3 (continued)

persuade. Here is a glimpse of Neustadt's views on the importance of presidential persuasion.

A President's authority and status give him great advantages in dealing with the men he would persuade. Each "power" is a vantage point for him in the degree that other men have use for his authority. From the veto to appointments, from publicity to budgeting, and so down a long list, the White House now controls the most encompassing array of vantage points in the American political system. With hardly an exception, the men who share in governing this country are aware that at some time, in some degree, the doing of jobs, *their* jobs, the furthering of *their* ambitions, may depend upon the President of the United States. Their need for presidential action, or their fear of it, is bound to be recurrent if not actually continuous. Their need or fear is his advantage. A President's advantages are greater than mere listing of his "powers" might suggest. The men with whom he deals must deal with him until the last day of his term. Because they have continuing relationships with him, his future, while it lasts, supports his present influence. Even though there is no need or fear of him today, what he could do tomorrow may supply today's advantage. Continuing relationships may convert any "power," any aspect of his status, into vantage points in almost any case. When he induces other men to do what he wants done, a President can trade on their dependence now *and* later. The President's advantages are checked by the advantages of others. Continuing relationships will pull in both directions. These are relationships of mutual dependence. A President depends upon the men he would persuade; he has to reckon with his need or fear of them. They too will possess status, or authority, or both, else they would be of little use to him. Their vantage points confront his own; their power tempers his.

The power to persuade is the power to bargain. Status and authority yield bargaining advantages. But in a government of "separated institutions sharing powers," they yield them to all sides. With the array of vantage points at his disposal, a President may be far more persuasive than his logic or his charm could make him. But outcomes are not guaranteed by his advantages. There remain the counter pressures those whom he would influence can bring to bear on him from vantage points at their disposal. Command has limited utility; persuasion becomes give-and-take. It is well that the White House holds the vantage points it does. In such a business any President may need them all—and more.

Are the Supreme Court Justices the Most Powerful Men and Women in America?

While the president and Congress are fighting it out over public policies, the Supreme Court quietly goes about its business of changing the face of America in the name of the Constitution. The nine men and women who make up the highest federal court in the country are the most mysterious power holders in the government. Most Americans do not know their names, their tenure in office, or the way they operate. They probably have some vague understanding that the Supreme Court is the country's court of last resort, but in general the Supreme Court is the "other" branch of government, and the Justices of the Court are those nine people who sit stoically in the front row during the State of Union address, never clapping for the president.

The Supreme Court is not just the "other" branch of the United States government. Ever since Chief Justice John Marshall established the power of the Court to declare a law of Congress unconstitutional (the principle of judicial review, established in the landmark case, *Marbury v. Madison*), the judiciary has expanded its role in national governance to the point where today it rivals the executive and legislative branches for leadership in the policy process. The Supreme Court does not make laws, yet it establishes policy; the Supreme Court does not speak for the nation, yet it serves as its conscience and legal guidepost; and the Supreme Court does not run for election, yet it defines the country's position on disputed issues. These paradoxical facts make the Supreme Court mysterious; they also give it the ability to shape the country in countless ways. That's power.

So what is the Supreme Court? From an organizational standpoint, the Supreme Court is the highest court in the federal judicial hierarchy. The Supreme Court, according to the Constitution, has original jurisdiction in specific areas, such as disagreement between states and cases to which the United States is a party. But most of the work of the Supreme Court is to hear certain cases on appeal from lower federal courts or from state supreme courts—cases in which a constitutional issue is involved.

The justices of the Supreme Court are very picky about which cases they choose to examine on appeal. From perhaps as many as 10,000 cases that seek resolution before the Court each session, the justices usually pick fewer than 100 cases to hear. It is not easy to know what moves the justices to choose one case over another, since those decisions are one of the closely guarded secrets of the Court. It is fair to say, however, that in many instances the justices want to bring a sense of closure to a particularly thorny issue of constitutional interpretation and application.

When the justices hear a case, it is nothing like a television drama. At 10:00 A.M. the nine justices in full robed regalia enter the courtroom and sit in order of seniority before the participants in the case. Lawyers from the contending parties present their sides of the case, while the justices constantly interrupt their remarks and interject comments about the validity of the argument that is being made. After about one hour of this legal harangue, the justices retire from the bench and the parties await their decision, which usually does not come until after some six to eight months.

During that period the nine justices, who have the equivalent of their own mini law firms, examine the case law (all the decisions other judges have made on similar cases) with their clerks in preparation for the key step in this process, the Wednesday and Friday conference. It is at these conferences that the justices in virtual secrecy hammer out a decision. Those who have had the opportunity to be present at these conferences report that there is plenty of give and take and raised voices as the justices attempt to put together a majority decision. Finally a vote is taken, and certain justices assume the responsibility of writing the majority opinion that will be the official response of the Court.

If there is a dissenting opinion representing the minority view of the Court, a justice on the losing side writes up a contrary interpretation of the case. In some cases one or more of the other justices may want to offer concurrent opinions to get their views into the record if their reasoning on the issues differs from the official opinion of the majority or minority.

The mechanics of Supreme Court decisionmaking is of course less important than how the justices viewed the particular case before them and applied pertinent federal law or constitutional principles to that case. It is this viewing of the case in relation to existing laws or the Constitution that gives the Court its power to make state and national policy. The way the justices approach this process of interpretation and application has been the source of some of the most heated debates about the role of the Supreme Court in American society. On one side are the strict constructionists, who see the role of the Court as following a literal comparison—taking the Constitution and matching it to the issue before them. If the Constitution is silent on the matter, then the strict constructionists see any action as an unwarranted bringing of modern values and predilections into the decisions. Whenever the strict constructionists find justices going out of their way to steer the Court into an area of interpretation and judicial policymaking that cannot be literally found in the Constitution, they raise a hue and cry over the contamination of our basic laws.

Opposed to the strict constructionists are those who believe the justices should use the Constitution as a means of expanding rights, addressing nagging social and economic problems, and taking the law in directions that the Founding Fathers never dreamed of. Those justices who are judicial activists are unabashed policymakers, who see their job as making the Constitution a document for the ages and not a kind of fundamentalist dogma that restricts the growth of the law as times and circumstances change. Needless to say, the willingness of some justices to find new rights or solve social and economic problems or develop new areas of law is the cause of great consternation among the strict constructionists, who see the activists as exceeding their authority and usurping the power of the legislative and executive branches to make public policy.

When the Supreme Court found the right of privacy in the Constitution by sewing together constitutional principles from the First, Fourth, Fifth, Ninth, and Fourteenth Amendments and then used that rationale to support abortion rights and other rights related to sexual orientation, the strict constructionists were quick to criticize what they felt was a faulty use of Court power. Nevertheless, the right to privacy is securely ensconced in our system of individual liberties, in large part because activist justices felt a responsibility to make the Constitution grow with the times and respond to the needs of American society.

This power of the Court to use the Constitution to respond to legal conflicts within American society and in the process make public policy is really limitless. The Court is faced with a range of challenges to existing laws, requests to apply constitutional principles to particular circumstances, and pressure to set legal precedents that will establish clear guidelines for any action, contract, or relationship that is protected by federal statute. This broad mandate has resulted in the Supreme Court issuing decisions that have had a sweeping impact on the way we live, work, and think in this country. From abortion rights for women to affirmative action procedures in the workplace to the rights of the arrested and accused, the Court has made its mark and changed the face of America in the process.

Of course, not every decision of the Court is a landmark case that will redefine the meaning of the Constitution; in fact many decisions of the Court are curt statements reaffirming a lower court decision. But in every session there are cases in which the participants and the nation await the outcome knowing full well that the decision made by the justices could shift the way Americans approach a difficult problem or deal with a contentious issue.

With all this power in their hands, it should come as no surprise that admission to the mysterious club of nine is not easy. As far as the process goes, the president of the United States nominates the justices for the Supreme Court and the Senate is responsible for providing advice and consent on the president's nomination. On the face of it, this does not seem to be a terribly difficult process, but becoming a justice of the Supreme Court has increasingly been marked by enormous political infighting, as liberals and conservatives in the Senate and interested groups in the country have made the nomination event into an ideological and cultural war.

The nomination of Robert Bork during the Reagan presidency began the recent politicization of Supreme Court nominees. Bork, a distinguished appeals court judge and former Solicitor General of the United States (the nation's official lawyer) was viewed by many Court observers as a strict constructionist who would likely vote negatively on future abortion rights issues and other attempts to read social change into the Constitution. The Senate hearings over the Bork nomination were the most heavily covered by the media in the history of the country.

Outside the Senate, groups supporting and opposed to Bork expressed their opinions with "friends of the court" briefs that provided opinions on the suitability or lack thereof of Justice Bork for the position. Liberal Democrats, who controlled the Senate, were successful in blocking the Bork nomination, but their success left a nasty gulf between those who believed the president should be able to appoint his choice for the high Court and those who felt an obligation to stop the nomination of someone whose judicial opinions were not popular.

The Bork nomination was only the first act in the battle over Court appointments. During the Bush presidency, Clarence Thomas was nominated to the high Court. Again, the hearings in the Senate became one of the most celebrated events in Court history. Thomas, a little known circuit court justice and an African American, was known to be a staunch conservative. In particular, his views questioning the merits of affirmative action policies and race-based hiring practices rankled many in the liberal community. Conservatives, on the other hand, saw Thomas as just the sort of justice who should be appointed to the Court, both a member of a racial minority and an unabashed conservative.

The whole nomination process entered its surreal phase when Anita Hill, a former employee of Thomas, testified that she was sexually harassed by Thomas over a number of years. Hearings went late into the night as Americans were glued to the television watching Hill and a parade of witnesses testify in favor of or against Thomas. Interest groups from across the political spectrum joined the controversy, as the American political system focused on a singular event. Liberal Democrats were not able to win the day this time as they did with Bork. Despite Hill's testimony, Thomas was approved by the Senate. Since being raised to the high Court, Justice Thomas has indeed joined the conservative wing among the justices and lent his vote to decisions that have been less than popular with the liberals.

As the Supreme Court is currently constituted, three justices can be categorized as making up the conservative bloc—Chief Justice Rehnquist, and Justices Scalia and Thomas. These justices fall into the category of strict constructionist—they see little basis for a constitutionally protected privacy right, and they have been highly critical of affirmative action programs and expanded federal power. On the liberal side are Justices Stevens, Ginsburg, and Breyer, who champion aggressive efforts to attain racial equality and are staunch supporters of abortion rights. The swing votes are held by Justices O'Connor, Kennedy, and Souter, who consequently make up a powerful section of the Court. The way they cast their votes in those secret meetings usually determines whether the Court sways to the right or to the left on the political spectrum.

If political power is defined as the ability to shape values and allocate resources, then indeed the nine members of the Supreme Court are powerful individuals. Whether it is ordering the desegregation of public schools or permitting women to have abortions or setting hiring standards for corporations, the Supreme Court of the United States must be considered a force to contend with in our governing

---

Box 5.4   *Who Are the Supreme Court Justices?*

	Appointed By
Chief Justice William Rehnquist	Nixon
Justice John Stevens	Ford
Justice Sandra Day O'Connor	Reagan
Justice Antonin Scalia	Reagan
Justice Anthony Kennedy	Reagan
Justice David Souter	Bush
Justice Clarence Thomas	Bush
Justice Ruth Bader Ginsburg	Clinton
Justice Steven Breyer	Clinton

- Seven of the nine justices were Appeals Court justices. One justice was a State Appeals Court judge. One justice was an assistant U.S. attorney.
- Justice Stevens is the oldest justice on the Court at 77. Justice Thomas is the youngest at 50.
- Three justices—Rehnquist, Scalia, and Thomas—make up the conservative wing of the Court. Breyer, Ginsburg, and Stevens are often viewed as liberals, which leaves Kennedy, O'Connor, and Souter as swing votes.

system. Granted that Congress makes the laws and the president exe-cutes the laws, it is the Supreme Court that protects the laws. Protect-ing the laws has come to mean that justices are expected to say what the law really means in countless specific circumstances. In this bring-ing to life of the words of the statutes and the Constitution lies the real power of the Court.

Why Do Bureaucrats Have Such a Bad Public Image?

Holding a job as a public servant is not what it used to be. In fact the term public servant is somewhat of a rarity, usually replaced by the more formal term bureaucrat or a range of more derogatory titles like "hack" or "public paper pusher." Working for the federal govern-ment in the minds of many Americans means being part of a bloated, costly, inefficient, and impersonal machine, in whose workings ridiculous rules and red tape have triumphed over reason. There are probably few in this country who cannot recount an experience with the federal government bureaucracy that was confusing, time con-suming, or just plain aggravating. Federal bureaucrats have become the target of much of Americans' anger toward the government. They are the people we love to criticize because they regulate our behavior, take money out of our pockets, and crank out all that paper.

Over the years the federal bureaucracy has been pushed and pulled by the forces of ethics, scandals, and professional reform. Presidential administrations from Jackson to Grant to Harding have been rocked by scandals involving government employees. One president, William Garfield, was assassinated by a disgruntled office seeker, prompting the Congress to pass the Pendleton Act in 1885, which created the modern civil service and established a testing procedure for entrance into federal employment.

In contemporary America there have been numerous episodes of what has come to be called whistleblowing, where government em-ployees blow the whistle on their bosses for malfeasance or on gov-ernment contractors for overcharging or producing shoddy work. For example, the internal criticism of the F.B.I. forensic lab by a former staff member (during the highly-charged trial of Timothy McVeigh for the Oklahoma City bombing) embarrassed the agency, but also stimulated reforms and increased professionalism. Also there have been frequent attempts to control the expansion and complexity of the bureaucratic process by establishing reform commissions, employing new budgeting and management techniques, and always seeking to decrease the amount of paper generated by the government. The Clinton administration is but the latest in a long line of reformers as it seeks to "Re-invent Government" by trimming $100 billion from the national budget and getting rid of needless paperwork.

But acts of Congress, whistleblowing, and new presidential initiatives do not seem to have much effect on bureaucratic behavior or performance. There always seem to be stories like the one about the $600 toilet seat purchased by the Air Force, or like the many about the mistreatment of taxpayers by the Internal Revenue Service and sufferings of business under the never ending rules and regulations of the Occupational Safety and Health Administration. The fact that the federal government and federal bureaucrats do much that is good, from defending the country to protecting the food we eat, often gets lost amid the weekly tidbits about incompetence that make the papers or television. The good that government bureaucracy does is quickly forgotten with one juicy story of bureaucratic excess.

There is of course no one reason as to why the government bureaucracy seems to be so often embroiled in controversy and scandal. It is important to remember, though, that implementing the laws of the land is no small venture and has not become any easier with time. As the U.S. Government has grown from fifty employees in three departments during Washington's time to the giant behemoth that it is today, the chances of tax dollars being misspent, bureaucrats exceeding their authority, and procedures for delivering public policy flying in the face of common sense have increased substantially. Size is no justification for incompetence or excess, but it certainly creates an organizational climate that is conducive to lax management.

At first glance the official organizational chart of the United States looks fairly neat and clean, with the three branches established by the Constitution, fourteen secretariats, and scores of independent agencies of government. In reality the operation of our nation's government is a complex and tangled web. This organizational web spends, according to one estimate, $1 billion every six hours, 365 days a year.

Given its millions of employees and billions of dollars in budgets, it is a Herculean task to bring some order and accountability to this vast governing organization.

Congress is charged with approving spending for the bureaucracy and investigating the performance of government workers, but it is often an uphill battle to get a clear picture of whether an executive department is doing its job as required by the law. Congress usually gets involved only after a major crisis has surfaced or a whistleblower calls attention to a particular problem. At that point it is usually a rearguard effort to clean up the mess, offer apologies (or excuses), and promise reforms.

The huge size of the federal bureaucracy and the prospect for disorder that size involves becomes clearer after the official organizational chart is broken down into its various parts. The fourteen executive departments that house most of the federal workers employ nearly 2 million people, from the smallest department, Energy, with nearly 20,000 employees, to the largest department, Defense, with nearly 900,000 employees. The remainder of the employees are in independent agencies such as the National Science Foundation (1200 employees), the National Aeronautics and Space Administration (22,000 workers), and the Environmental Protection Agency (18,000 workers). Bureaucratic entities such as the Central Intelligence Agency and the National Security Agency are supersecret organizations and do not report their budgets or the number of their employees.

In addition to these independent executive agencies there is a separate grouping of bureaucratic entities that regulate various segments of the economy such as trade, communications, nuclear power, and the stock market. These agencies employ a smaller number of people, but nevertheless their numbers range into the thousands. Finally, there are the government corporations, quasi-public organizations (a board of directors but no shareholders and no tax obligations) like the Postal Service and Amtrak. The Postal Service employs nearly 900,000 people; Amtrak, 23,000 people.

But the problems with the bureaucracy are not just a function of size; there is also the matter of how the bureaucracy is organized internally. For example, the Treasury Department is not just the bill payer for the federal government. Treasury borrows money, collects federal taxes, mints coins and prints paper currency, operates the Secret Service, and supervises national banks. In order to accomplish these broad tasks, the Treasury Department includes the Internal Revenue Service, the Bureau of Alcohol, Tobacco and Firearms, the U.S. Secret Service, the U.S. Mint, and the Customs Service.

Likewise, the Commerce Department is more than just the arm of the government that deals with the U.S. business community here and abroad. Commerce grants patents and trademarks, conducts the national census, and monitors the weather. To do these tasks, the Commerce Department controls the Bureau of the Census, the Bureau of Economic Analysis, the Minority Business Development Agency, the Patent and Trademark Office, the National Oceanic and Atmospheric Administration, and the U.S. Travel and Tourism Administration.

Many of the problems associated with the bureaucracy can be connected to size, specialization, and budget, but what most rankles many Americans is the regulatory role of the federal government. At various points in our history, Congress, responding to pressure from public opinion and interest groups, has passed legislation establishing several regulatory agencies charged with monitoring and controlling the actions of key sectors of the economy. Starting in 1887 with the formation of the Interstate Commerce Commission, which was designed to control the business and industrial sector, Congress has established (among others) the Federal Trade Commission (in 1914), The Federal Communications Commissions (in 1934), the Equal Employment Opportunity Commission (in 1964) and the Nuclear Regulatory Commission (in 1974). These regulatory bodies have been given broad powers to investigate their respective industries to determine whether laws have been broken or whether a specific industry is acting in ways that threaten the health, safety, or economic security of the American citizenry.

Establishing a regulatory arm of the federal government seemed a logical move as the United States became a more industrialized and complex country providing new services, new products, and new opportunities. But a regulatory agency's main mission is of course to regulate behavior and practice, and so corporate America, as well as many individual Americans, find these government entities intrusive.

In the late 1970s and 1980s, complaints about unreasonable paperwork, heavy fines for noncompliance, forced recalls of products, and endless rules to ensure adherence to the law increased to the point that these agencies became seen as not only enemies of business but a kind of Big Brother telling Americans how they should behave. Corporate America screamed that the Occupation Safety and Health Administration was requiring them to make millions of dollars in changes in the workplace to meet government safety rules; AIDS victims took the Food and Drug Administration to task for not permitting a speedier process of approving new drugs; and the Environmental Protection Agency became the target of industry wrath for its aggressive and costly efforts to clean up toxic waste dumps and limit air pollution.

The attacks on the regulatory agencies precipitated a move toward deregulation, the removal of regulatory restraints and the elimination of regulatory bodies. Starting during the Carter administration and reaching full steam during the Reagan presidency, the deregulation bandwagon moved forward, with the airline industry being freed from the restraints of the Civil Aeronautics Board (which set rates and determined routes). Budgets for many other regulatory agencies were slashed, thus making it difficult for these entities to perform their duties. The argument that regulation was harming corporate competitiveness and costing business enormous amounts of money had resonated with both Congress and the White House.

The drive to deregulate has not been as successful since the end of the Reagan presidency. During the Bush presidency the Americans with Disabilities Act, the Civil Rights Act, and the Clean Air Act all required heavy regulation in order to implement the intent of the legislation. During the Clinton presidency the Interstate Commerce Commission was eliminated, but there were renewed calls for more effective regulation of the food industry, as outbreaks of salmonella and other maladies brought attention to the ineffective regulation of the poultry and beef processing industry. Corporate America had the ear of Congress and the presidency during the 1980s, but the 1990s have seen a reversal of that trend, particularly in those industries that affect health and safety. Americans have welcomed the cheaper airfares created by deregulation of the airline industry, but when people get sick because the regulatory arm of the government is weak or asleep at the wheel, the call goes out for more and tougher regulation.

The contradictions present in popular attitudes toward regulation go to the heart of the problem of bureaucracy in this country. Americans do not like bureaucrats, but they regularly demand that they do something about polluted air, faulty products, tainted food, unsafe workplaces, and dangerous drugs. The federal bureaucracy has not grown because some secret cabal of bureaucrats have gotten together to fatten their budgets and expand their powers. Rather the federal bureaucracy has grown because interest group pressure and public opinion have convinced Congress and the president that the government needs to step into the private sector and do something to correct a problem.

The federal bureaucracy has a history of going overboard with our money and making our lives overly complicated. Moreover, the federal bureaucracy has amassed enormous regulatory power and on too many occasions has exceeded its authority and caused personal and financial harm to individuals and businesses. And yet the bureaucrats, those people we love to hate, are implementing the laws that Congress has passed and advancing initiatives the president has been charged with implementing. We may think that they are acting alone and driving up the cost of government, but whether we like it or not, they are performing the will of the people. They are us.

A Few Books You Should Read

Cooper, Phillip J. *Battles on the Bench: Conflict Inside the Supreme Court.* Lawrence, Kans.: Kansas University Press, 1995. An important discussion of how Supreme Court decisions are shaped and how the justices interact as they fashion decisions.

Davidson, Roger, and Walter J. Oleszak. *Congress and Its Members,* 5th ed. Washington, D.C.: Congressional Quarterly Press, 1996. A basic reference book on the members of Congress that is an invaluable tool for understanding the political environment of the House and the Senate.

Hargrove, Erwin. *The President As Leader: Appealing to the Better Angels of Our Nature.* Lawrence, Kans.: Kansas University Press, 1998. In this age of moral crisis of leadership, Hargrove dissects the modern presidency and the changing nature of presidential leadership.

Lazarus, Edward. *Closed Chambers: The First Eyewitness Account of the Epic Struggles Inside the Supreme Court*. New York: Times Books, 1998. As the title suggests, Lazarus tells about how the nine justices come to their landmark decisions. As Lazarus points out, there is a lot more politics, public opinion, and personality that goes into a decision than most thought.

Neustadt, Richard. *Presidential Power and the Modern Presidents: The Politics of Leadership from Roosevelt to Reagan*. New York: Free Press, 1990. An essential guide to the modern presidency by the most respected presidential scholar of our time.

Reich, Robert. *Locked in the Cabinet*. New York: Alfred Knopf, 1997. An insider's look at the Clinton cabinet and the Clinton administration by the former Secretary of Labor. A good behind-the-scenes view of government and governmental advisers.

Wiesberg, Herbert F., and Samuel C. Patterson. *Great Theater: The American Congress in the 1990s*. New York: Cambridge University Press, 1998. The most recent look at the Congress and the unfortunate partisan wrangling and ideological conflict that now characterize the legislative branch.

Wilson, James Q. *Bureaucracy: What Government Agencies Do and Why They Do It*. New York: Basic Books, 1998. An invaluable book on the bureaucratic establishment. A clear and concise examination of the way government agencies go about their business.

6

MAKING PUBLIC
POLICY DECISIONS

The marvel of all history is the patience with which men and women
submit to burdens unnecessarily laid upon them by their governments.
—*Senator William Borah, in a speech in the U.S. Senate*

How Does the Congress Work?

The initial response to this question is, "with great difficulty." When
presidents sit down at a table to sign a new piece of legislation they
are usually surrounded by smiling members of Congress. But to get
to that table is no easy task. The American legislative system is not
meant to be streamlined, quick paced, or one-dimensional. Instead it
is slow, plodding, obstacle-ridden, and filled with compromise, compromise, and more compromise. The finished product is a joyous oc-
casion in large part because the participants are just so glad that they
have been able to guide this new law through a minefield and still
come out with something to show the American public. Those smiles
on the faces of the president and the members of Congress are as
much smiles of relief as pride.

The key factors that contribute to this arduous legislative journey
are bicameralism, the committee system, and weak party discipline.
What the American legislative system is known for is a complex

blend of institutional competition, numerous pockets of power, and an independent voting culture. These characteristics do not breed cooperation or efficiency; in fact they create a legislative climate that is not conducive to radical lawmaking or quick response to public policy problems.

Bicameralism, better known as a two-house legislature, is not unique to democratic governance; in fact many of the advanced industrial nations have two legislative bodies. But in the American system the two houses have vastly different powers and responsibilities, which create points of tension. Members of the House of Representatives are more closely tied to a smaller electoral district and thus have a more parochial view of their responsibilities. They are more subject to interest groups and citizen pressure and to the pressures of election, since their term is only for two years. Senators, on the other hand, represent the entire state and come to their jobs with a broader perspective on the direction of the legislative agenda. They also have the luxury of holding office for six years, which allows them to avoid the wrath of a disgruntled electorate for a longer period.

Bicameralism can also be problematic because of party allegiance. As is currently the case, one political party (now the Republicans) may control both houses, but that unity does not guarantee cohesiveness. The government is still divided, since the current president is from a political party (the Democratic) that is in opposition to the party controlling Congress. With such a division, disagreements are likely to limit the prospects for speedy resolution of legislative issues. This condition of divided government has been the most enduring and frustrating characteristic of legislative-executive relations in America.

The tensions that can arise between houses of Congress and between the Congress and the White House often surface when a bill is working its way through the various legislative hoops. After legislation goes through the House of Representatives and the Senate, what often happens is that the Congress has two different bills on the same issue—a House bill that was constructed in a unique House environment of parochial interest, a more specialized committee structure, and restricted rules of debate and a Senate bill fashioned under a totally different set of circumstances, including a smaller number of voices, a more national approach to legislation, and very different rules of debate. At this stage a conference committee made up of representatives of both houses of Congress must be named to try and build a compromise version of the bill that will satisfy both the House of Representatives and the Senate. Compromise is indeed the order of the day, but often the final bill that comes out of the Conference Committee process is a brand new bill that differs dramatically from either the original House or Senate bill.

While the two legislative bodies have many differences, they share one critical ingredient, committee work, the core of the legislative process. It is often disheartening for visitors to the Capitol to find that there is not much going on in the House and Senate chambers when they walk through on the tour. The absence of members on the floor of Congress does not mean that they are out playing golf; rather they are conducting legislative business in committee sessions. Committees are the workhorses of the legislative process in our governing system.

Most members of Congress are assigned a number of committee positions by the leadership team when they begin the legislative session. Members of Congress seek out committee positions that will help them advance the interests of their district or state. They also have individual interests that they prefer to follow. A representative from a district with a large farming population would certainly seek an assignment on the Agriculture Committee, while a senator with a number of military bases back home might seek membership on the Armed Services Committee.

Whatever the composition of their constituency and their personal interests, members of Congress make great efforts to become experts in the area their committee handles and to bring that expertise to bear when legislation comes before their committee. A typical day for a member of Congress would include at least one legislative hearing on a pending bill. There may also be attendance at a "mark-up" session, where a bill that is moving through the process is actually written up and prepared for debate. At some point in their committee duties, legislators will be required to cast a vote on whether the bill is to be reported out for debate by the full House or Senate. Much of the work of legislators is thus rather tedious, and usually conducted in committee. The debate before the cameras is really only the frosting on the legislative cake, as much of the drama of legislation happens behind the scenes in committee sessions.

It is also important to remember that the legislative process is a highly partisan affair. But partisanship in Congress does not necessarily mean that party lines are clear and that members of the House and Senate will follow the dictates of their party or their legislative leaders. The U.S. Congress has a reputation as a legislative body with weak party discipline: Members are willing to break ranks with their party in order to respond to their constituents and their conscience. The independent quality of our members of Congress creates uncertainty about the legislative outcome. Majority and minority leaders are forever counting heads to see if they have the votes to pass a measure. Presidents also must work the phones of members from their own party to lobby for votes. There is no guarantee of cohesion or solidarity. The Congress is made up of Democrats and Republicans, but it is also made up of liberals and conservatives, southerners and northerners, men and women, blacks and whites, and legislators who follow the party sometimes, the people sometimes, and their conscience sometimes. It is, to say the least, a complex legislative stew.

When this exhausting process of legislating is complete, it is not really over. In our system of divided government, the president gets to play in this legislative game. With the power to sign or veto legislation, the president is a major player whose position on the proposed legislation cannot be ignored. Throughout the legislative process, the president and his staff are working closely with the Congress to see that the final product is something the president can support and sign. If the final product is not to the president's taste, then he can wield his veto pen and send the measure back to Congress for some reconditioning.

Most presidents do not enjoy using their veto because it further heightens the tensions between the legislative and executive branches. But some issues are so marked by division that it is impossible to avoid an impasse. The system does provide a way through the impasse: A veto by the president does not end the dance. The Congress can override the president's veto with a two-thirds vote of both branches. Getting that big a majority is not an easy task, but it is the only way of getting a vetoed bill through without compromise. There is just one more possible impediment to this legislative process that must be mentioned, and that is the role of the Supreme Court. Yes, the federal court system is also a peripheral player in lawmaking. Because the Court has the responsibility to protect the Constitution and the laws of the land, there have been laws passed by Congress and signed by the president that have been declared unconstitutional (and thus null and void) by the high court. The Constitution does not mention the Court's duty of judicial review, but it is implied in the duty of the Court to preserve the Constitution from illegal or ill-conceived legislation. Despite this power, the Court has been reluctant to overturn an act of Congress that has been signed by the president. Only about 150 federal laws or parts of laws have been overturned since 1804. (The Court has, however, declared over 1000 state laws unconstitutional.)

As is evident from this discussion, the legislative process set up by the Founding Fathers and institutionalized over two hundred years is a difficult journey. At numerous points along the way, the bill can be delayed, changed, or just plain killed. Out of some 10,000 bills introduced each legislative session, a mere two hundred or so ever make it out of this labyrinth. In fact, in the first half of the 105th session of Congress in 1997, 3,036 bills were introduced in the House and 1,568 were introduced in the Senate. Of the House bills, only 59 became law; of the Senate bills, only 19. Moreover, many of the bills passed were minor, such as amendments to the Atlantic Striped Bass Conservation Act and the awarding of a Congressional Gold Medal to Frank Sinatra. Some major pieces of legislation got through, such as the balanced budget and tax acts and the confirmation of the Chemical Weapons Convention, but in general the legislative productivity of the 105th Congress was unusually low.

This poor success rate has its defenders as well as its detractors. To some the low productivity of Congress is good, since it means that major changes are not moving through the system quickly but are the result of careful consideration and compromise. To others, however, the failure rate for legislation shows that the American legislation system is basically flawed, unable to respond to problems, and hopelessly immobilized by systemic deficiencies. This proclivity to create inefficiency and gridlock regularly gets on the nerves of the American people who bemoan all the partisanship and pettiness that leads nowhere. But secretly many Americans applaud the cautious nature of our legislative system. Because we are wary of government in the first place, a system of lawmaking that takes its good-natured time and is filled with compromise is seen as a fine check on power and the best we can expect from a governing system not meant to be speedy or terribly effective.

Who Makes the Laws?

Lawmaking is a messy business, with more than its share of behind-the-scenes manipulation, wheeling and dealing, and partisan intransigence. As the old saying goes, "There are two things you do not want to see made, sausage and laws." To get a finished product in the American legislative system requires that a number of important power contenders settle their differences and find some common ground. At the top of the list of these power contenders are the leadership teams of both the majority and minority parties.

In the House of Representatives, the Speaker, the majority leader, the assistant majority leaders (often called whips), and the chairman of the committee where the bill in question is sitting are responsible for negotiating the bill through Congress. Although the minority side of the equation is not in a position to control the legislative agenda, it nonetheless has a kind of "shadow team" of leaders whose job it is to counteract the maneuvers of the majority and make sure that both sides of the issue are heard.

With 435 members in the House, there must be restraints on the length of speeches and on the amending process. For example, the House members are bound by the five-minute rule, which limits their floor orations to five minutes. They can borrow time from a colleague, but the intent of the rule is to offer all the members a small opportunity to speak their mind. Unlike the Senate, the House has a specialized committee that acts like a traffic cop, guiding legislation through the House and setting the parameters for the all important debate. The Rules Committee schedules the vote, determines the number of speakers on each side of the issue, and decides how many amendments will be debated. The chairman of the Rules Committee has historically been one of the more silent but powerful members of the House, simply because he controls the all-important process of legislation.

In the Senate, the membership is smaller and rules concerning debate are less restrictive. No Rules Committee structures the debate in the Senate, nor are there significant restrictions on debate. The famous Senate filibuster, which uses the privilege of unlimited debate to block legislation, still exists, although a vote on cloture can end the endless talking. In this more open legislative atmosphere, the majority leader is the key player; he is looked to for setting the agenda, making the case for legislation, and convincing his fellow Senators to follow his lead.

As in the House, the majority party has its leadership team of whips (responsible for getting out the vote) and chairs of key committees. They meet regularly to discuss scheduling debate on a particular bill, what kind of amendments (if any) will be permitted, and how to respond to attacks from the minority leadership. Because party discipline in the Senate is uncertain, the leadership team must also count heads and plead for votes in order to guarantee a legislative victory. The effectiveness of the majority leader as the main legislative strategist and voice of the party in power is thus essential in this process. Any hint of weakness or failure to recognize what the other members of the majority are thinking could spell defeat and hand the minority party the opportunity to shape the legislation or if necessary kill it.

The party leaders in Congress are easily identifiable power contenders, but much also goes on behind the scenes, where other power contenders are hard at work shaping and directing the legislation. The most significant of these more anonymous power contenders are the staff members of the individual members of Congress. The reality of the legislative process in the United States is that Representatives and Senators are pushed and pulled in so many different directions that they rely heavily on their staffs to manage the hundreds of bills that must be voted on. Moreover, the common view that the member of Congress is the one who sits down and crafts legislation in response to the demands of constituents and pressures from interest groups is mythical. Staff members are the ones who have frequent contact with constituent groups and work closely with interest groups to take an issue and transform it into a legislative proposal.

In many instances members of Congress come in at the end of this legislative process to cast a vote on a bill that a staff member has briefed them about. That does not mean that the members are not prepared to debate the issue or are unfamiliar with the issue. Rather it means that the staff does all the leg work because it is physically impossible for their bosses to handle all the legislative requests and active bills that come before Congress. Needless to say, staff members have accumulated immense power in Washington as they become quasi legislators working behind the scenes.

Speaking of influential participants in the legislative process, the lobbyists who camp out outside congressional hearing rooms or the offices of members of Congress cannot be ignored. A good part of a legislator's daily schedule consists of meetings with representatives of special interests who want to make their case. If they can't get into the Representative's office, there is always the fund-raising/hors d'oeuvre circuit that begins around 6 o'clock on most days. Members of Congress are invited to meet with this or that group of interested citizens who are hosting a small get-together. Sometimes this get-together is a fund-raiser for the political party and sometimes it is a social event with clear political overtones. Whatever the motivation, the representatives of special interests rarely miss an opportunity to meet members of Congress and offer their insights on how legislation should be crafted.

Unlike the demonstrators who periodically stage massive demonstrations in Washington, the lobbyists work quietly in pairs or in small groups, present volumes of data to support their cause, and make earnest pitches for a piece of legislation. In most cases the lobbyists do not get an audience with an actual Representative or Senator (especially if the group is not a major special interest player) but must sit with a staffer who promises to inform the boss of the meeting. Again, staffers become the eyes and ears of the members of Congress and cultivating them is a critical ingredient for success in the legislative process.

The bureaucrats also have a hand in the legislative process. Legislation is not just an action that floats out there with no connection to any other part of government. Rather the bill passed by Congress will have to be implemented by the appropriate bureaucratic agency. It is in the agency that the money will be spent and the generalities of the law will be made clear by specific rules and regulations. As a result, representatives from the bureaucratic agency affected by the proposed legislation are important participants in the lawmaking process. Their expertise is crucial to the formulation of the legislation, and their insight on what may happen as the law meets the real world is invaluable.

Moreover, since most legislation calls for an appropriation of government funds, it is the bureaucrats who must provide the answers as to what is a workable dollar amount to attach to the law. In most instances the bureaucrats also act as lobbyists for the legislation, but in this case lobbyists for the interests of the government and their specific agency. Just like special interests, the bureaucrats have much at stake when a piece of legislation works its way through the Congress.

The involvement of the bureaucrats in the legislative process finishes off the three-sided "Iron Triangle" of American government. The interaction of legislative staff members, special interest representatives, and agency bureaucrats is at the core of the lawmaking process. Senators and Representatives rely on the interaction of these three groups to provide them with the outline of a bill that they then can put their own mark on and carry forward through the committee hearings, floor debate, and eventual vote.

The important role played by staff members, lobbyists, and bureaucrats, three nonelected groups, is bothersome to those who believe that lawmaking should be a democratic process in which elected representatives craft the legislation. The reality of the American legislative process is that the members of Congress are forced to rely on the "Iron Triangle" as a necessary evil in order to prepare the way for what will certainly be a long, complicated, and contentious road to that signing ceremony.

In any case, the work of the Iron Triangle does not mean that members of Congress are mere rubber stamps who come in and listen to the advice of their staffs, interested lobbyists, and government bureaucrats and then cast their vote. Senators and Representatives play their key roles when it counts, during the inevitable negotiations with party leaders and White House representatives once the bill is up for a vote. This is the stage when language is changed, amendments are added, the bottom line appropriation is adjusted, and favors are called in. The committee chair responsible for the legislation would likely be the critical power contender during these final steps, but certainly the majority leadership team would be highly visible as well.

Again, staffers, lobbyists, and bureaucrats may continue to play important roles in making their case to the Senators and Representatives, but now at crunch time, it is the elected members of Congress who must make a decision and cast a vote. And even when the vote is recorded, this process is not over, since in most instances a conference committee must be called in order to iron out differences between Senate and House versions of the bill. Once again, there is jockeying for influence (although among a more select group of leaders and experts on the bill) on the final language and the level of appropriation.

It should be evident from this description of the inner workings of Congress why passing legislation in our system of government is more than just the version that is broadcast on C-SPAN every night. The fact that the members of Congress are only the most visible power contenders in the legislative process means that the process of transforming a proposed bill into a law of the land is an intricate web of interactions, influence, and pressure. The complexity may be annoying, but it is a reflection of the openness of our system and the opportunities for participation by all the various interests associated with a particular piece of legislation. More than one critic of the American legislative system has lamented the inefficiency of the lawmaking process, citing the failure rate of legislation and the time line for successful completion of the obstacle course. There is no doubt that these critics are right on the money. The American legislative system is not an efficient process, it is more like a puzzle where all the pieces need to fit properly. But if we still hold to the view that laws are not to be whims of fancy but part of a democratic, competitive, deliberative process, then our system with all its annoyances, power struggles, quiet deals, and faceless participants is just right for us.

Box 6.1 Who's in Congress?

Who Are the Senators?

The Liberal Standard Bearer Senator Ted Kennedy of Massachusetts. The man liberals look to for leadership on causes associated with working men and women, minorities, and the poor.

Mr. Seniority Senator Strom Thurmond of South Carolina. At 97, Thurmond is still going strong, sure evidence of the power of incumbency.

The American Indian Senator Ben Nighthorse Campbell of Colorado. Once a Democrat, now a Republican, he wears his ponytail and cowboy boots with pride.

The Attack Dog Senator Jesse Helms of North Carolina. Never shuns an opportunity to stick it to the liberals and usually does so in an ornery manner.

The Millionaire Senator Herb Kohl of Wisconsin. Although being rich is not unusual for the Senate, Kohl is more than rich; his financial empire includes real estate, supermarket chains, and the Milwaukee Bucks—So why work for $135,000?

The Maverick Senator John McCain of Arizona. Hard to define ideologically, will criticize both Democrats and Republicans, especially on campaign finance.

The Prosecutor Senator Arlen Specter of Pennsylvania. Noted for his tough questioning and legal skill. Gained notoriety in the Anita Hill case and Clinton campaign scandals.

The War Twins Senator John Kerry of Massachusetts, Senator Bob Kerrey of Nebraska. War heroes from the Vietnam War, certain to test presidential waters in 2000.

The California Twins Senator Diane Feinstein and Senator Barbara Boxer. Female one-two punch in a heavily male-dominated Senate Club.

The Senate Gentleman Senator Richard Lugar of Indiana. Reserved, knowledgeable, and well respected—an example of what many Americans wish all the Senators were like.

(continues)

Box 6.1 *(continued)*

Who Are the Representatives?

Mr. C-Span Representative Mayor Owens of New York. Takes up the task of speaking on anything every evening. Title previously held by Representative Bob Dornan of California.

The Taxman Representative Bill Archer of Texas. Chair of the powerful Ways and Means Committee, which writes the nation's tax laws.

The Policeman Representative David Dreier of California. Chair of Rules Committee, which is the House traffic cop, scheduling legislation and setting rules for debate.

The Purse Strings Representative C.W. "Bill" Young of Florida. Chair of the Appropriation Committee, which controls all spending bills.

The Jock Representative Steve Largent of Oklahoma. New trend in Congress, the sports or celebrity figure who goes to Congress after a career entertaining the American people.

The Legacies Representative Patrick Kennedy of Rhode Island and Representative Jesse Jackson of Illinois. Both sons of famous liberals continuing the traditions of their fathers.

The Independent Representative Bernie Sanders of Vermont. Only member of Congress who is neither a Democrat nor a Republican.

Cong. Joe Sixpack Representative James Traficant of Ohio. Never a slave to fashion—Representative Traficant takes up the cause of working men and women.

Mr. Automobile Representative John Dingell of Michigan. Detroit's man in Washington, who usually gets his way protecting the Big Three.

The Congressional Voice of African Americans Representative Maxine Waters of California. Highly visible and outspoken representative of Black Americans.

How Does the Government Manage the Economy?

Go back, for a moment, to the dark days of the Depression. It is 1932. Unemployment is affecting 25 percent of the workforce; bankruptcies are accelerating at an alarming rate; foreclosures on farms are driving people off the land; and homeless men and women huddle next to fires in makeshift shanty towns (called Hoovervilles after President Herbert Hoover, who carried the blame for the economic downturn). National unrest is taking the form of frequent outbreaks of violence and calls for an end to capitalism.

Enter Franklin Delano Roosevelt, a Democrat elected in 1932 in a landslide victory. Roosevelt seeks to calm the nation by a promise of action. In the first hundred days of his administration, he transforms the role of government in the economy. Unlike Hoover, who avoided using the public sector to address economic downturns, Roosevelt constructs the model of an interventionist government that uses its power and influence to turn the country around. The New Deal, as Roosevelt calls his revolutionary program, is designed to restart the economy, saving a private sector economy by using the public sector.

With decisiveness and a flair for the dramatic, Roosevelt shut down the nation's banks and then permitted only the financially sound ones to open. Within a year, Congress had passed the Glass-Steagall Act, which set up the Federal Deposit Insurance Corporation to protect deposits up to $5,000. The Agricultural Adjustment Act was passed to boost farm income by controlling production. Roosevelt also established a series of so-called alphabet agencies with the express purpose of putting people to work. The Works Projects Administration (WPA) was charged with building parks, courthouses, and public buildings; the Civilian Conservation Corps (CCC) used the unemployed to restore national parks and protect natural resources; and the Public Works Administration (PWA) built larger projects like dams, bridges, and roads.

The American public was stunned by the speed with which Roosevelt involved the government in the economy, but relieved that action was being taken to address the economic ills of the country. The business community, however, was outraged at the interventionist policies of the Roosevelt administration. Many corporate and banking leaders remained steadfast in their belief that the government should stay out of the private sector economy and not attempt to end the Depression by being the employer of last resort, controlling prices and wages, and shaping the market system. Roosevelt was unconcerned by the criticism and firm in his belief that government should be the general manager of the nation's economy. His belief remained the bedrock of economic policymaking for years to come.

With the New Deal establishing the federal government as the manager of the nation's economy, subsequent presidential administrations, in concert with the Congress, continued to aggressively intervene to deal with inflation spirals, unemployment downturns, recessionary periods, labor-management disputes, international trade negotiations, and numerous other concerns associated with the growth and stability of our capitalist system. Presidents tinkered with wages and prices and jawboned business and labor leaders to reach amicable contract settlements; the Chairman of the Federal Reserve Bank became the single most influential manager of the economy through his direction of monetary policy—the control of interest rates and the supply of money; and Congress used its power of the purse and its taxing authority to influence the economy through budgetary decisions and legislation that increased or decreased taxes.

The federal government became the hub of America's economy, as corporate leaders, small businessmen, and the general public looked to Washington to guide the economic ship of state. What's more, Washington became the center of the economic influence game, as representatives from companies, banks, trade associations, and grass roots businesses descended on the Capitol to press their case for an endless stream of special interest considerations. The nation's economy is the sum of all the economic activity generated by the private sector, but as a result of Roosevelt's interventionist model, the federal government is at the helm steering the economy and controlling its direction.

To get a closer look at how the federal government currently participates in our nation's economy, it is helpful to examine the most recent developments in the formulation of tax policy and the determination of budgetary priorities. It is, after all, because of its impact on the checkbook and the pocketbook of the American public that the government as manager has created the most interest and controversy. In most years, Democrats and Republicans, conservatives and liberals, business and labor, the rich and the poor have all been at loggerheads at various times over how taxes should be used to influence the direction of the economy and how spending priorities should be established and then paid for from taxpayer revenues. Outside of war-making and issues of national security, no issues have energized the political process and divided the nation more than taxes and spending. To cut taxes or not to cut taxes, to spend or not to spend, these questions are at the core of the domestic policy debate in this country, and the debate has not been a quiet one.

Tax Policy

Before delving into the tax policy debate and what it says about how decisions are made in government, let's look at how the federal government raises revenue.

1. Individual income taxes constitute 41 percent of the total revenue collected by the government. Individual income taxes in this country are progressive: People with higher incomes pay larger percentages of their incomes than those with lower incomes.
2. Corporate income taxes make up 11 percent of the total revenue collected by the government. In the past this percentage has been higher, but because of congressionally mandated tax incentives, subsidies, and loopholes designed to enhance business investment and spur modernization and productivity, this total has remained well below that of the individual income taxes.
3. Social Insurance receipts, often termed payroll taxes, account for 33 percent of federal revenue. These receipts are the fastest rising source of federal revenue. They constitute a regressive tax: People with lower incomes pay the government a larger percentage of their income than those with higher incomes.

4. Excise taxes make up 4 percent of government revenue; they come from taxes on liquor, tobacco, airline tickets, and gasoline.
5. Customs duties and tariffs, often placed under the "other" category, have been decreasing since the United States moved toward embracing free trade with its trading partners and has pushed for a lowering or an end to such taxes.
6. Borrowing is also part of the revenue stream; the federal government needs money from nontax sources in order to balance its budget. Since 1969 there have been only four years when the federal government has not had to borrow money to cover a shortfall in revenue.

The policy debate in this country over taxes has focused primarily on the individual income tax. Politicians have been divided over issues such as whether cuts in taxes would energize the economy or feed the deficit. There has also been heated debate over who should benefit from tax changes—corporations, the wealthy, the middle class, or the working poor. These issues came to a head during the administration of Ronald Reagan. Reagan came into office with a mandate to cut taxes and reform the tax system. Within a few months of entering office Reagan began implementing his objective. In 1981 he got Congress to approve a tax cut, a move that he felt would help stimulate the economy. Reagan was influenced by supply side economics, a theory that stressed the importance of increasing the supply of money in the hands of individual Americans and corporations as the single most important catalyst for economic growth and prosperity.

Reagan continued to act on his belief in supply side economics by marshaling the 1986 Tax Reform Bill through Congress. The bill was the first major change in the tax laws in seventy years. In brief, the bill dropped the number of tax brackets from fifteen to two, reduced corporate deductions (such as the business lunch expenses), raised the personal and standard deductions, and simplified the tax code (at least that is what members of Congress said). Lobbyists for corporate and trade interests fought vigorously and successfully to ensure that special tax incentives for investment and plant modernization remained in the bill.

Since the 1986 tax law, the debate over tax cuts has continued and even intensified. The Democrats have been reluctant tax cutters, in large part because they fear that social programs would suffer from a diminution of federal revenues. The Republicans, with the Reagan model to build on, have championed tax cuts, especially those related to areas that would enhance investment. The Republicans have also been intent on avoiding the mistake of George Bush, who made the famous statement, "Read my lips, no new taxes," only to give in to congressional pressure and support a tax increase in 1990. In the Clinton administration, a Democratic president not fearful of raising taxes has faced a Republican Congress absolutely opposed to raising new revenues.

After making and then jettisoning a promise for a middle class tax cut, President Clinton in 1993 made an about-face and pushed for a tax increase on the wealthy (the so-called millionaires tax). By changing the marginal tax rate the Clinton bill raised taxes by $357 billion, an amount the president said was necessary to begin balancing the budget. The partisan wrangling over this proposal reached fever pitch, with both the Democrats and the Republicans bringing out their most impassioned rhetoric. The vote in the House in favor of the Clinton proposal was a slim 218 to 216. The vote was so close in the Senate that the vice president had to be called in to break the tie. Republicans excoriated the president for raising taxes and jeopardizing the tax policies of the Reagan administration. The Clinton administration responded that tax increases (coupled with budget reductions) were necessary in order to address the national debt, which continued to spin out of control.

Tax policy also became part of the 1996 presidential election campaign, as Republican Bob Dole proposed a six year cut totaling over $550 billion, including a major reduction in the capital gains tax (profits from the sale of stocks, bonds, and real estate), a 15 percent reduction in individual income tax rates, and child tax credits to middle and lower income families. President Clinton slammed the Dole proposal as further contributing to the deficit, but did counter with a college tuition tax credit.

Dole's defeat in 1996 did not mean the end of this tax cut debate, as the president and the Republican-controlled Congress agreed in

May of 1997 to a massive tax and budget agreement that included tuition credits, retirement savings incentives, and a cut in capital gains. Both the Republicans and the Democrats hailed this agreement and told the American people that the government was finally offering key sectors of the economy some tax relief. More on this later.

Budget Policy

We have looked at how the government takes money in; now let's see how they take all that money and spend it. Here is a list:

1. Direct benefit payments for individuals. This is the largest expenditure of the federal budget, 50 percent of the total. This money is for a range of entitlement programs, from Social Security and Medicare to federal pensions and family support. Because it is the largest segment of the budget, these benefits payments hold the answer to budget balancing.

2. Defense outlays. This used to be a sizable part of the national budget with allocations of 26 percent or more during the Cold War days. In the post-Communist world, defense garners about 15 percent of the federal budget, and the debate continues over how much defense is enough.

3. Grants to states and localities. These are basically transfer payments; taxpayers send money to Washington, which then sends money back to the states and localities for projects ranging from roads to subways to irrigation projects. These moneys are highly prized by legislators anxious to win friends and votes by bringing a popular project home.

4. Interest payments. As everyone knows, if you borrow money to balance the bottom line, the bill comes due in the form of interest payments. Much of the debate over balancing the budget surrounds these payments—balance the budget and the government has 15 percent of its revenue freed up for something else.

5. All other government operations. Even though many Americans complain about big government, only 5 percent of the federal budget goes for all the other programs and activities

of government from the FBI to running our embassies to managing our national parks and museums. Unfortunately, this 5 percent is where much of the budget cutting occurs, which doesn't leave much room to maneuver.

In 1997 the U.S. government spent approximately $1.6 trillion, while taking in approximately $1.5 trillion, leaving a deficit of about $100 billion. This enormous figure is still considerably less than the $290 billion deficit that occurred in 1992 during the Bush administration. With the federal government running in the red for most of the last thirty years and a national debt that is approaching $5 trillion, one of the hottest political issues in Washington has been how to move this nation into the black yet not jeopardize the programs and the spending priorities that have been agreed upon over the years.

Back in 1985 Congress passed the Gramm-Rudman-Hollings Deficit Reduction Act, which required the deficit to be reduced to zero by 1991. This effort by the Congress was a huge failure. The House and Senate were unable to control spending, in large part because they were unwilling to address the problem of reducing spending on the budget busters such as Social Security and Medicare, along with the various pork barrel projects that benefit their homes state or district. The Gramm-Rudman-Hollings Bill was revised and extended to 1995 with new targets, but again it failed to achieve its balancing objective. These failures led to a new approach, a Balanced Budget Amendment, which would use the rigidity of the Constitution to force the government to get its fiscal act together.

When first introduced in the Congress in the early 1990s, the Balanced Budget Amendment gained widespread popular support, because Americans saw the federal government's spending policies as no different from their own finances. The popular view was that if Americans had to balance their checkbook every month, then the nation's books should be balanced. The Republicans in Congress favored the Balanced Budget Amendment as the answer to our runaway spending. The Democrats were opposed, stating that a Balanced Budget Amendment would put the nation in a kind of straitjacket, unable to respond to emergencies. Moreover, the Democrats were concerned that many of the social programs that date back to the New Deal would be put on the chopping block in the name of fiscal order. Because a constitutional amendment requires a two-thirds vote of both Houses, the Republicans were never able to move the measure through the legislative process. Nevertheless, the defeat of the bill actually spurred Congress and the president to work in other ways to get into the black.

For much of 1996 and into 1997 Congress and the president were at war over balancing the budget. The goal was to achieve the balance by the 2002, but the means to achieve that goal were always the source of unprecedented partisan wrangling. Again the debate was over whether balance could be achieved in a way that did not gut major social programs. Cutting that 5 percent of the budget (called discretionary spending) that is the operational part of the total was not going to do the job. There was always a need to address Social Security and Medicare. The Republicans backed off their balancing proposals and reorganized their troops for another fight in 1997. Fortunately, in that one year the political landscape changed, with the reelection of Bill Clinton to a second term, and the economy continued to boom, thus increasing tax revenues.

In May of 1997 the White House and Congress agreed to a plan that would balance the budget by 2002 and actually earn a small surplus (in fact this goal was reached in 1998, with a $70 million surplus). There were smiles and handshakes all around as the debacle of the 1996 government shutdown was replaced by bipartisanship in 1997. The problem with the agreement to balance the budget by 2002 is that many experts feel that beyond 2002 the budget will again become unbalanced as Social Security and Medicare payments soar into the stratosphere. One estimate is that the deficit in 2010 will likely be 4.5 percent of Gross Domestic Product (the value of all the goods and services produced by the United States) and jump to a disturbing and dangerous 9.5 percent of Gross Domestic Product in 2025.

If these projections are correct, the debt burden on the United States economy will again be extremely troublesome, forcing a new round of cuts and a call for a resolution of the Social Security/ Medicare cost dilemma. As so often happens, the politicians solved the problem only by putting off the real problem for another day. A major budgetary meltdown will probably come sometime in the twenty-first century, but many of the politicians who smiled and shook hands in 1997 will not be there when the bill finally comes due.

Making fiscal policy in the United States has always been a risky proposition. Politicians tend to want to cut taxes in order to curry favor with the voters, but they don't want to hurt the programs the voters like. They also need to consider when to stimulate the economy through tax cuts and when tax cuts may overheat the economy. It is indeed a balancing act, with serious economic and political ramifications. Fortunately for the United States, the strength of the economy in the late 1990s made these decisions a little easier and politicians a little more popular with the voters. On the whole, managing the U.S. economy in this boom era has been marked by quiet tinkering from the Federal Reserve and a bipartisan commitment to keep the budget balanced—no major surgery, no major initiatives, just relief that all the key indicators are positive.

Box 6.2   The Toilet Regulations

One of the big complaints about government is that it regulates our life, even the most mundane aspects of our life. In 1992, Congress passed legislation requiring that every new residential toilet made in America use only 1.6 gallons of water per flush rather than the traditional standard of 3.5 gallons. In 1998, Congress, facing a wave of protest, began efforts to repeal the legislation. Apparently the new toilets make it necessary to flush more often and created clogged conditions. Congress is now intent on getting the government out of the bathroom.

There is another side to the story of what is becoming the great toilet war. Plumbing manufacturers and environmentalists support the regulations. One national standard is better than many state standards according to manufacturers, and water use has been down considerably in many communities. But protests against the new toilets are spreading, and a black market in the 3.5 gallon units has emerged. Because government regulations come with enforcement powers, there is now a $100 per toilet fine for manufacturing the 3.5 gallon toilet and in some communities a fine of $2,500 for violating building codes to install the old toilet. Should the government be in your bathroom?

How Does the Government Provide for the Health and Welfare of its Citizens?

It all started in 1940 when Ida Fuller of Brattleboro, Vermont, received her first Social Security check of $22.54. For the next thirty four years of her life she continued to receive a monthly check for that amount. In total Ida Fuller received nearly $21,000 in Social Security benefits. Although she had only contributed about $22 in payroll taxes, since the new program had only started four years before she retired, Ida Fuller became the first American to be able to count on the help of the government in her retirement. And now 42 million Americans receive on the average $745 a month in benefits.

The Social Security system, another legacy of Franklin Roosevelt's New Deal, is the most visible example of how the federal government has entered the business of providing Americans with a safety net of benefits to make their lives more secure. As we will see, this safety net has gotten bigger and more costly since the days of the New Deal, prompting a fundamental debate over just how much of a responsibility this country has to provide for the health and welfare of its citizens.

The concept of a federal safety net was not always embedded in American society and politics. Before the Great Depression and the victory of Roosevelt, this country responded to health and welfare crises on a more personal and local level. The family unit, the church or synagogue, the neighborhood, and a network of charity organizations were the primary sources of assistance to those in need. The idea that the government was the provider of last resort for personal well-being was largely a foreign idea. There were publicly funded poorhouses and some emergency relief from local governments, but the idea of federal government intervention in the form of national programs emanating from Washington and designed to offer a countrywide safety net was a radical innovation. The culture had always been one in which people took care of their own, rather than expecting the impersonal and distant arm of government to come to the rescue.

But then in 1928 the bottom fell out, and the economy continued to decline in the years that followed. People simply couldn't take care of their own any more—the problem had gotten too big. Roosevelt recognized quickly that not only the nation's economy required government intervention, but also the welfare of individual Americans, who needed not just jobs and financial security, but also a helping hand, especially the sick, the injured, and the aged. The New Deal thus came to include another form of aggressive, proactive government as the Roosevelt administration began to create a role for the federal government in the areas of health and welfare.

Taking the New Deal into the business of providing a safety net for many Americans initiated another divisive debate between those who felt that the state must provide a minimum level of well-being and those who felt Roosevelt was putting this country on the road to socialism. The idea of a large welfare state, where the government would take care of people, was to some perilously close to what was happening in the Soviet Union, where Joseph Stalin and his Communist comrades were expanding their reach into every area of national life. The specter of government-subsidized welfare programs raised fears especially among those in the upper classes that the Roosevelt administration was adopting a Big Brother mentality, and a costly one as well.

Once the first steps had been taken to develop a government-sponsored safety net by the Roosevelt administration, subsequent presidents and Democratic Congresses expanded the commitment to the nation's poor, disabled, sick, and aged. After his election in 1960, President John F. Kennedy announced a War on Poverty and introduced programs to assist the Appalachian region of Kentucky and West Virginia. President Lyndon Johnson expanded upon the Kennedy commitment by initiating the Great Society, an ambitious and costly legislative agenda that introduced health programs such as Medicare (for seniors) and Medicaid (for the poor), education programs such as Head Start (for preschoolers), and subsidized nutrition programs such as the Food Stamp Act.

Republican Richard Nixon continued the march toward strengthening the safety net by signing on to the Supplemental Security Income program (SSI), which established a minimum income for the elderly and the disabled. And in 1975 the Republican Ford administration, with Democratic support, approved the Earned Income

Credit program, which provided rebates of Social Security taxes to low-income workers. From 1962 to 1980, during Democratic and Republican administrations alike, the cost of government entitlement programs jumped from $144 billion to $490 billion, from 31 percent of government outlays to 48 percent of government outlays.

And then came the election of Ronald Reagan and George Bush. During the twelve year period from 1980 to 1992, entitlement spending increased by nearly $200 billion, but the percentage of government outlays for social programs increased only 2 percent, from 48 percent to 50 percent. The Reagan revolution was not only about keeping more money in the pockets of working Americans, it was also a determined effort to put an end to the New Deal–liberal democratic penchant for widening the safety net with new and costly programs. The Reagan administration, in particular, targeted the Medicaid program, Aid to Families with Dependent Children (AFDC), food stamps, and housing subsidies (so-called Section 8 housing), keeping their funding at the same level or giving only meager increases that did not keep pace with inflation. The days of generous budgets in entitlement programs directed toward the poor came to an abrupt end. Ronald Reagan touted the need for self-reliance and work for welfare recipients, while George Bush stressed the need for a volunteer approach (most notably in his famous "1,000 points of light" speech) to address the problems of those in need.

Democrats in Congress fought vigorously to protect these programs from the Republican knife, but the climate for social welfare spending was changing. The public mood was increasingly critical of entitlements that created a climate of dependency and limited opportunities to exercise personal responsibility. Politicians, ever willing to follow public opinion, became more vocal on the need to trim the government's entitlement commitments to the poor, setting up an inevitable reassessment of how this country takes care of its citizens who need extra help.

The issue of entitlements and the government's role in providing a social safety net came to a head during Clinton's second term, when Congress attacked the welfare system. As Bill Clinton started his second term, the political situation in Washington was significantly different; the Republicans controlled the House and Senate for the first time since the Seventy-first Congress (1929–1931). Conservative Republicans pressed hard to carry through on a major revamping of welfare, a promise made in 1994 in Speaker Newt Gingrich's Contract with America. The Republicans pushed for time limits for welfare recipients, a shift in responsibility to the states for running welfare, and again the all-important emphasis on moving from welfare to work.

Although welfare reform was promoted as a means of achieving considerable savings at the federal level (one prediction claimed a $55 billion saving by 2002), the driving force behind the push for change was the conviction that the answer to poverty was a job, not a government handout. The shift in Congress and ultimately in the White House was not just a matter of changing the eligibility rules, but steering public policy philosophy away from its long held beliefs that the government has a responsibility to care for a wide range of social welfare needs.

After first vetoing a welfare reform proposal in 1995, President Clinton was faced with intense pressure from state governors (many of whom were Republicans) anxious to implement experimental welfare reform programs that introduced concepts such as workfare, a two year cap on eligibility requirements, and restrictions on payments to teenage mothers. The president continued to have reservations about the impact of welfare reform legislation on children and legal immigrants, two groups that most welfare advocates were convinced would be hurt by reform efforts. He also was cognizant of the effect of his support for welfare reform on his own party and the African American community, both pressing him not to give in to Republican pressure.

Despite his reservations, President Clinton signed the Welfare Reform Act of 1996, pledging to work in the future to address the shortcomings of the Republican-sponsored bill. Again, another one of those bill-signing ceremonies, with Democrats and Republicans surrounding a smiling president. Only this time the president was being praised by the Republicans for his courage in bringing reform to the welfare system, while Democrats fumed that their chief executive had walked away from the New Deal philosophy of compassionate government.

Although welfare reform was touted as a long-awaited shift away from dependence on the government, the key element of the 1996 legislation was that welfare moneys from the federal government were channeled to the states in the form of block grants. These grants permit each state to use federal welfare moneys to construct its own unique welfare policy. As a result, welfare policy in the United States is now balkanized: Each of the fifty states fashions its own response to poverty. Significant differences exist among the states in terms of time limits, work requirements, demands on teenage mothers, and training programs.

Moreover, the success of the new welfare approach is built on the ability of states to create jobs, both public and private, to meet the needs of welfare recipients facing the end of their time on assistance. President Clinton has challenged the business sector to provide these jobs, but that may be wishful thinking, especially if the economy turns sour in the coming years. Also there is the issue of day care. Many welfare recipients are single mothers with young children. It is estimated that providing adequate day care for mothers who return to work may cost as much as $3,000 per child per year. Most states do not have adequate programs to provide for such care.

Finally, there is the issue of movement of people from state to state in search of a better welfare climate. Because there are fifty welfare programs in the United States, there is likely to be a good deal of shopping around (along with the normal movement of people from state to state). State officials are predicting a computer headache of major proportions, as state bureaucracies scramble to bring order to the welfare recipients establishing residence in their state.

True, there are some encouraging signs from the states; welfare reform is generating success stories. People are moving off welfare and into work. States are providing training programs to assist welfare recipients with the transition to the workplace. Day care programs are being instituted to assist mothers in this transition. And a new generation of nonprofit organizations and charitable institutions is emerging to supplement reduced government programs. But this optimism comes at a time when the American economy is in high gear, with low unemployment and low inflation. The fear of many in the human service sector is that when times become more difficult in terms of unemployment and inflation, the limits on welfare eligibility and the work requirements may have to be revisited. But what is certain and will likely carry over in the next century is the recognition by national political leaders that the New Deal approach to social problems, an approach that was highly popular and changed the landscape of American social welfare policy, is no longer accepted as gospel.

Box 6.3   Where Government Is Working/Where It Is Not

Percent of survey respondents saying government has succeeded:		Percent of respondents saying these are major problems:	
NATIONAL DOMAIN		Wasteful spending	76%
Space exploration	85%	Self-interested leaders	63%
Peace	80%	Unkept promises	63%
Economy	76%	Crime, poverty, and drugs	62%
ENVIRONMENT/HEALTH		Special interests	50%
Environment	70%	Long-term problems	48%
Medical research	69%	Lack of ethics	46%
Seniors' health	67%	High taxes	45%
Consumers/workers	64%	Poor public education	44%
CIVIL RIGHTS			
Individual rights	63%		
Race/sex discrimination	62%		

SOURCE: Council for Excellence in Government

How Has U.S. Foreign Policy Changed Since the Downfall of Communism?

On November 9, 1989, the Communist government of East Germany opened up the Berlin Wall and permitted people to pass freely from East Berlin to West Berlin. The Berlin Wall had since 1961 been the symbol of the Cold War, the ideological confrontation between the Communist world led by the Soviet Union and the free world led by the United States. There was a party atmosphere in this divided country, as both East and West Berliners tore the wall down amid fireworks, champagne bottles, and tears of joy. Although there were other milestones in the demise of Communism, it was this scene from Berlin that captured the imagination of the world and signaled to those who had championed the ideas of Marx and Lenin that capitalism had won. From this point on the way the United States conducted its foreign policy shifted dramatically.

We now live in what is commonly called the post-Communist world. This is a world without the tension and competition created by the two superpowers as they sought to spread their influence and their vision. The United States is now the unquestioned superpower, while the Soviet Union and its allies have renounced Communism and are largely free-market democracies, or at least attempting to become so. In this new world, the nuclear arms race has slowed considerably. The once great Soviet military power is a shadow of its former self, unable and unwilling to match the United States missile for missile.

Finally, in this new world, the order that accompanied the superpower competition has given way to a much more complicated and free-form international arena with multiple centers of power, new foreign policy players, and unexpected dangers from unforeseen sources. In short, the post–Communist world is in many respects more peaceful and stable than in the Cold War era, but at the same time it hides deeply troubling trends and forces that test the mettle of modern day governments, particularly the United States.

George Bush was the first president to preside over this post–Communist world. Bush coined the term New World Order to describe the changed relations and rules that emerged after the collapse of the Soviet Union. To Bush the New World Order seemed filled with hope. Without the threat from the Soviet Union, the United States could concentrate on domestic issues and enjoy a peace dividend as military expenses associated with the Cold War arms race declined.

The United States could also take the lead in transforming the world's economy as free-trade agreements and regional trading blocs replaced the protectionist, nation-driven policies of the past. And with the stability that the New World Order was expected to generate, there would likely be only brushfire wars, minor and localized conflicts that could be handled by either elite mobile units from the United States or multilateral peacekeeping missions under the direction of the United Nations. The New World Order was envisioned as a period in which the United States would become the preeminent leader in international affairs, working closely with international agencies, regional groupings, and traditional allies to chart a course of peace and prosperity.

And then came Saddam Hussein of Iraq. On August 2, 1990, Saddam Hussein's military invaded neighboring Kuwait and promised to annex the country as Iraqi territory. During the next days and months, President Bush mobilized the nation and our allies to respond to this invasion. The U.S. response to the Iraqi presence in Kuwait was to work in a multilateral fashion by using the United Nations to mount an attack on Hussein. As the United States moved closer to January 15, 1991, the deadline set for Hussein's retreat from Kuwait, it was clear that the president needed to convince the American people and the Congress that force was necessary and in our national interest.

The president used this time to describe the threat from Iraq in terms of its efforts to acquire nuclear weapons, Hussein's use of chemical warfare on his own people, and the dangers to neighboring Saudi Arabia, the number one oil producer in the region. Public opinion was by no means overwhelming in its support of Bush's decision to challenge Hussein. Americans felt that the number of U.S. troops sent to the region (570,000) was too large a commitment and that the financial contribution was disproportionate, considering what the other countries were providing.

Congress was equally reluctant to support the president, in part because of the belief that the proposed attack on Iraq violated the War Powers Act (a post-Vietnam law designed to limit the president's ability to use U.S. troops abroad), in part because of the multilateral nature of the forces, which meant that U.S. troops would be under the command of the United Nations. Despite these reservations, the president was able to carry his plan through and take the lead in a multination expeditionary force to drive Saddam Hussein out of Kuwait.

In quick fashion the American-led United Nations force defeated Iraq, freed Kuwait, and weakened Saddam Hussein's regime.

The quick victory of the multinational forces over Iraq and the enormous public opinion boost that President Bush received from the victory buoyed the administration. Nevertheless, the Persian Gulf War pointed out that despite the defeat of Communism, there were new dangers in the world and new adversaries that would have to be dealt with. Rather than one identifiable threat to American interests, there were now a range of threats coming in various shapes and sizes. After the Persian Gulf War, the United States faced ethnic warfare between Serbs, Muslims, and Croats in Bosnia-Herzegovina, military dismantling of democracy in Haiti, tribal warfare in Rwanda, and chaos in Somalia. Other threats as well: the specter of chemical and biological warfare, the migrations of thousands of refugees, renewed terrorist attacks, the proliferation of conventional and nuclear weapons in less developed nations, and ever expanding international drug activity.

As a result of the changes in the international environment, foreign-policy making bodies within the United States have been forced to make major adjustments not only in the way they operate, but also in the way they look at the world. Because the world has changed, government has had to change. The Central Intelligence Agency, once the core of our response to Communism because of its intelligence gathering and covert missions, faced a severe identity crisis in the post–Communist world. Its critics argued that, if there was no Soviet threat, it was absurd to spend an estimated $30 billion annually to spy on a weakened foe.

With no adequate answer to this argument,, the CIA slowly came to the realization that it had to redefine the mission of its supersecret organization by concentrating on the new challenges in the world, such as nuclear arms sales to rogue states, international terrorism, and even industrial espionage. This shift in focus was gradually accomplished but only after enormous soul-searching and organizational dysfunction brought on by the loss of its anti-Communist, anti-Soviet identity.

The State Department, long the most prestigious foreign-policy making agency in government, found its mission also in disarray, only this time as a result of a Congress desperate to make budget cuts and a White House (at least during the Clinton presidency) that had little interest in international affairs. Foreign-aid budgets, embassies and consulates, and foreign-service employees were given the ax as the country turned toward domestic concerns. From a high point of $37.5 billion in 1984, the international affairs budget for the United States, which includes the State Department, the U.S. Information Agency, the Arms Control and Disarmament Agency, and the Agency for International Development (AID), was reduced to $18.6 billion in 1996. Furthermore, between 1993 and 1996 the United States closed five embassies, twenty-three AID missions, and twenty-six Consulates and branch offices.

The focus of the State Department and foreign policy also changed dramatically during this period. Presidents Reagan and Bush focused on external matters, whether responding to Communist expansionism or dealing with the Middle East; President Clinton paid only lip service to the foreign policy agenda, making infrequent trips abroad and only occasional speeches on international issues, many of which were trade speeches that had a clear domestic connection.

Clinton's de-emphasis of the foreign policy agenda was a reflection of American public opinion, which shows little concern for matters abroad. Even with heart-wrenching pictures of ethnic warfare in Bosnia, genocide in Rwanda, and cruel military control in Haiti, the American people are in no mood to support overseas actions. The end of Communism has reintroduced a strange form of isolationism in the American political culture. Americans are willing to accept the concept of a global economy that requires new business and trade ties worldwide, but there is little interest in military expeditions or high profile diplomacy. Domestic politics have pushed foreign policy off the center stage.

The CIA and the State Department may have faced downsizing and mission reassessment, but the '90s also saw a resurgence in the United Nations. The phrase that kept coming into the international dialogue was multilateral peacekeeping. Rather than the major industrial powers engaging in bilateral responses to troublespots, the United Nations or other regional bodies (such as the North Atlantic Treaty Organization [NATO] in Europe, the Organization of American States in Latin America, and the Organization of African Unity in Africa) began to play a more active role in dealing with regional instability.

During the Bush and Clinton administrations, the Security Council of the United Nations became the locus of major debates over how to respond to instability in the world. If action has been taken by the Security Council, a multinational force has been sent to the troublespot, and the blue-helmeted UN troops in their distinctive white vehicles have placed themselves in between the warring parties. As of 1996, the United Nations had a total of 26,669 troops attached to thirteen missions, the largest being 8,500 troops in Bosnia. There are also a number of other specialized United Nations missions, such as the arms inspectors in Iraq and various human rights monitoring groups in countries where violations have been reported.

Even though these thirteen missions have been multinational in composition, the United States has remained the major participant in international peacekeeping operations and the major financial backer as well (although in recent years the United States has refused to pay all of its $1 billion assessment to the United Nations). This leadership role of the United States has led to a popular backlash. Public opinion polls show clearly that Americans do not want the United States to assume so much responsibility for international peacekeeping. Cooperation, shared responsibility, true multilateralism receive support, but Americans are growing in their concern that the United States is called upon too often by our allies to lead the charge into a foreign troublespot.

The front-line role for the United States in international peacekeeping operations has created another controversy; critics of the movement toward multilateralism feel that this country is surrendering its sovereignty by participating in missions controlled by the United Nations. Veterans groups are especially likely to feel that no U.S. soldier should be required to take orders under the United Nations flag. After problems arose in the United States mission to Somalia during the Bush and Clinton presidencies, the United States insisted on military control of its involvement in Bosnia.

The multilateral nature of U.S. involvement in world affairs has also raised the issue of what is properly defined as national interest and national security. During the Cold War, it was very easy for the foreign policy establishment to define our national interest and our issues of national security—the Soviet Union was a powerful adversary that required a response. Take the Soviet Union out of the picture, and the United States in the last fifteen years has had great difficulty in deciding how it should operate in the international arena.

Of particular difficulty has been the debate over the U.S. response to humanitarian issues. Should the United States send troops into a country where massive human rights violations are occurring? Should the United States come to the aid of a nation threatened by a military overthrow? Should the United States try to bring stability to a land in chaos?

Many leaders in Congress believe that the United States should not become involved in troublespots like these. From their perspective, national interest and national security mean that the United States becomes involved diplomatically and militarily only when there is a clear threat to our nation, our people, our economic interests. To make humanitarian pursuits part of our national interest, so the argument goes, will take us too deep into problems that are none of our business.

On the other hand, the proponents of expanding national interest and national security principles to include humanitarian concerns state that this country has a moral obligation to use its resources, influence, and power to right wrongs in the world, especially now that we are the sole major power in the international arena. This debate has become the core of the foreign policy dialogue in the post-Communist world and is likely to continue on into the next century.

No part of national public policy has undergone such major reevaluation and redirection as foreign policy. The end of Communism has forced the United States to look at how it intends to interact with the rest of the world. There are equally powerful arguments for looking inward and paying attention to the domestic agenda and for taking an active role in the world, since without our presence political instability and increased danger may raise their ugly heads. This dilemma has already been partially resolved, as the United States cooperates with other countries to bring peace, while aggressively pursuing its global strategy of market-based demo-cratization. But just as in 1990, another day will come

FIGURE 6.1   The Government of the United States

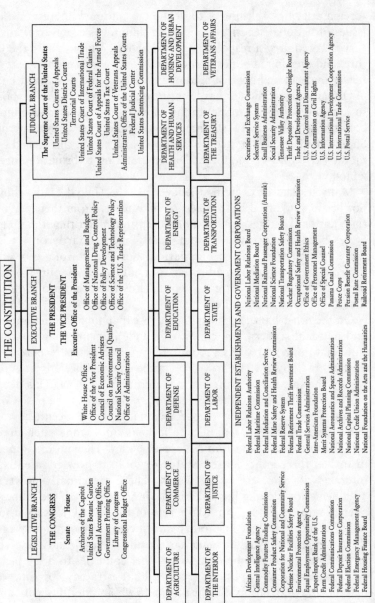

SOURCE: U.S. Government Manual.

when a country or region of the world is threatened by a bully like
Saddam Hussein, and the United States will be looked to for leadership. The debate over the question of what policies are in our national interest and which crises constitute a threat to our national security will again take center stage.

A Few Books You Should Read

Dye, Thomas. *Understanding Public Policy*, 9th ed. Saddle River, N.J.: Pren-
tice-Hall, 1998. Remains the standard text for making sense out of the
public policy process in the United States.

Kuttner, Robert. *Everything for Sale: The Virtues and the Limits of Markets.*
New York: Alfred Knopf, 1996. A balanced yet critical view of the relationship between government and the economy in the post-Communist,
globalized world.

Landy, Mark. *The New Politics of Public Policy.* Baltimore: Johns Hopkins
University Press, 1995. The author explores the so-called environmental
influences on public policy making, such as culture, demographics, and
socio-economic pressures.

Lieber, Robert, ed. *Eagle Adrift: American Foreign Policy at the End of the
Century.* New York: Longman, 1997. A series of articles on the world's
hot spots and issue areas that is timely and also readable.

Moynihan, Daniel Patrick. *Miles to Go: A Personal History of Social Policy.*
Cambridge: Harvard University Press, 1991. One of the key architects of
contemporary social policy in this country talks about how the U.S. government has responded to the needs of its people.

Peters, Charles. *How Washington Works.* Reading, Mass.: Addison-Wesley,
1992. An insider's view of the Washington political establishment. Written
in an easy style with many anecdotes.

Phillips, Kevin. *The Politics of the Rich and Poor: Wealth and the American
Electorate in the Reagan Aftermath.* New York: Random House, 1990. A
disturbing examination of how public policy decisions benefit those at the
top of the economic ladder, while ignoring those at the bottom of the economic ladder.

Schick, Allen. *The Federal Budget: Politics, Policy, Process.* Brookings Institution, 1995. There is no way of making the budget exciting reading, even
though Schick does a superb job. Nevertheless, a book on the budget is essential reading.

7

CURRENT POLICY DILEMMAS IN AMERICAN GOVERNMENT

These are the times that try men's souls.

—Thomas Paine

How Much Defense Is Enough?

Politics always involves setting priorities and making choices. Political leaders and governmental officials are constantly faced with questions about where to allocate scarce public resources. This is no easy task, since the demands made on government are considerable and are often made with great passion. The powerful and well-connected use their influence to capture the public resources, while the weaker competitors either lose out in this contest or must settle for the crumbs. This is a game of raw political power with much at stake, especially since the U.S. budget is no longer an open spigot with dollars flowing freely. Public policy formation and implementation is a mad scramble, as departments and agencies of government are pitted against each other and inevitably meet head on as they make their case for funding.

This mad scramble is nowhere more evident than in the U.S. defense establishment. The collapse of Communism and the end of the Soviet threat have put an end to the philosophy of defense at any cost that dominated the country after World War II. As the Cold War progressed from the days of nuclear brinkmanship in the 1950s and the 1960s to Ronald Reagan's description of the Soviet Union as the "evil empire," the generals in the Pentagon and the defense contractors who supplied them with the latest inventions of war were able to convince presidents and members of Congress that more is better.

Enormous military budgets were approved with nary a hint of criticism, newfangled weapons systems appeared regularly, and the armed forces were held up as the premier institution in American society. During most of the Cold War period the defense budget dominated government spending with nearly 30 percent of the pie and as much as 10 percent of the Gross Domestic Product. One factoid worth remembering—from the beginning of the Cold War to 1996, one estimate put United States military spending at a whopping $3 trillion.

A popular and growing defense establishment was good for American business. Contractors such as Boeing, General Motors, Mac-Donald Douglas, Raytheon, Northrop Grumman, and Lockheed Marietta made billions off of government contracts for jet planes, radar equipment, and sophisticated weapons systems. The unholy alliance between the Defense Department and defense contractors that President Eisenhower warned against in his farewell speech in 1960 (Eisenhower termed it the military-industrial complex) simply got stronger and stronger over the years, evolving into a lobbying machine that rarely experienced defeat.

The success of the military-industrial complex was also good for the American worker. At its high point in the early '80s, an estimated one in ten Americans was employed as a result of defense contracts. The economies of areas where a military base was situated became boomtowns, and states like California, Florida, Texas, New York, and Massachusetts, where defense contractors were headquartered, reaped the benefits of a powerful defense spending machine.

But good times do not last forever, and the defense spending machine eventually met the end of the Cold War and the inevitable question, why does this country need so much defense? In contrast with Ronald Reagan's call for a 600 ship navy, a trillion dollar Star Wars defense, and B-1 Stealth bombers at $280 million a plane, the leaders of the 1990s inaugurated a time of peace dividends, base closings, and military downsizing. By 1997 the defense budget was a greatly reduced $248 billion, or 17 percent of the spending pie. The number of men and women in the armed forces had also declined from a high of approximately 2.4 million during the Reagan years to 1.6 million.

What has changed the most with respect to defense policy in this country is the climate of military escalation and one-upmanship that characterized the Cold War. The disturbing expansion of the nuclear arsenals of the United States and the Soviet Union (a combined total of 60,000 warheads during the 1980s) that fostered a deterrence strategy aptly named MAD—Mutual Assured Destruction—has given way to a succession of treaties and agreements that have provided for cuts in short range, medium range, and the dreaded intercontinental ballistic missiles. The culmination of this process was the signing of the START II treaty (Strategic Arms Reduction Treaty) in Moscow by George Bush and Russian president Boris Yeltsin in 1993. With this treaty both countries agreed to begin the process of taking nuclear weapons and nuclear missiles out of commission.

Also during this period the United States and the Soviet Union agreed to a reduction in conventional forces in the European theater, the center of superpower tension since the end of World War II. This commitment solidified the growing spirit of cooperation between the United States and the Soviet Union. With over 500,000 U.S. military personnel in Europe during the height of the Cold War, it also had a marked effect on military spending and military personnel needs. The process of making painful base-closing decisions in the United States followed close on the heels of conventional force downsizing in Europe.

By 1994 President Clinton and Russian President Boris Yeltsin were agreeing to speed up the reduction and destruction of nuclear arms, and in 1995 these same two leaders pledged to work together on peacekeeping missions such as the one in Bosnia. A far cry from the days when Premier Nikita Khrushchev and President John Kennedy brought the world to the brink of nuclear war during the Cuban Missile Crisis. The two superpower adversaries were becoming military allies and pledging to bring an end to the insane competition for military supremacy.

Of course these gestures of conciliation and harmony were achieved because the United States had become the clear victor in the Cold War and the Russians quietly and quickly accepted their fate. Both nations remained nuclear powers with sufficient weapons to destroy each other, but the adversarial relationship had ended, and more importantly the justification for huge outlays of budget resources had disappeared. The defense establishment would have to find other rationales for continuing the spending machine. This would not be a difficult task.

The American people and the American military establishment got a glimpse of what the future rationale for spending on defense would be tied to when Saddam Hussein invaded Kuwait in 1990. The invasion signaled to the United States that the wars of the future would not necessarily be fought in Europe against a Communist foe, nor would U.S. defense depend on huge nuclear arsenals and a nuclear deterrence strategy based on the capacity for mutual assured destruction. Instead Iraq's aggression pointed up that the United States would have to develop more mobile military forces that could respond to crises in a variety of hot spots around the world.

It would also be necessary to utilize the latest in technological breakthroughs to create "smart" weapons that would provide ground, sea, and air forces a high level of mission success and optimum protection from retaliation. Pentagon planners and defense industry executives began stressing the need to build a new generation of weapons that would provide the military with that all-important edge in the battlefield of tomorrow.

The Persian Gulf War also alerted the U.S. military to the very real prospect of chemical and biological warfare. Because Hussein had already used mustard gas in his successful campaign to squelch a rebellion by Kurdish separatists and was known to have hidden stockpiles of chemical weapons, the coalition of forces involved in the invasion of Iraq had to learn a new brand of warfare. They were issued gas masks and protective gear in case the dictator unleashed a chemical weapons attack.

The Pentagon reminded Congress that the U.S. military must be prepared to respond to a new style of warfare, one that allowed a much weaker opponent the ability to threaten and perhaps even immobilize a superior military. Although the United States easily defeated Iraq and hemmed in Hussein's military by establishing no-fly zones and aggressive weapons inspections, the Persian Gulf War revealed that the era of nuclear competition and confrontation had most likely been replaced by a different type of threat requiring new and costly types of preparation.

A further rationale for continuing to develop a sizable military machine in the post–Cold War era is tied to domestic jobs and the protection of our defense industries. The Pentagon and defense industry lobbyists have been working Congress to convince legislators that it is necessary to keep production lines active by building new weapons systems for both the U.S. military and for foreign markets. A new so-called triad of government, defense industry, and foreign buyers has emerged as a powerful force for garnering scarce federal dollars. Using the argument that it would be foolhardy to close down a production line employing thousands of highly paid and skilled workers even though future military challenges are undefined, members of Congress have been successful in increasing the defense budget and keeping on line a number of weapons systems that were destined to be phased out as unnecessary. According to John Tirman, the author of *Spoils of War: The Human Cost of America's Arms Trade,* "Congress is piling on as many new defense purchases as the balanced budget limits will permit. It added $5 billion to the military budget in the 1997 budget cycle. And more is coming. The Pentagon says modernization will cost 50 percent more in four years, up to $68 billion, and will include two new types of fighter jets, an attack helicopter and an attack submarine."

Perhaps the best example of keeping a weapons system alive in order to maintain domestic employment and production objectives is the Black Hawk helicopter made by Sikorsky Aircraft of Stratford, Connecticut. Despite the Army's attempt to stop production of the Black Hawk, the Connecticut legislative delegation led by Senator Christopher Dodd was successful in restoring fifteen Black Hawks at a cost of $150 million. Sikorsky Aircraft has sold 500 Black Hawks to twenty foreign buyers, including Turkey, Israel, Romania, Mexico, and Colombia.

Also not to be denied is Lockheed Aircraft, which is positioning itself in this new triad by pushing the military to buy more of its new F-22 fighter planes. At the same time, because there is a lucrative foreign market, Lockheed is pressuring Congress to support the $70 billion program as a way of lowering unit costs and making its product more attractive overseas. Currently, thirteen countries are in the F-16 program, and they are prime candidates to upgrade to the new F-22, and of course help Lockheed increase its profits.

What has occurred then in the post–Cold War defense environment is a short term downswing in military spending and military personnel followed now by a gradual but steady increase in budget resources headed for the Pentagon and defense industries geared toward foreign production. Military spending is once again on the way up, and grand plans are being made to introduce a number of new weapons systems that a few years ago were viewed as excessive and unnecessary.

Defense spending is one of those areas of government that is still able to ride out the storm of budget cuts. The lobbying groups in place for the new triad are proving that they can rebound from some lean years to emerge again as a powerful budget force. Even though peace may have broken out in the world, many are willing to be convinced that more and better protection from an adversary is required. It is important to remember that in the preamble to the Constitution "providing for the common defense" is mentioned before "providing for the general welfare." This positioning of priorities accurately foreshadowed how the U.S. government answers the question of how much is enough defense.

Box 7.1 Defense Spending

Per Capita (In dollars, 1997)

DISTRICT	$5,137
VA.	3,227
HAWAII	2,681
MD.	1,420
MAINE	1,200
MO.	1,143
WASH.	1,111
GA.	1,074
COLO.	1,070
MISS.	992

SOURCE: General Accounting Office

Largest Increases/Decreases
(In billions of dollars, 1988–1997)

GA.	$1.5
VA.	1.0
FLA.	0.5
KY.	0.4
HAWAII	0.1
CALIF.	−7.1
N.Y.	−4.2
MASS.	−3.6
CONN.	−2.9
OHIO	−2.4
DISTRICT	−0.4
MD.	−0.6

SOURCE: General Accounting Office

Can the Government Really Keep the Budget Balanced?

Benjamin Franklin once said, "Beware of little expenses. A small leak will sink a great ship." And former Illinois Senator Everett Dirksen said, "A billion here, a billion there, after a while it adds up to real money." Both these quotations get at the heart of the budget debate that seems to preoccupy government in the 1990s. The goal of trying to balance the federal budget is on the surface a simple concept—ensure that the amount of money the government spends each year is matched by the amount of money the government takes in every year. The reality is not so simple.

Although Americans often approach the budget process of the government as if it were like their monthly ritual of balancing the family checkbook at the kitchen table, the government of the United States is not like the family checkbook. Not only are the dollar amounts in the millions and billions of dollars, those millions and billions of budget dollars represent programs and initiatives that have been lobbied for by interest groups and grass roots organizations on behalf of their membership. They quite simply represent the fruits of the democratic process in this country.

Because there has been steady and heavy public pressure on the government to address national needs, Congress and the president have been unable and unwilling to say no to the military lobby, the welfare lobby, the environmental lobby, the education lobby, the agricultural lobby, the space lobby, and on and on and on. All these lobbies have experienced some lean years, when budget increases were kept to a minimum, but for the most part programs and initiatives of the federal government have been moving upward while tax revenues have not been expansive enough to keep pace with this spending spree. The result—yearly deficits of gargantuan proportions and a national debt with many zeroes.

When government decided to do something about its bottom line, there was general agreement that balancing the budget was a good thing. Politicians stood on their soapboxes and demanded that the United States government get its fiscal house in order. And so the great budget crusade began in earnest, with Democrats and Republicans both trying to lead the way and take the credit for getting the

U.S. fiscal house in order. The only problem with this noble task of putting our fiscal house in order was that no budget item that had been on the books for a generation was going to go softly into the night, and no constituency that had benefited from government largesse was going to willingly give up a program.

The task of balancing the budget thus became a huge headache and a political football, as Congress and the president debated where to make the cuts in a way that would not sink the ship of state. This is when the budget battle became a game of high stakes showdown to see who would blink first on what budget items to cut and who was willing to be a model American and make a sacrifice for the good of a balanced bottom line.

After many false starts and painful deadends, in 1997 the White House and the Congress achieved the budget deal discussed in the previous chapter. The agreement was a surprising mix of liberal expansion of social programs, conservative tax relief, and the inevitable "putting off till tomorrow" tactic. For liberals, the White House and GOP negotiators agreed to spend $24 billion over five years in payments to states to expand health care coverage for uninsured low-income children. There was a small increase in Medicare premiums and some expansion of services for seniors. For conservatives, there was a child tax credit of $400 for families with incomes as high as $110,000, a tuition tax credit for low and middle income families, and a reduction in the capital gains tax.

Even though the budget deal of 1997 was hailed as a breakthrough in bipartisan compromise and visionary politics, the real surprise came in 1998 when it became clear that the words "budget surplus" had quietly slipped into the political lexicon. A Congressional Budget Office report in early 1998 predicted that the budget deficit for the year would be a mere $5 billion (actually there was a surplus). But the more important prognostication of the Budget Office was that the strong economy had expanded tax revenues so much that the federal government could even expect small surpluses and that "the federal budget is likely to be essentially balanced for the next 10 years *if current policies remain unchanged*" (author's italics).

"If current policies remain unchanged" is one of those "citizens beware" signs that should be posted in the halls of Congress and the entrance to the White House. What is happening in this new era of balanced budgets and anticipated surpluses is that politicians are now directed not towards budget cuts, but rather toward managing the extra money. President Clinton and the Republican Congress are agreed that there should be a concerted effort to bring down the national debt, which is somewhere in the range of $5.4 trillion, obviously no small amount of money, even by Senator Dirksen's standards. The yearly debt service on that $5.4 trillion is approximately $245 billion or 15.2 percent of the national budget. Putting surplus money into drawing down that debt would allow budget resources to be channeled into other accounts.

But it is after this agreement on the debt that the president and the Congress part company. President Clinton has gone on record in favor of expanding social programs that benefit the poor such as Medicare, child care, and educational training. In particular, he used his State of the Union address in 1998 to push for a Medicare expansion that would greatly benefit poor seniors not yet 65 who are without health care benefits. The Republicans in Congress have predictably set their sights on a far different goal—tax cuts. In effect the Republicans are seeking to transfer the budget surplus directly to the taxpayers in the form of what they term a broad-based income tax reduction.

Expanding social programs or offering broad tax cuts, however, would ignore the warning that budget balancing can be attained "if current policies remain unchanged." What will be happening in the coming years is that sound financial and economic principles related to budget balancing and debt management will run head on into the art of politics, as politicians try to make friends and influence policy with what will likely be a period of surplus revenue. With a projected surplus of $14 billion in 2001 and $138 billion in 2008, politicians have a kind of dream scenario after years of nightmares—extra money to advance their particular agendas.

Already Republicans and Democrats are taking positions on what to do with the surplus. Senate Budget Committee Chairman, Republican Pete Domenici of New Mexico, has said that "now is not the time to start passing a raft of new federal programs," while New Jersey Senator Frank Lautenberg, Democrat, commented on the Republican penchant for cutting taxes, "We have to make sure this doesn't represent Christmas in springtime."

This fight over what to do with windfall moneys is a classic tug of war between those who believe that it is important to use new resources to address longstanding and neglected problems and those who feel that if there are excess funds available, the taxpayers should get a refund and use their money as they choose. Because this tug of war will be played out within the liberal-conservative nexus, the surplus issue does raise a basic question of what the role of government revenues is to be in the United States of the twenty-first century. Should it use its tax resources and its surplus to improve the lives of its citizens, or should it treat the hoped-for windfall as a kind of profit and return that profit in the form of a dividend payment to the taxpayers?

There is a third option, however, in this debate, and the Congressional Budget Office is quick to remind the White House and the Congress of another way of looking at the surplus. The government could establish a rainy day fund, in case the economy should enter a recession, or it could address the future needs of Medicare and Social Security, which will place huge demands on the budget in the period around 2020. That's a long time away, but the Congressional Budget Office recommends that the politicians think not in terms of new programs or tax cuts, but rather what the country might need in the distant future.

So where do you fall in this emerging tug of war over found money? Are you a "program expander," a "tax returner," or a "future planner"? Your answer in large part depends on whether the projections of the Congressional Budget Office are indeed correct, whether politics will take precedence over sound fiscal policy, and whether the economy continues to perform well. Projections are reasoned (but not infallible) visions of the future and the "roaring '90s" of economic prosperity can quickly come to an end due to uncontrollable forces in the vast and interconnected global economy. In short, where the American people stand on program expansion, tax givebacks, and twenty-first century planning may be less important than how the economy fares in this new global business environment.

Box 7.2 *What's in the Federal Budget?*

The federal budget for fiscal 1999, as presented by President Clinton, called for spending a total of $1.743 trillion. That mind-boggling sum of money goes to fund social services, Medicare, national defense, federal pensions, and a litany of so called discretionary programs from the National Park Service to higher education grants to environmental cleanup. But included in the 2,514 pages of the budget (weighing in at 11 pounds 3 ounces) are the following not so well known allocations that you the taxpayers are being asked to fund:

- $2 million to protect elephants in Asia and Africa
- $15 million to maintain the federal helium supply
- $33 million to build roads in the Polynesian mini state of Polaw
- $15 million to help restore the Hawaiian Island of Kaho'olowe because the Navy for 50 years nearly destroyed the island on its bomb training missions
- $11 million to operate the president's family living quarters
- $2 million for the adopt-a-house program
- $2 million for the office staffs of the four remaining living presidents

Is There a Fair Way of Collecting Taxes?

One of the most unpleasant duties of an American citizen is paying taxes. Most of us grumble as we bump up against that April 15 deadline and head to the post office before midnight. Some of us get really creative and use an army of accountants to ensure that we pay the IRS as little as possible. Some of us even refuse to pay Uncle Sam his due, claiming everything from the unconstitutionality of the Sixteenth Amendment (authorizing Congress to levy a direct income tax on individuals) to our God-given right to keep what is ours. There is no more controversial public policy in this country than the tax system and no more hated bureaucracy than the Internal Revenue Service. In biblical times the tax collector was a persona non grata, and nothing has changed since then.

Although paying taxes and dealing with the Internal Revenue Service stimulates a rush of emotions and passions in the American public, the tax code and the tax collection system are a necessary part of what political scientists call extractive policy. Although the term extractive sounds rather harsh, like going to the dentist to have a tooth pulled, government would certainly not be able to function and provide the current level of service to the American people without the funds it takes from the taxpayers.

Over the last few years, however, there has been more and more talk about what is wrong with our extractive policy. Congressional Republicans have transformed tax reform into a crusade, and they have also begun a campaign against the Internal Revenue Service, calling for hearings to bring to the fore IRS arrogance and malfeasance in extracting taxes from American citizens. At the fringes of American politics, militia groups and tax protesters have been given extensive media time to present their skewed vision of a federal government out of control, taking their hard-earned money and causing them financial hardship.

Certainly there is little disagreement about some basic problems. Members of Congress seem to agree that the current tax code is much too complex, with thousands of pages of rules and regulations creating a nightmare for tax filers. They also agree that the current tax collection system has broken down, with the IRS using antiquated computer systems to track taxpayers and increasing numbers of Americans either refusing to pay taxes or entering the underground, where cash is the means of payment and no taxes are paid. Estimates of money lost because of evasion of taxes approach $80 billion a year, and estimates of revenue lost to the underground economy range from $400 billion to $1.2 trillion a year. But when it comes to spelling out specific alternatives to the current tax code and tax collection system, there is hardly agreement. In fact, tax reform is a classic political football—politicians keep passing the issue among themselves without taking the ball over the goal line.

The key reason for the inability of Washington policymakers to come to agreement on tax reform is the issue of fairness—changing the federal code to bring relief to a certain class of Americans or to simplify the process of paying taxes may not benefit another class of Americans. A specific proposal for reform is likely to engender a counterproposal by a competing group who feel that the reform will make their tax burden greater or give someone else a tax windfall.

The problem behind this competition is that legislators have shaped the tax laws in response to constituency and special interest pressure. As a result, the federal code is a complex labyrinth of exemptions, incentives, loopholes, and credits, none of which are easily removed. Whenever the issue of taxes comes before Congress, the halls outside the House Committee on Ways and Means (which writes the tax laws) is awash in lobbyists working to ensure that their clients' interests are represented in the federal code. Moreover, this tax labyrinth has given birth to an ever expanding industry of financial advisers and tax attorneys who have made careers out of interpreting the code and offering advice to their clients on how they can best achieve the goal of most Americans, paying as little in the way of taxes as possible.

In the 1996 campaign for president, the tax reform issue surfaced in the campaign of Republican candidate Steve Forbes, who proposed a flat tax as the centerpiece of his platform. Forbes presented his flat tax as a means of simplifying the federal tax code. It would establish a flat tax rate of 17 percent permitting Americans to simply subtract the appropriate exemption (for example interest income from home mortgage payments) and multiply the rest by the flat rate. Forbes also stated that there would be a threshold under which individuals and families would pay no income tax and promoted it as a means of putting a dent in the estimated $50 billion industry associated with preparing tax forms.

The flat tax proposal immediately ran into a storm of criticism from those who felt that there would be a shortfall in government revenues, especially during times of economic recession when there would likely be a need for increased spending on social welfare programs. Also the Democrats raised the suspicion that the rich would benefit from the flat tax, while the bulk of the government's revenue extraction would be placed on the shoulders of the middle class. Proponents of the flat tax countered that the simplification would not impact government revenues at all and in fact would encourage more people to pay their taxes. Also the flat tax would likely increase economic growth, because people would put more money into savings and businesses would channel more of their profits into investment.

Steve Forbes' candidacy for the White House went nowhere in 1996, but his flat tax plan remains popular, particularly among conservatives who see the change as a long overdue simplification of the code and as an economic stimulus. The flat tax debate that Forbes began in 1996 led to other innovative proposals. A national sales tax has been proposed as a replacement for the income tax. There have also been discussions of a Value Added Tax (VAT), which taxes an item at every stage of production. The VAT has become a major source of government revenue in Europe. There has even been talk of creating a national lottery to tap in to the nation's craze for getting rich quick while providing government with the revenue it needs.

Despite the flood of new ideas and reform suggestions, Congress has been reluctant to engage in the radical surgery necessary to move to a flat tax or any of the other proposals. What is most likely to happen in coming legislative debates is an effort to chip away at some of the tax laws that affect the middle class, for that is where the votes are. One of the areas that is certain to get a closer look is the so-called marriage penalty. Simply stated, the current tax laws extract more taxes from a married couple who both work and file jointly than from a couple who file separately. The marriage penalty has been criticized for years as an unfair tax on working couples, and a reform of the tax code relative to married couples would enhance the standing of those members of Congress who favored the change. Unlike changing the capital gains tax, which has often been viewed as a narrow benefit to the rich, removing the marriage penalty appeals to a large segment of the voting public.

Besides making adjustments to the tax code, Congress will no doubt focus attention on reforming the collection procedures of the Internal Revenue Service. During congressional hearings in 1997 and 1998, the American public witnessed evidence that IRS managers set quotas on the collection of back taxes, took overly aggressive steps to force taxpayers into compliance, made countless errors in audits, and then refused to acknowledge those errors. The IRS was painted as a vindictive bureaucracy with little internal control and little sympathy for the taxpayer. As a result of these hearings, Congress approved a $18.3 billion overhaul of the IRS, including an oversight board and protection against abusive conduct by IRS agents.

Since 1969 the Congress has passed five tax reform bills designed to reduce the tax burden and simplify the process, but in reality these laws have been classic examples of special interest politics. In each case the reformers engaged in incremental policymaking by tinkering with the existing law—cutting a marginal rate here, adding a credit there, and offering relief to a particular industry, group or class. The reforms, however, have never properly addressed the issue of how wealth affects how much tax one actually pays. Even leaving tax policy out of account, those at the higher end of the income scale have an advantage simply because they can hire experts who will advise them on strategies to legally avoid a heavy tax burden. Add to that tax breaks for the rich, and a system that claims to assess a fair level of income extraction from all taxpayers has been rendered unfair by the realities of wealth, influence, and power. The same can be said for corporate taxation—effective lobbying mixed with contributions to campaign coffers of legislators has led to those loopholes that businesses use to limit their tax bill. In the end it is the middle classes, blue collar and white collar, who pay the freight in terms of providing the government with the revenue it needs to function. According to a study by Citizens for Tax Justice, tax reform legislation from 1977–1990 decreased the tax burden of the richest 19 percent of the population by 36 percent and increased the tax burden on middle income families by 7 percent.

In fact, much of the taxpayer anger over taxes is associated with the middle class awakening to the fact that the wealthy and the corporations have carried the day in terms of winning exemptions, incentives, credits, and loopholes from Congress. In 1966 the *National Journal* estimated that 124 tax breaks cost the government $100 billion a year. Increasingly, Congress has come to recognize that it must provide the middle class with real tax relief if it is to avoid further angering the American taxpayer. As a result there has been more emphasis on college tuition tax credits for middle class parents, expanding the standard deduction for children, continuing the Earned Income

Credit for the working poor, and providing other incentives that are popular with middle class families, such as deductions for day care.

With five tax reform bills in the last thirty years, it is safe to say that extractive policy will continue to be a hot button issue in this country. Whenever the government dips into people's pocketbooks and takes their hard earned money, it is bound to create controversy. But because taxes are such a volatile issue and change is played out in the political arena, it is unlikely that this country will ever conduct radical surgery on the way it raises money to pay its bills. What is certain is that Americans will complain about the tax collector and do whatever is possible within their means to keep that tax bill to a minimum. But at least we can hope for a somewhat fairer way of collecting taxes, especially if the middle class continues to demand it.

Box 7.3   Key Points of the 1998 IRS Reform

- Shifts the burden of proof from the taxpayer to the IRS in civil court tax cases.
- Establishes nine-member independent IRS board of directors to oversee operations of the 102,000-employee agency.
- Allows taxpayers to sue the government for up to $100,000 for civil damages caused by IRS negligence.
- Creates a Treasury inspector general to help improve the administration of the tax code.
- Prohibits the IRS from seizing a taxpayer's home if taxes owed were less than $5,000.
- Limits liability of "innocent spouses" for tax problems caused by former spouses.
- Reduces the 18-month period for holding stocks and other assets to 12 months in order to qualify for a lower capital-gains tax rate.
- Makes many employer-provided meals tax-free, a provision inserted by lawmakers from Nevada, where many casinos provide meals to workers.

SOURCE: From News Reports

Are Free Trade Agreements Good for the American Economy?

One of the more memorable verbal images created in recent American politics was presidential candidate Ross Perot's description of the North American Free Trade Agreement. Perot said that NAFTA would lead to a "giant sucking sound" as American jobs headed south of the border to Mexico. Although Perot was not able to use his opposition to free trade to galvanize his campaign for the White House, the debate over whether free trade and free trade agreements are right for American business and the American worker continues today.

Even before the passage of NAFTA, corporate America had embraced the concept of the global marketplace and was reshaping its investment, its marketing, and its production in order to benefit from the movement of countries toward free trade. Working through the United Nation's General Agreement on Tariffs and Trade (better known as GATT), the United States has joined 111 other countries in reaching agreements on a wide range of tariff reductions designed to enhance free trade. The most successful round of talks, called the Uruguay Round, attained some major breakthroughs in tariff reductions worldwide and helped sustain the momentum for continued expansion of the global economy. The world today is increasingly being defined in terms of trading blocs that cover identifiable regions, such as the European Community (EC), which is currently transforming twelve European nations into an economic powerhouse.

But the GATT, EC, and NAFTA initiatives for eliminating tariff barriers and encouraging the formation of a global economy have had their drawbacks, particularly in their lack of protection of domestic industries and workers from low cost foreign competition. In America, these drawbacks have raised serious questions about whether pursuing free trade is in the best interests of the nation and forced the issue into the political arena. The signing of the North American Free Trade Agreement in 1994 created intense opposition from those who felt that the benefits of free trade far outweighed the costs, particularly the human costs.

NAFTA and the policy of pursuing free trade has fostered a classic labor-management, old industry–new industry, Democrat-Republican schism in this country. Free trade supporters point to the opportunities for new jobs and a more vibrant economy that comes with opening up America to the world. President George Bush hailed NAFTA, calling it "an extraordinary enterprise that would create the largest, richest, and most productive market in the entire world: a $6 trillion market of 360 million people that stretches 5,000 miles from Alaska to the Yukon to the Yucatan Peninsula." Free trade critics argue that agreements such as NAFTA destroy jobs, factories, and cities in the name of corporate profitability. House minority whip David Bonior of Michigan echoed the criticism of many of his Democratic colleagues when he said, "The working people who stand to lose from this treaty don't have degrees from Harvard. And most of them have never heard of Adam Smith. But they know when the deck is stacked against them. They know it's not fair to ask American workers to compete against Mexican workers who earn $1 an hour."

What has made the political debate over NAFTA and free trade especially divisive is that President Clinton has been one of the most vigorous supporters of tearing down the tariff barriers. Clinton has often joined with Republicans to fashion legislative coalitions to advance free trade agreements, and in the process alienated Democrats from states and districts that have been hard hit by the economic impact caused by that "giant sucking sound."

Despite the ill-will toward him from Democratic members of Congress and the labor union movement, President Clinton is undaunted in his support of NAFTA and free trade. As he said during the debate over NAFTA's passage, "We need not only to reduce trade barriers, but to prepare our entire work force not only to compete in the global economy, but to live with the changes in it and to make sure nobody gets left behind. I am convinced that the North American Free Trade Agreement will generate jobs and growth on both sides of the border."

The reality lies somewhere in between the promises of the free traders that agreements like NAFTA would generate 600,000 new jobs because of newly opened markets and the dire predictions of the critics that 900,000 jobs would be lost as U.S. companies took advantage of lower wage and tax rates across the border. Globalization of national economies offers both opportunities and dangers. Free trade has indeed been the catalyst for new industrial growth, as companies tap into foreign markets. U.S. exports are up dramatically; this country is now the leading export nation in the world. But even though we are the export leader of the world, we continue to import more than we export due in large part to our insatiable desire for foreign goods. This country carried a balance of trade deficit of $162 billion in 1996 as proof that trade is a two way street.

Also the prediction that free trade would destroy the industrial base in this country just has not come true. There has been job loss due to U.S. firms contracting work outside this country, but the loss of old industrial jobs has been made up for by new high-tech jobs (many carrying good wages). One study out of California found that NAFTA's impact on workers had meant the loss of an estimated 28,000 jobs, but NAFTA also created an estimated 31,000 new jobs to handle the increase in demand from Mexico. In many instances these new jobs require training, and government programs to ease the unemployed into new areas of work have not been forthcoming. Nevertheless, many displaced workers have started new careers in industries that are far removed from the metal-bending jobs of the past.

Moreover, the predictions that free trade would bring economic ruin to factory towns have come true only in the short term. Cities in the Rust Belt hard hit by the exit of major industries, such as Racine, Wisconsin, Bethlehem, Pennsylvania, Gary, Indiana, and Brockton, Massachusetts, are enjoying slow but steady growth as new smaller high tech companies, tourism, gambling, and an ever widening number of service and retail companies replace the smokestack industries. It is true that the transition caused by NAFTA has not been easy for many Americans. There have been long periods of unemployment in many of the factory towns, and when employment did rebound, it was often not in skilled positions or at the same rate of pay as before. Nevertheless, on the whole the news has been good.

And yet despite the solid evidence that free trade has been more of a boon than a bust to the American economy, the debate over jobs versus corporate profits continues unabated. The latest struggle occurred in 1997, when the Clinton administration sought to get so-called fast track negotiating authority to close a deal that would bring Chile into the North American Free Trade Agreement. Chile is one of

Latin America's most developed nations and a natural for inclusion in NAFTA. A vote in favor of fast track negotiating power would have permitted the Clinton administration to negotiate a trade deal with Chile that could only be voted up or down by the Congress—no amendments, no deals, no ability to shape the final agreement.

To the surprise and dismay of free trade advocates, the Democratic opponents of fast track were able to defeat the president and stop the extension of NAFTA to Chile. Congressman Richard Gephardt of Missouri, a long time critic of NAFTA, took the lead in the campaign to stop fast track. Gephardt not only marshaled union support to accent the job loss associated with free trade agreement, but linked NAFTA with increased drug trafficking from Mexico and with the failure of U.S. companies to honor environmental and workplace safety regulations in their factories across the border.

Gephardt pointed out that increased truck movements associated with a more open economy were creating a new problem, as eighteen-wheelers were bringing across tons of marijuana and cocaine undetected by U.S. authorities. Gephardt also castigated U.S. firms who have built plants in the maquiladoras (the Mexican version of industrial parks) that emit untreated wastes into the groundwater, provide Mexicans with few protections from workplace dangers, and in general reflect a climate of unfettered capitalism, putting profits over social responsibility.

The media campaign and the internal lobbying over the fast track authority was intense, with the president making the case that the United States would lose its competitive edge in the new global economy if his administration was not able to expand NAFTA. Gephardt and the other Democrats on his side made their arguments against fast track in more populist tones, presenting it as a result of an economic philosophy that was not in the interest of the American worker and a strategy designed only to enrich corporations and permit them to increase their profitability at the expense of worker security. Gephardt and a bipartisan mix of legislators concerned about the impact of globalization on the workplace carried the day. The president and his Republican supporters recognized that the vote was not going to give them fast track and delayed the final tally until the next session of Congress.

But while the issue of free trade is debated by politicians, the global marketplace continues to expand and to attract new players. Free trade may be one of those economic juggernauts that is impossible to stop or contain; there is just too much money to be made and too much time and money already invested to have the international system return to the days of protectionism and domestic driven economies. What may occur in terms of global trade agreements is a kind of time out period, during which countries will draw a deep breath and deal with the impact of globalization on society and politics. The defeat of fast track and NAFTA expansion was a signal that many Americans are not comfortable with the rush to a global marketplace. The debate is certain to continue about free trade and free trade agreement, but the juggernaut appears to be unstoppable. Because there is a consensus among key political and corporate elites that free trade is essential to a growing economy, those opposed to globalization may win a few battles but will ultimately lose the war.

Box 7.4   The NAFTA Agreement

The North American Free Trade Agreement (NAFTA) has been one of the most hotly debated public policy issues in recent history. Most Americans know that NAFTA is about free trade and that Mexico and Canada are now part of a regional trading bloc. What most Americans don't know about NAFTA is exactly how it operates, particularly in Mexico, in order to advance free trade. Below are the key parts of the agreement:

1. Tariff elimination: About 65 percent of U.S. industrial and agricultural exports to Mexico will be eligible for duty-free treatment.
2. Reduction of motor vehicle and parts tariffs: Cars and light trucks will have easier access to Mexican markets.
3. Auto rule of origin: Only cars and trucks "with substantial North American parts and labor" will benefit from tariff cuts.

(continues)

Box 7.4   (continued)

4. Expanded telecommunications trade: The agreement opens up a potential $6 billion market for telecommunications equipment and services.
5. Reduced textiles and apparel barriers: Upwards of 20 percent of tariffs on U.S. exports of textiles and apparel will be eliminated immediately, and an additional $600 million worth of exports will be freed from controls in six years.
6. Increased trade in agriculture: Mexican export licenses, which cover 25 percent of U.S. agricultural exports, will be eliminated.
7. Expanded trade in financial services: The opening of Mexico's financial services will allow U.S. banks and securities firms into the Mexican market.
8. New opportunities in insurance: U.S. insurance companies will be permitted to obtain 100 percent ownership of Mexican companies by 1996.
9. Increased investment: U.S. firms will be treated for the first time like Mexican firms; this will allow U.S. firms to invest without promising to export goods.
10. Land transportation: The agreement allows U.S. trucks to carry international cargo to Mexico by 1995.
11. Protection of intellectual property: NAFTA will provide a higher level of protection for intellectual property—patents, copyright, and trademarks.

SOURCE: U.S. State Department

Is Affirmative Action Necessary to Help Achieve Racial Equality?

We Americans have had a difficult time with the concept of equality. Because this country was born out of a quest for independence and liberty, there has never been much debate over the place being free has in our society. Patrick Henry's cry of "Give me liberty or give me death" occupies a prominent spot in the memory bank of quotations of most Americans. It is equality, that "other" value at the core of our system, that has caused problems. Although equality has a prominent place in the Declaration of Independence and has been the theme of important presidential speeches from Abraham Lincoln's Gettysburg Address to Lyndon Johnson's civil rights address to Congress, there has always been disagreement over exactly what is meant by equality and how best to achieve it.

Over the years, Americans have latched on to two acceptable definitions of this important concept. First, equality has been linked to opportunity, equality of opportunity, which has come to mean providing everyone with the chance to succeed and reach the American dream. Equality of opportunity suggests that what all Americans are entitled to is a shot at making money and improving their social position. Equality of opportunity fits nicely into the American economic system, which is based on individual initiative and the promise that anyone who participates in the national marketplace can reap the benefits.

The phrase equality under the law has also taken a prominent position in our political vocabulary. Americans take great pride in showcasing Lady Justice standing blindfolded with the scales of justice balanced. Statements such as "no man is above the law" and "we are a country of laws, not men" provide clear evidence that equality under the law is enshrined in our system of government. Although Americans know that equal justice may occasionally break down, allowing the rich to get off where the poor go to jail, there remains a solid faith that the blind lady and the balanced scales will win out most of the time.

Even though equality of opportunity and equality under the law are commonly accepted as baseline guarantees of treatment, this does not mean that all is well in achieving the standard set in the Declaration of Independence and reinforced in the Gettysburg Address. The struggle against injustice and discrimination is a key part of our social and political history. From the scourge of slavery to the tragedy of the Civil War to the fight for racial justice in our own time, the popular belief that we are a country of equal opportunity and equal justice has been belied by the sad reality of Americans treating other Americans unfairly.

In response to the failures of equal opportunity and equal justice, particularly with respect to African Americans, the government has taken steps to redress the grievances of its people—Lincoln freed the slaves, Truman integrated the armed forces, Eisenhower began the desegregation of public schools, and Johnson pushed the Civil Rights Act and the Voting Rights Act through Congress. These have all been milestones in the struggle to ensure that the American dream applied equally to all Americans. But tucked away among these milestones of attaining racial equality is the series of guidelines and regulations that have come to be known as affirmative action. Title VII of the Civil Rights Act of 1964 prohibits discrimination in employment based on race, color, religion, gender, or national origin. In order to ensure that Title VII would actually be an effective tool against old habits of discrimination, the Johnson administration began issuing affirmative action guidelines and regulations in 1965.

Once in place, those guidelines and regulations began to set antidiscrimination hiring goals and timetables for companies doing more than $10,000 worth of business with the government (which included most of the Fortune 500 companies and thousands of smaller companies). Also labor unions were added to the affirmative action process, since they often controlled hiring at job sites and in the factory setting. The Equal Employment Opportunity Commission (EEOC), which grew out of the Civil Rights Act of 1964, was charged with monitoring compliance with affirmative action plans. Its primary charge was to see that companies and unions gave special consideration to minorities and disadvantaged individuals as one way of responding to past discrimination. The key words here are "special consideration" and "responding to past discrimination." Affirmative action became a powerful tool in the hands of the government as it pressured the business and labor community to take measures that would bring minorities into the workplace.

Almost from the beginning the concept of affirmative action and affirmative action guidelines were the source of disagreement and division in this country. White Americans, in particular white male Americans, criticized the program as denying them job and career opportunities while showing preference to African Americans and females. A new term, reverse discrimination, entered the lexicon, with

the meaning that whites were becoming the group that was discriminated against by employers forced to implement preferential hiring
procedures to comply with affirmative action. Companies and unions
also entered the fray by complaining about affirmative action as creating an unworkable quota system whereby employers were forced to
reach racial goals no matter whether the job applicants were qualified
or not.

In the political arena, conservatives and liberals clashed over the
appropriateness of affirmative action. Conservatives zeroed in on the
practice of tying employment opportunities and career advancement
to race rather than to more traditional standards such as merit, test
scores, time in service, and performance evaluations. To conservatives, affirmative action was a blatantly unfair means of attaining
equality that placed one specific group in a selected category and then
pressured employers to hire individuals from this selected category.
Liberals, on the other hand, accented the clear evidence of past discrimination: minorities and women had been denied employment and
advancement because of racism and sexism and were at a disadvan-
tage in the workplace. Without programs such as affirmative action,
and the force of government to back up the program, liberals argued
that there would be little if any progress in getting minorities ever
widening job and career opportunities.

Eventually, the issue of affirmative action reached the United States
Supreme Court. In 1978 the Court rendered a landmark decision involving a white Vietnam veteran who was denied admission to a California medical school because a certain number of seats in the program were reserved for minorities. In *Regents of the University of
California v. Bakke,* the justices held that Bakke had indeed met the
admission requirements for entrance into the medical school and the
school's rejection of his application was illegal because racial quotas
had been used. The Court did state that race could be taken into account by the medical school, but it could not base admission or de-
nial of admission solely on racial grounds.

The Bakke decision opened up the floodgates of litigation related
to affirmative action programs and claims of discrimination on the
part of whites. As long as the Court retained its liberal majority, the
decisions that were delivered generally supported affirmative action

programs. For example, the Weber case out of Louisiana validated a union training program that showed preference for minorities. However, with the ascension of Justice William Rehnquist to the position of chief justice in 1986, the Court began to reexamine affirmative action. Gradually they chipped away at programs that tried to achieve equality by supporting racial preference guidelines. Many of these cases involved white public employees, firefighters, teachers, and government workers, who were denied employment or laid off in order to advance or protect a racial preference system. The decisions made it more difficult for minorities to prove discrimination and gave whites greater leeway in challenging affirmative action programs.

Because the tide was turning on affirmative action, minorities began looking to Congress for relief. In 1991 Congress passed another Civil Rights Act, which responded to the conservative trend in the court on affirmative action. The Act made it easier for those alleging a grievance to sue for discrimination, it expanded racial harassment provisions, and it put an end to challenges of existing court judgments that set goals for hiring minorities. The Civil Rights Act of 1991 made some adjustments to the law to deal with issues before the Supreme Court, but it did not address the critical issues of whether affirmative action was an appropriate means of reaching racial equality in this country.

In fact since the signing of the Act by President Bush, the Supreme Court has continued refining its understanding of how affirmative action squares with the language of the Fourteenth Amendment to the Constitution in which Americans are entitled to "equal protection of the laws." In an important decision out of Texas in 1996, the Supreme Court took serious issue with a race preference admission program at the University of Texas Law School refusing to look at a lower court decision that stated the minority preference program violated the equal protection clause. The Texas Law School decision was looked on as the beginning of the end of affirmative action as a constitutionally protected approach to expanding equal rights in this country.

In 1995 the debate over affirmative action shifted from the Supreme Court and the halls of Congress to the states. The Regents of the University of California decided not to consider race as a factor in any facet of university affairs from employment to admissions to purchasing. This decision, which was viewed as a complete about-face from policies in the 1970s that had aggressively pursued preferential treatment for minorities, led to major protests on the campuses of the state system.

One year later the voters of California passed a highly charged referendum, Proposition 209, which made California the first state to forbid governmental agencies to pursue policies based on preferential treatment. The intent of Proposition 209 was clearly to put an end to affirmative action at the state level, no matter what was happening, or not happening, at the federal level. The constitutionality of Proposition 209 has yet to be tested in the federal courts, particularly in light of the Fourteenth Amendment charge to provide all Americans with equal protection of the laws. Nevertheless, momentum continues to build against affirmative action, as evidenced by the success of a referendum which ended preferential hiring and race-based college admissions in the state of Washington.

At the heart of the debate over affirmative action is the question of whether we as a people have progressed so far in terms of race relations and commitment to equality that we no longer need intrusive government programs to force us to do the right thing. Many white Americans are convinced that affirmative action has outlived its usefulness and is a vestige of the civil rights movement of the 1950s and 1960s. But many African Americans believe that without the force of government, white Americans will quickly slip back into subtle (if not blatant) racism and show an unwillingness to give minorities access to jobs and career advancement.

The debate over affirmative action, thus, is about what we have become as a people. If those are right who believe that we can now use standards such as excellence and merit in personnel decisions rather than racial and gender preferences, then affirmative action programs should be phased out and we can move forward to enjoy a colorblind society where equality is not just a vision. If, however, the opinion of many in the minority community is correct that racism will always be with us and that no matter how vigorously Whites protest, there will always be a climate of unfairness toward people of color, then affirmative action still retains its validity.

As a result of the referendums in California and Washington, affirmative action and affirmative action programs are fighting a rearguard action. Those who voted for those referendums, and many others, want decisions based on merit rather than on making up for past mistakes, whereas minorities constantly point to the upward mobility experienced by people of color that would not have happened without the force of government policy. In particular, recent studies of college admission policies under affirmative action show the tangible successes of guidelines that take race into consideration. But no matter where this debate over affirmative action takes the country, Whites and Blacks still have a long way to go toward achieving some consensus on equality and the American dream.

If there is a lesson to be learned from affirmative action it is that relying on the force of government to attain racial equality has its limits. There comes a point in time when public laws, regulations, and programs begin to lose their rationale or their base of support. What wise political leaders must do then is to reexamine the validity and appropriateness of these laws, regulations, and programs in a changed world. This is what is occurring now with respect to affirmative action. One can only hope that wisdom will prevail.

A Few Books You Should Read

Adams, Charles. *Those Dirty Rotten Taxes*. New York: Free Press, 1998. An interesting and valuable discussion of the history of citizen rebellion against what is perceived to be unfair taxation.

Bowen, William G., and Derek Bok. *The Shape of the River: Long-Term Consequences of Considering Race in College and University Admissions*. Princeton: Princeton University Press, 1998. Based on a wealth of data, these two former college presidents (Princeton and Harvard) show that affirmative action programs have had significant positive results for minorities admitted to prestigious colleges.

Eckes, Alfred E. *Opening America's Market: U.S. Foreign Trade Policy Since 1776*. Berkeley: University of California Press, 1995. From the early competition with Britain and France to the North American Free Trade Agreement with Canada and Mexico, the author explains how we have formulated and implemented trade policy and dealt with the domestic and international repercussions of trade policy.

Hart, Gary. *The Minuteman: Restoring the Army of the People.* New York: Simon and Schuster, 1998. Former Senator and presidential candidate, Hart presents the argument for a new, scaled-down, but effective military machine that is prepared for the challenges of the twenty-first century.

Kettl, Donald F. *Deficit Politics: Public Budgeting in Its Institutional and Historical Context.* New York: Macmillan, 1997. One of the most critical issues of government in recent years is explained in a readable manner. There is no exciting way to present the deficit story, but Kettl does an admirable job.

Orme, William J. *Understanding NAFTA: Mexico, Free Trade and the New North America.* Austin: University of Texas Press, 1996. A balanced account of this controversial trade agreement that also describes the future impact of open borders on both the United States and Mexico.

Pollack, Sheldon. *The Failure of U.S. Tax Policy.* University Park: Pennsylvania State Press, 1998. The author presents the arguments and the evidence that show the enormous disenchantment with current taxation policy. An essential guide to the intricacies of tax failure and tax reform.

Thernstrom, Stephen, and Abigail Thernstrom. *America in Black and White. One Nation, Indivisible: Race in Modern America.* New York: Simon and Schuster, 1997. A highly controversial book, which takes on the issue of affirmative action. The authors, conservative in persuasion, make powerful arguments that cannot be ignored.

8

THE CHALLENGES
FACING AMERICAN
GOVERNMENT

Don't stop thinking about tomorrow.
—Fleetwood Mac, Bill Clinton's Campaign Song

Is Social Security in Trouble?

"Save Social Security First!" This was the challenge posed to the Congress by President Clinton during his State of the Union Address in 1998. Although the words of the president sound something like a bumper sticker slogan, his call for the Congress to address the spiraling costs of taking care of the retirement of America's seniors points to a real need. Projections from various government and independent sources show that by the year 2013 the number of Americans retiring will be so large that the cost of providing monthly checks to seniors will far outstrip the money coming in to the Social Security system. Currently it takes 2.7 workers paying Social Security taxes to support the system, but by 2013 it will take 3.3 workers to provide the same support. By 2032 some prognosticators assert that the Social Security system will be bankrupt and unable to meet its financial obligations to the American people.

2032 is a long way off, and most Americans pay little attention to such distant problems. But the president has reminded Congress of the need to take whatever moneys are available from future budget surpluses and target those dollars to help bolster a program that remains the most popular social program initiated by the government. Even if the Congress goes along with the president and puts aside surplus money for Social Security, the added funds (anywhere from $73 billion to $200 billion) would only delay the predicted collapse of the program by two years. Social Security, after all, is an enormous program serving 27 million retirees, 5.4 million widows and widowers, 4.4 million disabled, and 3.8 million children of deceased or disabled persons. Currently, Social Security and its companion health care program Medicare cost $529 billion. By the year 2030 the number of Americans eligible for Social Security will have risen to over 70 million, and the additional taxes that will be necessary to fund the increase in recipients is estimated to be $1 trillion, in today's dollars.

Social Security funding is in fact a critical policy problem: The costs that will be incurred as the baby boom generation becomes eligible for retirement are huge, yet there is little agreement on what needs to be done in order to meet this funding challenge. A thirteen-member panel of experts has been charged by President Clinton with finding ways to deal with the Social Security funding issue, yet the experts themselves have been divided on how best to find a way out of this demographic morass. The first area of disagreement is over whether taxes should be raised or benefits cut in order to ensure the financial solvency of Social Security. Needless to say, either option is filled with political dangers, especially since seniors, who vote regularly, do not want their nest egg tampered with; they object fiercely to receiving a diminished benefits package. When talk of not tying the yearly cost of living increase to the Consumer Price Index was broached in Washington in 1996, seniors were outraged and let their legislators know that in no uncertain terms.

One possible option that might be palatable to seniors is to push the retirement age from sixty-five to sixty-seven, or perhaps even seventy, as a means of holding off the inevitable financial pressures in the Social Security system. With seniors living longer and healthier lives, advancing the official retirement age and the eligibility for Social Security benefits is a change that seems workable. And yet there are counterpressures related to age. President Clinton is on record as supporting a change in Medicare eligibility that would allow Americans as young as 55 to buy into the program. The president supports this change primarily because there are millions of Americans who are either retired or lose their jobs in this age grouping and may therefore need the health benefits of Medicare.

A more controversial option than fiddling with age and retirement is investing Social Security assets in the stock market. Since the stock market has been growing during the last few years at a rate of over 20 percent annually, there is a case being made that the answer to the problem is on Wall Street. And yet many in Washington and on Main Street America are concerned with the unpredictability of the market. Fluctuations in the stock market over time and the prospect that a crash cannot be discounted has raised deep skepticism about the advisability of this idea. Nevertheless, supporters of the stock market approach point out that since huge revenue streams need to be raised by 2032, it is far better to rely on the vagaries of the stock market than go to the taxpayers for the money. Despite early opposition from President Clinton, the idea of using the stock market to help save Social Security has not faded; in fact, the president suggested late in 1998 that he saw some merit in the proposal.

The most radical reform suggested for Social Security is to abandon the program in favor of individual retirement accounts. Increasingly younger Americans are recognizing that in the years leading up to 2032, those FICA taxes (Federal Insurance Contributions Act) that they see on their pay stub will likely move up and up. At present, roughly two-thirds of Americans pay FICA taxes, and those taxes now exceed income taxes as the largest source of revenue extracted from American citizens. Because of the growing tax burden from Social Security, polls point to a growing willingness to replace Social Security with individual responsibility for the retirement nest egg. With new laws making contributions to Individual Retirement Accounts (IRAs) more attractive, Americans are asking why they should be paying taxes to a governmental program that is growing out of control and may not be financially sound in the future.

Although scrapping Social Security is not in the political cards, there are examples of what life would be like without this gigantic program. In the early 1980s, when laws permitted it, the City of Galveston, Texas, took its employees out of the Social Security system and started a private retirement system based on stable and secure bond investments. The experiment has worked well and the employees are satisfied to see their retirement portfolio grow at a rate beyond inflation. Critics of the Galveston experiment admit that for full-time employees the abandonment of Social Security may work, but they point out that Social Security also provides assistance to the disabled and to children of recipients who have passed away. For these groups, a privately-funded system may not provide the kind of benefits they've been getting from the government program.

Somewhere along the line a president and Congress will have to make the difficult choice among the options. None of the current options hold the key to solving the shortfall, and all of them carry serious problems. Although the dire predictions of a collapse of Social Security get the most attention, the scariest scenario involves the deepening of generational differences as the generations compete for resources.

The political battles of the next twenty to thirty years in this country may very well be associated with the issue of where government directs its budget moneys. Should government take care of that giant bubble of baby boomers who will be moving into retirement or the younger generation, who, if the current system remains the same, will be placing ever higher amounts of their tax dollars in programs that they receive little or no benefit from? Deciding where government should direct its energy and resources may be the most difficult policy decision of the next century.

When Social Security was inaugurated in 1935, a retirement age of sixty-five was the norm, and life expectancy was around seventy. Those who benefited from the system were receiving roughly the same amount they had put in. Today, however, much of the money that retirees put into Social Security is used up while they still have many years to live, meaning that for the rest of their life the younger generation is paying for the older generation. Because the young will likely continue to pay for their elders, there will be an inevitable showdown over who is responsible for taking care of grandma and grandpa. What started out as a well-meaning program to support the retirement needs of seniors has evolved into a potential budget and tax disaster that is quickly creating a gulf between the young and the old.

In 1983 Congress supported a major overhaul of Social Security because it was becoming clear that payments to recipients were outstripping contributions. Those reforms helped to put the system on more solid financial ground. In 1993, the last time the Democrats controlled the Congress, new taxes on some Social Security recipients were passed despite Republican opposition. At that time an army of senior citizens came out to show their opposition to the increase, but the vote prevailed.

During the balanced budget debates of 1996 and 1997, some members of Congress called for including Social Security in the discussion over cuts aimed at meeting the goal of balance by the year 2002. But as the talks over the balanced budget progressed, the Republican majority recognized that making real reforms in Social Security was political dynamite. Social Security was taken off the negotiating table. Thankfully for politicians reluctant to face the wrath of the senior lobby, the strong economy in the 1990s has allowed Congress to buy more time before it is forced to fix Social Security.

Delay is a common tactic in American politics, but the demographic projections about the baby boomers heading into retirement are accurate, and the cost projections will not go away. The bill will come due, whether it is in 2010 or 2020 or 2032, and when it does come due there is likely to be a political tussle of grand proportions. What Social Security has become is a trillion-dollar hot potato with the young and the old at odds over the costs and the benefits of the program. It will take all the best bargaining skills of political leaders to take the country through this generational minefield.

Why Has Resistance to Immigration Risen (Again)?

There is perhaps no more inspiring sight in this country than the Statue of Liberty in New York harbor. For over one hundred years

Lady Liberty has been welcoming new arrivals to the United States with upraised torch, that beacon of light that symbolizes the hope and opportunity that are the bedrocks of this nation. Many of those arrivals were not just tourists on vacation, but immigrants seeking to start a new life in a country that has so much to offer. The poet Emma Lazarus said it best when she put these memorable words into the mouth of Lady Liberty—"Give me your tired, your poor, your huddled masses longing to breathe free." That poetic refrain has served as the basis of how we as a people view immigration and indeed how we define our country. We are a nation of immigrants, and we continue to open our shores to the tired, the poor, and those huddled masses longing to breathe free. Yet it's also true that we have always placed limits on immigration, and now there is a growing demand to reexamine who should be permitted into this country and how we should respond to the problems that arise when new people step onto our shores.

Despite the powerful poetry of Emma Lazarus, the arrival of immigrants to America has never been based on pure altruism. Although over the years we have provided people with protection from repressive regimes and offered those without anything a new home, America has opened up its gates for largely economic reasons—we needed cheap and eager workers to help drive our economy forward. Whenever we put out the "Help Wanted" sign, it was quite easy to attract workers, first from Ireland, then from central and southern Europe, and now from Latin America and Asia. What is different today and why there is growing concern about immigration is that many new arrivals are entering our country without the financial means for settling here (or a network of financial supporters). The result is that these new arrivals are in need of some form of government assistance. This need for assistance has driven up legal, social, medical, and educational costs associated with settlement to the point where state governments are crying for relief and angry citizens are saying enough is enough.

At present there are about 20 million foreign-born persons living in the United States, which is 9 percent of the total population. It's a large number, but the ratio of immigrants to total population is actually less now than during the heyday of migration between 1880 and 1920, when nearly 30 million people came to the United States and made up 14 percent of the population. Today, however, the number of immigrants in this country has created a backlash against our tradition of open arms and generosity. Another reason for the backlash is that approximately one third of the new arrivals each year come here illegally. Often crossing the border from Mexico into California or Texas or slipping in by boat from Cuba or Haiti, immigrants who are desperate to leave economic hardship or political repression brave capture by the U.S. Border Patrol or Coast Guard in order to enter the United States.

Historically there have always been problems associated with foreign-born people seeking employment in this country, from the stark signs in factory windows during the 1840s, "No Irish Need Apply," to the terrible conditions endured by Asian workers on the railroads and in the mines of the West. Today the problem is not so much discrimination against immigrants in the workplace, especially since there is a high demand for their services; the problem is rather the fear that the presence of immigrants in this country poses a job and salary threat to those already here.

The pressure points have been at the lower end of the job scale, with representatives of native minorities and labor unions claiming that the new arrivals, legal or illegal, are responsible for keeping wages low and for limiting access to jobs for Americans. Above all, the tension has been between the immigrant community of Hispanics and Asians and the African American community, which claims that immigrants take jobs away and then accept poor wages, depressing wages for Americans.

Although the argument that new arrivals to this country have limited the employment prospects of Americans has been at the center of the anti-immigration debate, a number of recent studies have shown that foreign-born persons have not had a negative impact on jobs and wages. In fact the studies show that immigrants often take jobs in areas of the economy that Americans have no interest in or feel are beneath them, such as the garment industry, fast food, domestic jobs in hotels, gardening, and housepainting. And new arrivals have not only taken menial jobs essential for the continued growth of the economy, those immigrants who are skilled and educated have proven to be valuable contributors to the key areas of computers, technology in general, biomedicine, and scientific research. Many in the business and academic sectors say without hesitation that the new arrivals, many with so-called critical need visas, have filled important employment gaps that were going empty because of the shortage of American job applicants.

While the issue of job loss and wage depression associated with immigration has been quieted somewhat, in large part due to a booming economy, the immigration debate has shifted to the burden that government must assume in order to house, educate, and provide for the overall health and welfare of the new arrivals. As many as 30 percent of foreign-born citizens who arrive in this country tap into some form of government services, at least initially. The cost of these services, which may even be directed toward illegal immigrants (educating, for example, the children of illegal immigrants), has caused citizens in states like California, Texas, and Florida to lash out at the growing bill for immigrant services.

This lashing out has been most pronounced in California, which passed Proposition 187 in 1994. This state referendum, supported by a solid majority of the residents, prohibited access of illegal aliens to public services, including education, and nonemergency health care. The referendum was a hotly debated ballot question that divided the state along racial and ethnic lines, with natives of all ethnic groups claiming that state resources should not be provided to illegal immigrants. Immigrant groups responded, stating that this was a heartless and racially motivated vote that would hurt the sick and the children of illegal immigrants born in this country.

Despite the controversy surrounding Proposition 187, the anti-illegal immigrant mood eventually hit Washington, where Congress went so far as to deny most forms of public assistance even to legal immigrants. The rationale behind the congressional vote was based on a provision in the Immigration Reform Act of 1996, which mandated that sponsors of immigrants coming to this country must have an income that is sufficient to provide for the new arrivals.

The passion that is inherent in the immigration debate is seen best when the matter of language is brought into the mix. Because of the influx of immigrants from Latin America and Asia in the last twenty years, whole separate communities have developed within urban areas. Little Havanas, Koreatowns, MexAmericas have sprung up as islands of ethnic identity amid the dominant native landscape. Sections of cities where only Spanish or Creole (Haiti's language) is spoken are now common. Movement through Los Angeles and Miami is like traveling from mini-country to mini-country—it requires multilingual talents and an appreciation of cultural diversity. Moreover, pressure from ethnic groups has been successful in convincing governments and school systems to honor this diversity and ethnic pride with policies that permit the use of foreign languages in all public business and encourage bilingual education as a fundamental instructional approach in the classroom.

This diversification of America has led to a highly charged debate about immigration. At its roots, the debate is about whether this country will hold to its traditional "melting pot" vision of immigration. As the term suggests, immigrants coming to this country have been expected to melt into the culture and become Americanized, which means learning the language, pushing into the background the old ways of their former country, and taking pride in being American. Today's immigrants appear to be less interested in melting in and more interested in preserving their heritage and their language. But to many critics of immigration, this refusal to become completely American carries the threat of societal fragmentation, with the United States becoming not one country created out of many people, but scores of countries with no unifying nationhood.

For some critics of this ethnic diversity, the answer is the English First movement, which seeks to mandate an official language for the United States. A number of groups, primarily in California, Arizona, Texas, and Florida, have organized to put on the ballot proposals that would end policies that create multiple language application forms for governmental business or mandate multilingual education in the public schools. While the English First movement has support in border states, it does not have enough strength nationwide to become a viable public policy issue. The United States has never had an official language as some countries have and has always thought of itself as a nation where English would be accepted by new arrivals.

Immigration is one issue area that is filled with emotion, patriotism, and an occasional dash of prejudice. Because we are a nation of immigrants, the ebb and flow of new people arriving on our shores is nothing new. What is new, however, is that some of these immigrants are climbing the fences and fording the rivers to get here illegally; some of these immigrants are not interested in melting in; some of these immigrants are pushing social welfare spending skyward; and (although this is not really new) some of these immigrants threaten the established ethnic, racial, and social arrangements in the communities where they reside. Because this immigration is viewed as different by the American public, the call has gone out to limit and control entry.

Government is getting the message. In 1996 another immigration reform act was passed taking the place of the landmark reform bill of 1986. This new legislation doubles the number of border guards, increases penalties for smuggling and document fraud, quickens the deportation process, and mandates programs to help verify the immigration status of foreigners. The bill is directed above all toward dealing with illegal immigration from Mexico, which has been one of the major sources of citizen complaints. The Mexican-U.S. border has become something of a war zone, as the Border Patrol and now military units engage in daily roundups and occasional firefights as illegals seek entry into the United States. 12 foot walls with glass shards on top have been built, huge ditches to limit automobile traffic dug, and miles and miles of fences erected, all in an attempt to keep out illegal entry.

And still they come, perhaps as many as 1 million a year. Many illegals cross the border as if it were a daily trip to work with a return crossing at the end of the day. Others are here for months, working to get enough money to support family back in Mexico. What is important to remember is that these illegals come into the United States because there is a job waiting for them with a business run by an American seeking cheap labor. Moreover, the same Americans who complain about illegal immigration most likely have been served in some way by illegal immigrants, whether as housepainters, gardeners, or creators of wearing apparel.

And so the trek to America continues. This country remains the preferred destination of the immigrant looking for a new life. As in the past, the arrival of immigrants has created problems of assimilation, primarily because new people with new languages and customs need time to settle in a new country. The most recent immigrants, however, have created a new set of problems for Americans, largely because they come from different parts of the less-developed world. But what remains essentially the same is that this country continues to be an immigration magnet, and that fact is unlikely to change, however much it may be accompanied by difficulties for American society as the new arrivals settle here.

Box 8.1 *Hispanic Population Figures*

States with a Higher Percentage of Hispanics than the National Average

New Mexico	38.2 percent
California	25.8 percent
Texas	25.5 percent
Arizona	18.8 percent
Colorado	12.9 percent
New York	12.2 percent
Nevada	10.4 percent
New Jersey	9.6 percent

The Ten Cities with the Largest Hispanic Populations

New York	1,784,000
Los Angeles	1,391,000
Chicago	546,000
San Antonio	520,000
Houston	450,000
El Paso	356,000
San Diego	230,000
Miami	224,000
Dallas	210,000
San Jose	208,000

SOURCE: U.S. Census

Can the Government Win the War on Drugs?

The drug war hasn't created the tragedy of tremendous loss of life like World War II, or divided the nation like the Vietnam War, or stirred up pride in the armed forces like the Persian Gulf War. The war on drugs is a different kind of war. It is a war measured in tons of cocaine seized, acres of marijuana burned, and scores of convictions of smugglers and kingpins. It is also the longest war that this country has been involved in, dating back to the early years of the Reagan administration. It was during this time that the government declared that it would end the "scourge of drugs" and promised to use the full weight of its power to bring those responsible for this illicit trade to justice.

Finally, it is a war that has serious social impacts, since continued drug use creates an estimated $1 trillion worth of costs in terms of work loss, hospitalization, crime, and property damage, not to mention the inestimable cost of emotional distress caused to families and loved ones. Because of the social and medical problems associated with drug use, this country currently spends over 12 billion tax dollars to fund this war. And yet despite the obvious dangers and sadness associated with drugs, this war has shown no "light at the end of the tunnel," a phrase often used in discussions of our last military quagmire, in Vietnam. Small victories are no consolation in a war without end.

The war on drugs may very well go down in history as our most serious defeat. There have been victories to be sure—drug seizures are at an all-time high, our prisons are bursting at the seams with members of drug organizations, and high-profile operations around the world attest to the commitment of our allies to work with us to win this war. But the war is far from being won. 25 million Americans spend $50 billion a year to purchase marijuana, cocaine, heroin, and a pharmacopoeia of hallucinogenic pills. Although we have only 5 percent of the world's population, we consume 50 percent of the world's illicit drugs. And what may be the most telling disappointment of the war is that drugs remain plentiful and cheap. The average cost of a kilo of cocaine in 1981 was $70,000; in 1995 it was $20,000. Moreover, while the federal antidrug budget increased by

300 percent during the Reagan years, the supply of cocaine multiplied ten times. It is now claimed that there is enough cocaine produced in northern Mexico alone to provide every person on this planet with a line of the drug.

Yet the war continues, with the Coast Guard chasing down drug "fast boats" in the Caribbean, U.S. Customs agents checking cars, trucks, and planes for drug contraband on the Mexican border, and the Drug Enforcement Agency (DEA) working with their counterparts around the world to destroy cocaine labs and poppy fields and track illegally laundered money through the international banking system. Because these are hard working and dedicated antidrug warriors, smugglers are captured, drug shipments intercepted, and whole organizations brought down. But for all the effort, most agree that the successes in the war are only the tip of the iceberg. It has been widely reported that government agents stop only about 5–10 percent of the illegal drugs destined for the United States. With over 88,000 miles of coastline and 300 ports of entry, the task of trying to control what enters this country is, to say the least, daunting. Add to this the normal human traffic of over 500 million entering the country each year along with 128 million vehicles and 586,000 aircraft, and the task goes from daunting to impossible.

Although there are signs aplenty that the war on drugs is not going well, no one in government is calling for some kind of negotiated settlement with our sworn enemies, the drug organizations, and certainly no one is willing to use the word surrender. We remain determined to stop the entry of drugs into our country and to prosecute those individuals who break our drug laws. Those who talk of decriminalizing the use of drugs (which would essentially mean that drug users would pay a fine for possession of small amounts of drugs) or legalizing drugs (and putting drugs in the same category as cigarettes and alcohol, with of course the taxes going to the government) are portrayed as permissive fools who would give up the fight and turn this country into a nation of druggies.

The current policy of interdiction, militarization, and incarceration tends to be the main focus of news coverage, making it seem that the only alternatives are harsh military tactics or surrender. Yet prevention and rehabilitation are also options in the war on drugs, options that the government, at the national and state level, is pursuing, with equally mixed results. Programs have always existed, particularly at the state and local level, to provide counseling and medical attention to drug addicts and drug abusers, but the beginning of extensive federal involvement in the prevention and rehabilitation side of the drug war began in 1986, with the signing of the Omnibus Anti-Drug Act. The $1.7 billion bill was designed to combat drug abuse not only by tough laws and law enforcement, but also through educational programs and rehabilitation initiatives. President Reagan at the signing ceremony called the Omnibus Anti-Drug Act the "vaccine" to respond to the "epidemic" of drugs in America.

Although the Reagan-sponsored legislation recognized that prevention and rehabilitation must be part of the mix in the war on drugs, the vast majority of government resources during his administration were targeted to interdiction, militarization, and incarceration. When the Reagan administration did move away from its law enforcement strategy and toward domestic demand, it was criticized for halfhearted efforts. Nancy Reagan, the President's wife, caused a stir when she called on young people faced with the temptation to use drugs to "Just Say No." The First Lady's advice was seen by most drug counselors and experts in the field of drug abuse as simplistic and unrealistic. What was needed, so the critics stated, was more money for prevention and rehabilitation, not slogans.

The arrival in the Oval Office of George Bush did nothing to advance the cause of prevention and rehabilitation. In fact it was President Bush who attended numerous drug summits in Latin America and pushed through the Andean Plan, a $2.2 billion program to assist countries like Peru, Bolivia, Ecuador, and Colombia to prevent drug cultivation and fight the drug trade. The Bush years were marked by open criticism of countries that did not cooperate with the United States in the war on drugs. Major operations like Operation Blast Furnace in Bolivia, in which U.S. military units were employed to destroy cocaine manufacturing labs and coca fields, were initiated. But operations like Blast Furnace and programs like the Andean Plan had limited success, largely because drug organizations became more sophisticated in their ability to limit their losses and to protect their businesses. Drug lords like Pablo Escobar of Colombia developed their own private armies to protect their investments and used corruption of public officials and terror against their own people to remain in business. The Bush administration could do little about the internal situation in a drug-producing country and had to settle for an occasional big strike that was only a small inconvenience to the drug organizations.

It was not until the Clinton administration that the government began to bring more balance to strategies for dealing with illegal drugs. One of President Clinton's first official acts was to scale down the staff of the White House Office of Drug Policy and to publicly emphasize the need for more programs to deal with the public demand for drugs in this country, rather than focusing on the supply and the suppliers outside our borders. There were fewer high-profile operations by the Drug Enforcement Agency and the U.S. Customs Service and more emphasis on educating the young to the dangers of drugs. Federal moneys to local communities and school districts, particularly in urban areas, increased dramatically during the Clinton administration.

By the mid-1990s there were some encouraging signs that the educational and prevention programs were getting results. Nationally, drug use was down 50 percent from its highest level in 1979. Most encouraging, cocaine use among young people dropped dramatically and the crack cocaine wars in the urban areas subsided. But while cocaine use was on the decline, marijuana, a new generation of mood enhancing pills, and heroin were being used with more regularity among the young. Despite the constant barrage of antidrug messages and the thousands of drug rehabilitation programs available at the local level, young people were again turning to drugs for recreational purposes and as a dangerous habit.

These drugs were making their way into not just urban areas, but the suburbs as well (and even small rural communities). Perhaps even more disturbing was the youth violence that accompanied the drug trade. Urban and suburban gang membership climbed dramatically during the 1990s and the drug wars took on a new meaning as gangs battled each other for drug supremacy and the riches that came with supremacy.

The renewed interest in drug use among the young has prompted a new political debate. In large part the debate centers on President

Clinton's announcement of a ten-year drug strategy to reduce drug use and availability by 50 percent. The White House program is based on a series of performance targets that government agencies will be kept to as they advance the drug war. The program began with a $17 billion appropriation for fiscal 1999, which added 257 new drug control agents and included the largest percentage increase to date (15 percent) for programs to help youths deal with drugs. President Clinton used the language of war and family responsibility as he introduced the new program, saying that the fight against illegal drugs "must be waged and won at kitchen tables all across America. . . . Even the world's most thorough antidrug strategy won't ever do the job unless all of us pass on the same clear and simple message to our children—drugs are wrong, drugs are dangerous, and drugs can kill you."

Republicans immediately jumped on the ten-year program, charging that President Clinton had neglected the drug war for most of his presidency, particularly interdiction, and was now taking much too long to implement a strategy. House Speaker Newt Gingrich criticized the president for providing the drug cartels with some breathing space, allowing them to regain the initiative in the drug war. As the Speaker stated, "This President would have us believe that with all of the resources, ingenuity, dedication, and passion of the American people, we can't even get halfway to victory in the war on drugs until the year 2007—nine full years from now. This is not success. This is the definition of failure."

And so the drug wars continue, along with the political rhetoric. The ingredients remain the same—more money, more programs, more arrests, more talk, and some progress. It is easy to criticize the government for its failures with respect to drug use, but the problem is really a reflection of societal decay. When billions of taxpayer dollars go yearly into the drug wars and the results are, to say the least, mixed, questions inevitably must arise as to whether the war is worth the effort.

The problem is that the alternative is to allow drugs to be used openly and legally, an option that has never been accepted by the American people. Most Americans see drugs as an evil and remain in a fighting mood when faced with calls for decriminalization and legalization. Yet despite this brave talk, we are a nation of drug hypocrites; we are the world's leaders in using prescription drugs; we continue our love affair with the cigarette, and we would never consider putting a ban on alcohol, perhaps the most dangerous of the drugs available. Under these circumstances, it is no surprise that the war is not going well. Government cannot win a war the American people only halfheartedly support.

Box 8.2   *Federal Counternarcotics Intelligence Centers*

Number		Location	Established
Department of Defense	1	Key West, FL	1989
	2	Alameda, CA	1990
	3	El Paso, TX	1989
	4	Cheyenne Mountain Air Force Base, Colorado, Springs, CO	1989
Defense Intelligence Agency	5	Arlington, VA	1967
	6	Arlington, VA	1989
Drug Enforcement Agency	7	El Paso, TX	1974
	8	Arlington, VA	1989
Federal Bureau of Investigation	9	Washington, DC	1984
U.S. Coast Guard	10	Washington, DC	1984
	11	Miami, FL	1990
U.S. Customs Service	12	Riverside, CA	1988
	13	Oklahoma City, OK	1989
U.S. Coast Guard/	14	Miami, FL	1987
U.S. Customs Service	15	Miami, FL	1986
	16	Gulfport, MS	1987
Southwest Border Committee	17	Buffalo, NY	1987
Department of Treasury	18	Washington, DC	1990
Central Intelligence Agency	19	Washington, DC	1989

SOURCE: Office of National Drug Control Policy

What's Wrong with Our Health Care System?

The answer to this question depends on who is being asked. For most Americans the health care they receive remains the best in the world. Our hospitals and medical research centers are on the front lines of providing the latest in patient care and breakthrough procedures. When it is time for the Nobel Prizes in Medicine to be awarded, it is likely that the recipients will be either Americans or foreign nationals associated with the American medical community. Perhaps the most glowing endorsement of our health care system is the number of world leaders and dignitaries who come to the United States for care rather than remain in their own country.

But if we consider who has access to that excellent health care, all is not well with the American health care system. Between 1992 and 1998, the number of medically uninsured Americans has risen from about 40 million to 43 million. Of that 43 million, 10 million are children, many of whom are losing their federal disability coverage; 3 million are between 55 and 64 and have no coverage due to corporate downsizing and 30 million are the working poor, who have jobs but receive no insurance with those jobs. Americans who do have medical insurance are now being pushed into health maintenance organizations (HMOs), which have limited cost increases (at least for the moment) but have also trimmed access to a range of procedures and created a kind of private medical bureaucracy that at times appears more interested in profits than patient care.

Until quite recently, medical treatment for Americans was not a front burner issue. After 1993, when President Clinton accepted the defeat of his attempt to pass the Health Security Act, the American public was lulled into accepting the view that the private health care system had made significant reforms and that federal intervention on a grand scale was not necessary or wise.

But now the American people are not so confident about their health care system; they are concerned about the issues of quality medical care, spiraling medical costs, and the general health of our young, our old, and our poor. One sign of this creeping loss of confidence is a call for greater governmental intervention to ensure that Americans are not harmed by the restructuring and bottom-line efficiencies that have overtaken the health care industry. Once again, what happens between patient and doctor in hospitals around the country has entered the political arena.

One early sign of the increasing reliance of the American people on government to take a more active role in health care was the furor raised over policies set by many hospitals that women giving birth must leave the hospital within twenty-four hours of delivery. This common policy was largely an economic one, as health maintenance organizations (HMOs) were conscious of the costs associated with stays longer than one day. Many pregnant women and their doctors were outraged at the time limit and approached Congress with the proposal to make it mandatory for HMOs to pay for a stay of up to two days after delivery, if the woman so chooses. The twenty-four hour policy alerted many Americans to the changing nature of health care in this country, where budgetary concerns could override reasonable health care treatment.

The concerns created by limitations on the hospital stays of pregnant women and the negative response to the business model of health care delivery have given rise to a broad-based reform movement of HMO practices. This spirit of reform is best represented by the Health Care Bill of Rights for Patients and Physicians. Proposed by Senator Edward Kennedy of Massachusetts, the Bill of Rights would, in the words of the Senator, guarantee that, "Insurance company accountants should not be allowed to practice medicine. No woman should be denied the right to see a gynecologist or forced by a health insurance plan to undergo a drive-by mastectomy. No doctors should be subjected to gag rules, or bribed with financial incentives, or threatened with financial penalties that prohibit or discourage them from giving patients the best medical care and advice." The Health Care Bill of Rights for Patients and Physicians is loaded with guarantees that the health care industry would likely find onerous, but just as with the Taxpayers Bill of Rights, there is growing pressure from the American public to ensure a certain level of care, no matter what the cost.

Not only is there more focus now on using government to make reforms in the health care industry, political leaders are also keenly aware that in the not too distant future the Medicare program for seniors will create enormous budgetary pressures. Medicare, the health program for seniors receiving Social Security, has two parts—Part A, which covers hospitalization, some nursing home care, and home health services, and Part B, an optional component that covers payment for physician services and many outpatient and diagnostic services. Part A Medicare is financed by a payroll tax of 1.45 percent paid by employee and employer; Part B costs the senior a monthly fee, which has increased steadily each year.

Starting in the 1980s, Congress has become more and more aware of the rising costs associated with taking care of seniors. In 1983 Congress made its first major attempt to cap expenses by paying hospitals a set amount for the services they provided. With less money coming in from the government, hospitals reduced the stay of its patients and limited access to seniors of certain procedures. Nevertheless, the costs of Medicare have not subsided. In 1994 Medicare costs were $163 billion; in 2000 the program is projected to cost $247 billion. As seniors live longer and make more use of advanced technological procedures, the Medicare program, like Social Security, is destined to be a budget buster that will have to be addressed. The reform that is being discussed will not be popular with seniors, since options such as higher premiums and less coverage dominate the discussion.

Right behind Medicare as a budget buster is the Medicaid program. Started at the same time as Medicare, Medicaid provides many of the same health care options as seniors receive, only these options are made available to those of any age who qualify as financially needy. In 1994 the Medicaid program cost $89 billion, and like Medicare its projected cost will be substantial in the year 2000. Estimates now show that Medicaid costs will jump to $136 billion. These dollar figures are somewhat misleading, in that Medicaid is jointly financed by national and state governments. Although the federal government pays up to 79 percent of the costs of Medicaid, it is the states that set standards for eligibility and benefits. The contribution of states to Medicaid varies, with Mississippi at the low end of contribution and Massachusetts at the high end. But whatever the level of contribution from the states, Medicaid is also a costly program that is certain to grow. But there is one major difference between Medicare and Medicaid. Historically, Medicaid has been the target of budget cutters, while Medicare has remained sacrosanct.

A poll taken during the Clinton health care debate found that an overwhelming number of Americans viewed health care as a basic right. Moreover, those same Americans, again by an overwhelming number, felt that they should get the treatment they need, even if the costs are astronomical. As a nation we have come to expect that quality health care will be available, no matter the cost. The only problem with this view is that health care is taking an ever larger slice out of corporate benefit packages and an even larger slice out of government budgets. Health care costs now take up over 14 percent of the gross domestic product, and we are now in the trillion dollar range of total health care costs in this country. There is no end in sight.

And while the costs of providing the current level of health care for Americans are skyrocketing, there are renewed calls to expand the pie even further. Already a number of states have taken the lead in adding mental illness to insurance coverage, and it is expected that the push will be made at the federal level over the next two years. Also the intent of the original Clinton Health Security Act, to ensure that all Americans have access to health care, is regaining strength. A group of Democrats led by Senator Kennedy is seeking to make universal coverage a campaign issue in future elections. The Democratic argument is that with the economy so healthy and the need so great, the country should build on the foundation of Medicare and Medicaid and add universal coverage to its social welfare agenda. As Senator Kennedy stated in his defense of universal coverage, "If this country can't fulfill the hopes and answer the needs of average families in a time of peace and prosperity, when will we ever do so?"

Inspiring words indeed, but expanding coverage to all Americans got waylaid in 1993 amid charges by critics that universal health care would not only create a huge financial burden, but would also lead to a huge national medical bureaucracy. The mood in this country remains skeptical of developing another major social program that uses taxes to take money from some and redistribute it to others in order to attain a defined social good. Nevertheless, the medical needs of 43 million Americans are real, and rising costs will likely prohibit those

43 million from access to the treatment they need. This country has some critical health care challenges to face in the coming years—containing costs, providing for the growing needs of the aged, the young, and the poor, and ensuring that those who do have health care coverage do not become a casualty of the corporate bottom line. How we deal with these challenges will say much about how we value the health, welfare, and lives of our citizens.

Box 8.3   Health Care Bill of Rights and Responsibilities

President Clinton created the thirty-four-member Advisory Commission on Consumer Protection and Quality in the Health Care Industry on March 26, 1997, charging it with recommending such measures as may be necessary to promote and assure quality and value and protect consumers in the health care industry. The Commission is cochaired by Secretary of Labor Alexis Herman and Secretary of Health and Human Services Donna Shalala. The Commission submitted its final comprehensive report on creating a quality framework to the president, through the vice president, on March 30, 1998.

The Commission's consumer bill of rights consists of the following rights and responsibilities:

1. Access to Accurate, Easily Understood Information about health plans, facilities, and professionals to assist consumers in making informed health care decisions.
2. Choice of Health Care Providers that is sufficient to ensure access to appropriate high quality care. This right includes providing consumers with complex or serious medical conditions access to specialists, giving women access to qualified providers to cover routine women's health services, and ensuring continuity of care for consumers who are undergoing a course of treatment for a chronic or disabling condition.
3. Access to Emergency Services when and where the need arises. This provision requires health plans to cover these services in

(continues)

Box 8.3   (continued)

situations where a prudent layperson could reasonably expect that the absence of care could place their health in serious jeopardy.

4. Participation in Treatment Decisions, including requiring providers to disclose any incentives—financial or otherwise—that might influence their decisions, and prohibiting gag clauses that restrict health care providers' ability to communicate with and advise patients about medically necessary options.

5. Assurance that Patients are Respected and Not Discriminated Against, including prohibiting discrimination in the delivery of health care services based on race, gender, ethnicity, mental or physical disability, and sexual orientation.

6. Confidentiality Provisions that ensure that individually identifiable medical information is not disseminated and that provide consumers the right to review, copy, and request amendments to their medical records.

7. Grievance and Appeals Processes for consumers to resolve their differences with their health plans and health care providers—including an internal and external appeals process.

8. Consumer Responsibilities provisions that ask consumers to take responsibility by maximizing healthy habits, becoming involved in health care decisions, carrying out agreed-upon treatment plans, and reporting fraud.

What Is the Government Doing to Protect the Environment?

Actually the government has done a great deal to protect the environment, which has pleased those Americans who want strict laws limiting man's ability to threaten nature. Not everyone is happy, however. Powerful corporate interests are upset with the interventionist role of government because they believe this use of government to guard our natural resources has resulted in too many regulations and far too much taxpayer money. Protecting our environment—the air we breathe, the water we drink, the land that we live and play on—would seem to be one of those areas of public policy that engenders widespread support. And yet the efforts of the government to pass legislation and implement rules and regulations has led to some of the most contested debates and votes in the political arena. Nevertheless, environmental politics is only now really coming into its own as the critical issue of the next century.

The United States has a long tradition of concern for the environment. From the establishment of the Department of the Interior in 1849 to the most recent Clean Air Act in 1990, this country has taken a leadership role in the world in responding to threats to the environment both at home and abroad. In the last thirty years Congress and the White House have worked out agreements that have created a laundry list of legislation designed to address particular environmental concerns such as soil conservation, land reclamation, water quality, protection of endangered species, pesticide control, toxic substance regulation, and hazardous waste clean-up. These laws have led to the formation of an ever widening environmental bureaucracy charged with implementing the intent of the legislation. From the Bureau of Land Management to the Environmental Protection Agency, the government has created powerful voices for environmental policy.

The laws and the bureaucracy that accompanies them have had a substantial degree of success in responding to environmental threats. By most objective standards the quality of the environment has improved—the air is cleaner, the water is purer, and the land, from coastal beaches to mountain ranges, has been preserved and protected. Furthermore, the visibility and understanding of environmental issues has increased dramatically over time. Environmental scientists and the heads of government agencies involved in environmental issues have been more and more successful in bringing their concerns into the policymaking arena.

Their concern has been matched by interest from the American public, who are now much more conscious of the environment and demand information on the impact of corporate policies on natural resources. On the local level, recycling of paper, bottles, and other household refuse has now become commonplace, and Earth Day celebrations have increased significantly since the first event in 1970. Also, the number of Americans who cite environmental protection as a major national interest has skyrocketed to over 70 percent. In response to the public interest in the environment, a range of media outlets regularly provide information to the American public on topics such as global warming, toxic waste dumps, air pollution, and recycling. During the 1998 El Nino weather disturbances, not a night went by on network television without a segment on the impact of weather on the environment or the connection between environmental change and the weather.

But with greater concern for the environment and greater scrutiny of the connection between economic development and the environment, disagreements have also increased over the extent to which government should take measures that may be environmentally sound but can also have a deleterious impact on corporate profitability. Some of the more serious public battles have been over automobile emissions and the responsibility of car makers to build an environmentally friendly product. Acid rain pollution from Midwest factories and its effect on the water, the forests, and the wildlife of Canada has created tension between this country and its northern neighbor. Global warming, especially the connection between industrial production and the slow but potentially dangerous increase in world temperature, has led to prickly debates between environmentalists and political conservatives. And the preservation of natural resources such as timber forests (and the endangered species that live in the forests) versus the jobs and income of workers who depend upon logging for their livelihood has separated some communities into two hostile camps.

As a result of tensions between environmental protection and economic impacts, government, at both the national and state level, has been the target of pressure from groups and organizations anxious to make their case. Some of the more active interest groups in American politics are the Sierra Club (650,000 members) with major concerns for preserving wetlands and endangered species and reducing air pollution, the Wilderness Society (370,000 members) with primary interest in access to public lands, and the Natural Resources Defense

Council (168,000 members) with emphasis on reducing air and water pollution. Facing the pressure of these groups is a wide array of trade groups and corporations, such as the National Association of Manufacturers, the Northwest Timber Growers, and the Big Three Automobile companies. These organizations are often leading the fight against environmental regulation and the business costs that accompany regulation.

Increasingly, the focus of environmental politics in this country is on the response to global warming. Although there still remains some dispute about whether the earth is warming and whether emissions from automobiles and factories (primarily from the United States) are the source of the warming, the debate is already on over how to properly respond to this phenomenon and how to avoid serious economic repercussions should regulatory measures be implemented. Because the United States produces nearly 25 percent of the greenhouse gases commonly viewed as responsible for global warming, there has been constant pressure on government leaders in this country to take measures to reduce these emissions.

The United States took a major step toward reducing emissions of greenhouse gases during the presidency of George Bush. Pledging to be the "environmental president," Bush pressed for the passage of the Clean Air Act of 1990. Despite opposition from members of Congress representing industrial states like Michigan and Ohio, Bush was able to fulfill his promise on clean air. The Clean Air Act placed stronger controls on fuel use by automobiles. The legislation required automakers to install pollution devices on cars to reduce dangerous emissions. The Act also addressed emissions from factories. Industrial plants that emitted a certain level of gases were required to install devices (commonly called scrubbers) that would clean the air. Paying for what has been called the costliest clean air in history, the yearly $25 billion price tag associated with the intent of the Clean Air Act was seen as a necessary step in order to address those areas of environmental regulation that had been neglected. While some business leaders complained about the new level of regulation, the Clean Air Act of 1990 was viewed as a watershed of vigorous environmental policy.

The victory of the Bush administration in its domestic environmental agenda was not easily transferable to the international arena. The

United States became the target of many less developed nations, who felt this country was demanding that poor nations restrain their economic growth in the name of environmentalism, while the rich nations continued to threaten the planet with their emissions. The Earth Summit in Rio de Janeiro in 1992 brought into clear view the debate between the United States and the less developed world over who would make energy sacrifices. The United States, along with 166 other nations, reluctantly signed a treaty that would require this country to place a limit on emissions of these greenhouse gases at 1990 levels by the year 2000.

While many less developed countries doubted whether the United States would meet the requirements of the treaty, the Clinton administration began taking policy steps to achieve emission controls. In Clinton's first term, a broad-based energy tax was proposed as a way of meeting this goal. Republicans opposed the measure, arguing that the administration really wanted the tax for the sake of deficit reduction rather than to prevent global warming. The tax went down to defeat. The Republicans, however, found out quickly that their victory on the tax was hurting them with the voters, who saw them as anti-environment. With public opinion polls suggesting that as many as 60 percent of Americans support regulation to protect water and air, the Republicans began to show more interest in environmental issues, especially in those states where House or Senate victories were tied to environmental issues.

In the second Clinton administration the debate over global warming, clean air, and greenhouse emissions became more heated, as new pressure was placed on the United States by the less developed world. In 1998, at another United Nations Conference on the environment held in Kyoto, Japan, the Clinton administration took a controversial position, supporting more stringent emission controls as a way of responding to the threats from global warming. Vice President Al Gore, representing the United States at the conference, linked the extreme weather conditions recently experienced in the world and the beginning of polar icecap meltdown as signs that the world community of nations must take serious measures in limiting emissions. Business leaders responded quickly to the Gore position, arguing that the economic vitality of the nation depended upon the continued productivity of our industrial base and that emission controls would cripple what has become the longest and most sustained period of economic growth in U.S. history. The lines between environmentalists and supporters of economic growth had been clearly drawn, with the government at the center of the debate.

Meanwhile, efforts continue to finish the work of cleaning up our country's water, air, and soil. One important objective is cleaning up toxic waste. In the early 1990s the government targeted 1,245 sites as toxic waste dumps worthy of cleanup under the Comprehensive Environmental Response Compensation and Liability Act, better known as the Superfund legislation. Since its inception, the Superfund has spent over $11 billion to clean up the toxic waste sites. There has been criticism, that too much of the money in the Superfund, which is money from insurance companies to settle claims, has gone for lawyer fees. But with the Environmental Protection Agency stating that over one thousand cancer cases a year are associated with hazardous waste sites, strong support continues for Superfund spending. Unfortunately, the cleanup of the sites is a slow process, and it will likely take decades before the danger from these hazardous waste dumps is completely ended. In the meantime, waste products are seeping into the ground water or fouling the air and creating serious health and safety problems.

Despite the controversy surrounding global warming policies and the unfinished business of toxic waste sites, there are tangible examples of success in improving our environment. As a result of an international agreement called the Montreal Protocol, harmful chlorofluorocarbons used in refrigeration and air-conditioning and responsible for the depletion of the ozone layer around our planet are being brought under control. There have also been agreements on the dumping of sludge in our oceans, along with a number of initiatives to protect endangered species in rainforests and other ecologically threatened regions of the world.

Environmental protection is not only about what the government has done or intends to do. Rather environmentalism is a way of life, a recognition that citizens have a responsibility to protect the earth. There is now a greater consciousness among the American people that we live on a fragile and threatened planet. This consciousness has already led to greater pressure on political leaders to make up for years of neglect. This pressure is not likely to abate. There is in fact an emerging consensus among Americans that we must be faithful stewards and leave to future generations a cleaner, healthier, and safer earth. The clearer that consensus is, the more likely it is that the government will act effectively.

Box 8.4   *The Clinton Plan to Fight Global Warming*

President Clinton has proposed spending $6.3 billion over five years to fight global warming. Here are some highlights of the administration's plan:

- $3.6 billion in tax credits for energy efficiency, including:
- Up to $4,000 per individual for purchasing highly fuel-efficient cars.
- Up to $2,000 per individual for rooftop solar electricity and hot water systems.
- Up to $2,000 per individual for home improvements that save energy.
- $2.7 billion in new research and development spending, including:
- A $277 million increase in funding to develop "new generation" vehicles that are as much as three times more fuel-efficient than today's cars and trucks.
- A $100 million boost for research on renewable forms of energy, including wind, solar, and biomass.

SOURCE: White House

A Few Books You Should Read

Ball, Robert M. *Straight Talk About Social Security.* New York: The Century Foundation, 1998. As the title suggests, the issues raised by Social Security—future costs, future coverage, and future reforms—are presented in a readable manner.

Benjamin, Daniel K., and Roger Leroy Miller. *Undoing Drugs: Beyond Legalization*. New York: Basic Books, 1993. The authors present the arguments swirling around the drug debate, including the ramifications of legalization. Some solid analysis of what options are available to stem the tide of drug use.

Conca, Ken, and Geoffrey D. Pabelko, eds. *Green Planet Blues: Environmental Politics from Stockholm to Kyoto*. Boulder, Colo.: Westview Press, 1998. A comprehensive primer on the public policies related to environmental protection with special emphasis on U.S. involvement in international conferences and the impact of those conferences on domestic politics.

Easterbrook, Gregg. *A Moment on Earth*. New York: Viking, 1995. A clear and concise discussion of what has been achieved and what remains to be done in the area of environmental protection.

Harris, Nigel. *The New Untouchables: Immigration and the New World Order*. New York: St. Martin's Press, 1996. A thorough account of the movement of peoples in search of work and prosperity in the global economy.

Johnson, Haynes, and David Broder. *The System: The American Way of Politics at the Breaking Point*. Boston: Little, Brown, 1996. Two of America's most accomplished journalists describe how the Clinton health care reform effort went down to defeat.

Rushefsky, Mark, and Kant Patel. *Politics, Power and Policy-Making: The Case of Health Care Reform in the 1990s*. New York: M. E. Sharpe, 1998. A more scholarly approach to the health care policy debate than Johnson and Broder. The authors provide a detailed discussion of the policy options that have made up the health care debate.

Scott, Peter Dale, and Jonathan Marshall. *Cocaine Politics: Drugs, Armies and the CIA in Central America*. Berkeley: University of California Press, 1995. A look at the drug issue from the Latin American perspective, with special emphasis on the role that United States agencies such as the CIA play in the war on drugs.

CONCLUSION:
GOOD CITIZEN,
BAD CITIZEN,
INDIFFERENT
CITIZEN

America! America! God mend thine ev'ry flaw,
Confirm thy soul in self-control,
Thy liberty in law.

—Katherine Bates, *"America the Beautiful"*

Are you a good citizen? I ask my students this question at the beginning of my American politics class each semester. Invariably the response is an overwhelming yes. Confidently and with nary a hint of reluctance the students join millions of other Americans in patting themselves on the shoulder for a job well done.

A few dissenters in the crowd, however, state rather sheepishly that they aren't very good citizens. They don't really know why they are bad citizens, but they have this lingering suspicion that they must be doing something wrong or, worse yet, not doing anything right when it comes to being an official American.

It doesn't take me very long to sow the seeds of doubt among the "good" crowd when I begin to ask them whether they have voted recently, whether they belong to a politically active group, whether they attend public meetings or write public officials or help out in electoral campaigns. After about ten minutes of this line of questioning, the class is abuzz with debate over what really defines good citizenship. The good crowd falls back on the argument that they pay taxes, obey the laws, inform themselves about the issues, and support their country in a patriotic way.

At this point the "bad" citizens begin to take the offensive and tell their friends with the white hats that citizenship involves more than the kind of couch potato brand of involvement in politics that the "good" citizens claim to practice. And moreover, so their questioning goes, who doesn't try a few sleight-of-hand tricks with the IRS or break the speed limit regularly or forget the words to the national anthem? As accusations fly through the air with dizzying speed, the definition of citizenship becomes murkier and murkier. Just what does citizenship entail, and how can we tell whether we really are good citizens?

Since I have a responsibility as a teacher to explain the world of politics rather than leave my students confused, I begin telling the story of what it means to live in a democracy, to have the opportunity to influence public decisions and solve public problems. I start with the ancient Greek, Pericles, who in his renowned funeral oration declared that the citizens of democratic Athens had attained the highest glory of man. I then tell them about Cincinnatus, the Roman citizen/farmer, who left his plough to save his country and then went back to his plough, and so became a symbol of the proper balance of private interest and public involvement in a democracy. I remind them of the terrible times in history when dictators like Stalin and Hitler saw citizens as mere slaves to be used to advance their own power. I end my story with the quote from President John F. Kennedy's inauguration speech in which he challenged Americans to "ask not what your country can do for you, but what you can do for your country."

From these little stories I begin to build the case that being a good citizen somehow involves a relationship between people and their government. I remind them that if democracy is to be preserved, it will require that the people who live in that democracy, the citizens, take responsibility for their government, which includes participating in public affairs, supporting the institutions of government, working to solve public problems, and protecting this system of popular rule from those who would weaken it or destroy it.

By now the class is in that think mode where they are struggling to find themselves and define their own citizenship. Few change their minds about their own status, since most of the "good" citizens can find some redeeming quality in their own relationship to the government and the "bad" citizens seem resigned to the fact that they just don't possess the interest and energy required to meet their government half-way.

As they head out into the hallway and back home, some of the students continue the debate, but most revert back to the topics of the day—sports, music, and movies, heroes, villains, and celebrities. Academic debates about democracy and citizenship are not their cup of tea. How citizens interact with their government, what level of commitment people make to the country they live in, and what responsibilities are associated with citizenship are questions really only worth about fifty minutes of classroom time. The lesson learned in that classroom is not so much that there are good citizens and bad citizens, but rather that most citizens just don't care; they are indifferent citizens.

But there is hope, as there is always hope. While indifferent citizenship is the norm, that does not mean that we have become a nation devoid of commitment to government and our democratic way of life. In 1996 95 million people voted, a number that has often been criticized as woefully low but one that nevertheless outdistanced the combined viewing audience of the television shows, *Friends*, *Seinfeld*, and *Home Improvement*. Moreover, the number of hits on government-related Internet sites and the use of e-mail communications with the White House and the Congress is growing dramatically, suggesting that Americans are interested and interacting with the government, albeit in a more high-tech manner.

And finally, the anti-Washington attitude toward politics that has permeated America for so long is slowly receding as jobs expand, downsizing diminishes, and the economy becomes more stable. The number of Americans who express satisfaction with government is on the rise. Even the salacious details of the Clinton-Lewinsky affair have had little bearing on the president's job approval rating. There is nothing like more money in the ol' pocket to make government and politicians look a little better.

But much needs to be done if we are to realize the ideal expressed by Pericles of citizenship as the highest calling and good citizens to be found everywhere. The dizzying pace of American life has not been kind to citizenship. Most people are just too busy and pulled in too many directions to give of themselves in public matters; just keeping their private lives in order is a monumental task. And then there is the disastrous mix of money and sex that has wreaked havoc on our public confidence. Political scandals now seem the norm rather than the exception in America. Finally, government in our country has become so overwhelming, costly, and interventionist that people are sick and tired of this colossus hanging over the heads and say enough. As they retreat from government, they find answers in sports or popular culture or personal relationships and leave the community, the state, and the country behind. It is unfortunate, but not at all surprising.

Politics for the most part is serious business, with complex problems that require complex solutions. Politicians try to jazz up the process of public decisionmaking, but alas it is no contest when the latest debate in Congress is faced with competition from professional sports figures, the movie glitterati, and of course all the stuff that is on television. To most Americans, politics is plain and simple an uninteresting activity that is endured but not enjoyed. There is just too much competition out there for people's attention, and politics doesn't have what it takes today to capture America's heart and mind.

What is most serious about the lack of interest in good citizenship is the long term impact of that lack of interest on good government. As we turn our attention away from the political arena, we also begin to lose respect for public officials and public servants. We start to tell ourselves that breaking the law is O.K.; we try to avoid simple duties like being on a jury; and we feel no great impulse to offer our services for the good of the nation. It's a long road from failing to vote to becoming a really bad citizen, but losing that civic virtue that involves a deep sense of responsibility to give back to one's country is the first step on that road.

All is not lost. There are some things even busy people can do to make themselves better citizens, and they aren't terribly complicated, although they do require a willingness to move off the couch, leave the bunker mentality behind, and get involved in the world outside. Here are some helpful hints that may help ordinary Americans get back on the road to citizenship:

Helpful Hints

1. Start Small—Don't Try to Save the Country All at Once. Most Americans have convinced themselves that participation and good citizenship mean that they have a responsibility to take on world peace, nuclear disarmament, the end of hunger, and environmental protection. Good citizenship, however, starts with that one small step out the door and towards the improvement of the neighborhood, the strengthening of the public school, the building of a playground. Take your citizenship in small doses; that way your participation will be manageable and in the end more meaningful.

2. All Politics Is Local. There are enough people trying to save the world, but not enough people who are interested in saving their street. Former Speaker of the House of Representatives Tip O'Neill coined the phrase that all politics is local, and he hit it right on the nose. Politics is an activity that builds up from a citizen base. Sure there are leaders and powerful people at the top, but in a democracy what happens at the bottom is ultimately very powerful. Start your involvement at the bottom and work your way up the ladder of power.

3. You Can Still Make a Difference. Don't let anyone tell you that people don't matter in politics. There is just an overwhelming mountain of evidence that voting matters, sending letters to elected representatives matters, signing petitions matters, and protesting injustice matters. One of the tragedies of the current downswing in citizen participation is the big lie that popular involvement does not have an impact on public affairs. The lie is obvious: There have been too many elections won by a handful of votes and too many causes started by a lone voice to go on believing that lie. Remember, the system does work if you know how to work the system.

4. Politicians Are People—Some Are Good, Others Are Not So Good. Too often we fall into the trap of believing that everyone in the public sector is corrupt, but virtue and goodness reside in the private sector. GET REAL. The world doesn't work that way; humans are

humans whether they are elected officials or corporate executives. One of the best steps back into good citizenship is to see the world as it is rather than hold on to the stereotypes of politicians as lower than the low. Talk to your elected officials, and you will quickly find that they are for the most part dedicated public servants doing a difficult and often thankless job. When you do find a rotten apple in the political arena, then do something about it with your vote. Complaining only blows off steam. Voting is power.

5. Politics Is about Power, So Being Political May Require You to Be Tough. Don't be shy about getting into the political arena. Rather see the experience as an thrilling ride with a few bumps along the way. Remember that participating in politics means that you are at the very epicenter of human activity. Whether we think about it or admit it, everything is political, and it is political power that directs society. As science fiction writer Robert Heinlein put it:

> Politics is just a name for the way we get things done . . . without fighting. We dicker and compromise and everybody thinks he has received a raw deal, but somehow after a tedious amount of talk we come up with some jury-rigged way to do it without getting anybody's head bashed in. That's politics. The only other way to settle a dispute is by bashing a few heads in, and that is when one or both sides is no longer willing to dicker. That's why I say politics is good even when it is bad, because the only alternative is force . . . and somebody gets hurt.

> —Uncle Tom in *Podkayne of Mars*

Box 9.1   Helpful Internet Sites on American Government and Politics

Congressional Quarterly

http://www.cq.com/
   The most informative and nonpartisan news about Congress.

(continues)

Box 9.1 *(continued)*

The Gallup Organization

http://www.gallup.com
The most reputable polling organization in the world.

American University's Campaign Contribution Site

http://www.soc.american.edu/campaign/
Since money is the mother's milk of American politics, this is an indispensable site.

The CIA World Fact Book

http://www.odci.gov/cia/publications/nsolo/wfb_all.htm
Perhaps one of the longest Internet addresses, but worth it. A wealth of information about every country in the world through American eyes.

Democratic National Committee

http://www.democrats.org/
News and notes about the Democrats.

Republican National Committee

http://www.rnc.org/
News and notes about the Republicans.

The White House

http://www.whitehouse.gov/
Send the President an e-mail.

(continues)

Box 9.1   *(continued)*

C-Span

http://www.c-span.org
    Remains the most respected source of information on the activities
of American government.

U.S. Election Map Bank

http://www.worldmedia.fr/elections/
Anything you ever wanted to know about elections in America.

Yahoo/Index: Government

http://www.yahoo.com/government
    The Big Kahuna of search engines on U.S. government. If you can't
find it, look here.

A Few Books You Should Read

Barber, Benjamin. *A Place For You: How To Make Society Civil and Democracy Strong.* New York: Hill and Wang, 1998. Some solid advice on how
to transform our apathetic political system into something more dynamic.

Lerner, Michael. *The Politics of Meaning: Restoring Hope and Possibility in
an Age of Cynicism.* Reading, Mass.: Addison-Wesley, 1997. As the title
suggests, Lerner also has helpful hints on how to heal the current political
malaise.

McKenna, George, and Stanley Feingold. *Taking Sides: Clashing Views on
Controversial Political Issues,* 10th ed. Guilford, Conn.: Dushkin, 1997.
An essential guide to the key political issues of the day. Organized into pro
and con sections, the text is helpful in forming political opinions about
what matters in American society.

Osborne, David, and Ted Gaebler. *Re-inventing Government: How the En-
trepreneurial Spirit is Transforming the Public Sector.* Reading, Mass.: Ad-

dison-Wesley, 1992. Now viewed as the bible of governmental reform. Chock full of ideas on how to make government work better and smarter.

Rubin, Barry. *A Citizen's Guide to Politics in America*. New York: M. E. Sharpe, 1997. A helpful handbook on the ins and outs of making your voice heard in the halls of government.

Sandel, Michael. *Democracy's Discontent: America in Search of a Public Philosophy*. Cambridge: Harvard University Press, 1997. An important book that lays out how the ideas and the ideals of good government and good citizenship are being defined in America today.

Schudson, Michael. *The Good Citizen: A History of Public Life*. New York: Free Press, 1998. A must read for anyone interested in finding out how those who came before them participated in public life.

Sinopoli, Richard C. *The Foundation of American Citizenship: Liberalism, the Constitution and Civic Virtue*. New York: Oxford University Press, 1992. An interesting examination of American citizenship from the perspective of the Founding Fathers. The author explores the roots of American citizenship.

EPILOGUE

Politics is the art of looking for trouble, finding it everywhere, diagnosing it incorrectly, and applying the wrong remedies.

—*Groucho Marx*

You're probably wondering why I haven't devoted more space to the Clinton-Lewinsky scandal? After all, if there is any event in recent American politics where anger, boredom, and confusion intersect, it is in the sordid affair involving a flawed, but popular president, a starry-eyed intern, a relentless independent counsel, a deeply divided Congress, and an American public begging for an end to a constitutional soap opera.

The basic reason for placing the presidential scandal at the very end of the book is that this national morality play is so fresh and so prone to high emotion that it is difficult to provide sober and fair analysis. While the essentials of the scandal are known—a presidential sexual dalliance, charges of perjury and obstruction of justice, a politically charged impeachment, and a tense Senate trial—what remains for political analysts and historians is to sort out the meaning of this mess and more importantly its impact on the body politic.

Perhaps the best place to start is by focusing on what can be called the "democratic gap" that developed between the Congress and the American people. Throughout the scandal a solid majority of the American people seemed unfazed by the charges leveled against President Clinton. Even though Independent Counsel Kenneth Starr was able to convince Republican members of the House Judiciary Committee that the president lied under oath and obstructed justice, a steady 60 percent of the American people remained opposed to the extreme constitutional sanction of impeachment. Public opinion polls pointed clearly to the concern of Americans with saving Social Security, funding education, and continuing the long period of economic growth.

But while the American public wanted to change the agenda of government, the Republican majority in the House of Representatives was adamant in its belief that the president's actions met the standard for "high crimes and misdemeanors" as laid out by the founding fathers. With the Republicans in the majority and able to hold most of their members in check, impeachment was a foregone conclusion. Bill Clinton became the Andrew Johnson of the twentieth century. Once the focus turned to the Senate, where the trial was conducted, the position of the American people did not change significantly. There was an increase in the percentage of respondants in polls who felt the president should resign, but still no turn around in the basic belief that removal from office was the wrong solution. The Senate put a less strident face on the trial proceedings, but did not vote for an early dismissal of the charges. The Republican majority was committed to carrying the process through—no matter what public opinion was saying.

This apparent disconnect between the American people and Congress raises a key question—If the vast majority of Americans did not want their president impeached and put on trial, then why didn't Congress listen? The principle of representative democracy would appear to have been violated in this instance as members of Congress overruled the American people and voted for a process that had only been fully implemented once before. The members of the House of Representatives who voted impeachment and the Senators who insisted on a full-blown trial may have taken that course with the highest intentions of upholding the rule of law and constitutional principles. Yet, what about democracy? Doesn't the clear intent of the American people mean that elected politicians should follow the wishes of their constituents?

The answer may lie in the enormous ideological gulf that separates President Clinton and the Republican Congress. In this case there is more than the usual partisan disdain that often accompanies divided government. The liberal Clinton, child of the sixties, a womanizer without military service, is far removed from the conservatives in the Republican majority who are repulsed by both the permissive values and the outrageous behavior of the chief executive. On the surface this may be a constitutional struggle over the rule of law, but the subtext is a clash of cultures. Within such a climate of distaste it should come as no surprise that public opinion polls are inconsequential to the Republicans. In many respects this is a war to put an end to all that Bill Clinton stands for.

Then there is the issue of presidential character. More than just a tawdry sex scandal at the highest level of government, the Clinton-Lewinsky affair forced this country to think about what kind of president they want in the White House. Many Americans found themselves asking another question—

Is it more important to have a president who is morally upstanding or politically effective? Apparently the American people knew what they were getting into when they elected Bill Clinton and then reelected him. Despite the outrage of some who saw the disinterest of Americans toward the president's sexual peccadilloes as a sign of societal and legal decline, it was clear early on in "Monicagate" that the general public wanted a leader who kept the nation peaceful and prosperous. The president's sex life, even though it broke the bonds of marriage and compromised legal principles, was viewed by many Americans as a private matter and certainly not the business of Congress. In many respects, Americans were becoming more "Europeanized" in that they were able to separate private sexual behavior from public performance. In their minds, Bill Clinton might be a scoundrel, but he was an effective scoundrel.

Despite the lack of public outcry over the president's behavior, most Americans remain deeply disappointed in Mr. Clinton. There was enormous sympathy for Mrs. Clinton and Chelsea and a collective longing for someone in the White House who could be viewed as a role model, but like the division between polls and Congressional support for impeachment, the American people were divided over whether to rock the boat during the most sustained period of peace and prosperity in our history. If polls accurately portrayed the views of America, a disreputable Bill Clinton in office was better than creating a constitutional nightmare over an affair.

Unfortunately, while Washington politicians were engaged in the partisan trench warfare over Bill Clinton, something else was going on outside the beltway. Americans were moving further and further away from an appreciation of politics. The American people are smart enough to know that politics is a tough business and that democracy is imperfect. But what they will not tolerate is when politicians take their eye off the target and engage in behavior that weakens the country. This is a recipe guaranteed to create anger, boredom, and confusion. Americans are angry with Clinton's philandering and the Republican moral crusade, bored with the legalistic double talk and interminable hearings, and confused about why such an obviously intelligent president would provide his political adversaries with the means to destroy his presidency.

Yes, Americans continue to be angry, bored, and confused, but the whole Clinton mess has added another element. Americans are now also tired—tired of politicians, tired of hypocrisy, tired of lies, tired of unfulfilled promises, and tired of the game of politics. When the cloud of tiredness covers the American people it can have far-reaching consequences. Not only is there a lack of interest in matters of state, but there is a sharp drop-off in what can be considered political spirit. In short, Americans become disheartened; they begin to lose focus and look elsewhere for something to bring meaning to their lives. One of the more memorable nuggets of analysis during the entire Clinton scandal was Geraldo Rivera's comment that the reason Americans were not focusing in on the impeachment hearings was "they're all at the mall." If the fallout from the Clinton scandal is that we have become a people who find the answer in the mall, rather than in the town hall, then we are in big trouble.

INDEX